COLLABORATORS, REBELS AND TRAITORS

COLLABORATORS, REBELS AND TRAITORS

Dissenters from Frontiers React to the Indian Union

AWADHESH C. SINHA

MANOHAR
2024

First published 2024

ISBN 978-81-19139-86-6 (hardbound)
ISBN 978-81-19953-44-8 (ebook)

Published by
Ajay Kumar Jain *for*
Manohar Publishers & Distributors
4753/23 Ansari Road, Daryaganj
New Delhi 110002

Typeset by
Ravi Shanker
Delhi 110095

Printed and bound in India

To

SANGEETA

and

PRATEEK SINHA

Contents

List of Illustrations 8

Preface 9

Acknowledgements 11

PART A: BACKGROUND

1. Introduction: Historical and Geographical Background of the Study 15
2. Geographical and Historical Background of the Frontiers 24

PART B: LOCALE

3. Naga Hills District in the Province of Assam 45
4. The Princely State of Jammu & Kashmir 79
5. Lushai, No Mizo Hills District of Assam 94
6. The Indian Protectorate of Sikkim 113

PART C: THE PERSONAE

7. Zaphu Angami Phizo and the Naga National Council 143
8. Sheikh Muhammad Abdullah and the (Jammu and) Kashmir Quagmire 177
9. Pu Laldenga and the Mizo National Front 226
10. Palden Thondup Namgyal, the Last Maharaja of Sikkim 243

PART D: PERFORMANCE

11. Indian Strategy of Accommodation and Defence against the Dissenters 265
12. Collaborators, Rebels and Traitors: Were the Dissenters Collaborators, Rebels or Traitors? 286

Index 305

Illustrations

Figures

1. Zaphu Angami Phizo 144
2. Sheikh Muhammad Abdullah 178
3. Pu Laldenga 227
4. Palden Thondup Namgyal 244

Maps

1. Indian States & British India 34
2. Notional Map of Naga Hills 46
3. Notional Map of the Princely State of Jammu & Kashmir 80
4. Notional Map of Lushai Mizo Hills 95
5. Notional Map of Sikkim 114

Preface

The British withdrawal from India led to formation of a Muslim Pakistan and an economically, ethnically, linguistically and religiously diverse India. Makers of the Indian Constitution envisaged a multi-ethnic, multi-lingual, and secular republic of Indian Union. While there was a provision of a strong Federal Government, the provinces were provided with resources for their all round development. However, dissenting voices emerged from the frontier regions from the very beginning leading to insurgency in some cases. The book proposes to study these dissenting voices as dissenters in the form of collaborators, rebels or the traitors. The presentation has four parts. Part A examins the scheme of the study and historical and geographical background of the frontier regions under study. Part B provides details of the four locales of Naga Hills District of Assam, Jammu and Kashmir, Mizo Hills district, and the princely state of Sikkim in four chapters from where the dissention emerged. Part C evlauates roles of the four state leaders, who were all non-Hindus from minority communities in the next four chapters and in fact some of them took to the arms. In Part D I have surveyed the administrative and constitutional response of the Federal Government to the issues raised from the states. I have assessed the types of leadership among the forntier dissenterd and noted that two were collaborators at their terms, one was an out and out rebel and the fourth one was a rebel of his own type. Lastly, I have surveyed why some dissenting movements, which succeeded and others, whic continue to exist at the cost of men and materials. One of the issues emerges loud and clear that these leaders saw Indian Union predominantly as a Hindu state in which they did not see themselves secured with their unique background. However, it goes without saying that the federal government has always tried to rise to the occasion to resolve the issue on hand. In fact, one of the worst suffer of the insurgency, it is the Mizoram, which is forging ahead in every walks of life among the Northeastern States of the Indian Union. Not only that, one feels that there is regional fatigue with the insurgency and common man wanted peaceful co-existence for a normal living condition. A large many well wishers came out to help me out to make the study possible instantly.

New Delhi
10 June 2023

AWADHESH C. SINHA

Acknowledgements

While teaching in North Eastern Hill University, Shillong with campuses at Kohima in Nagaland and Aizawl in Mizoram, I had to visit various parts of the region and interact with the colleagues and students and learnt a lot from them. I used to make it a habit to pay my respects to their elders by visiting them at their residence. Similarly, I learnt a lot from my students in the university about their culture, history, politics, and social set up from 1976 to 2004, when I was a member of the faculty and I still maintain my contacts with at least some of them. Then I conducted field research in Sikkim, Bhutan and much less in Nepal and Darjeeling and came in contacts with a huge number of valuable friends and associates, who did not only provide valuable data for the research, but they also turned out to be my links with the region for a variety of purposes. At home, Arav and Ahan, my grandsons, used to get intrigued: 'What does Dada go on writing?' and my better-half, Krishna, would demand: 'is it (the writing) over?' So it is over for now after about a two-year long involvement. Similarly, many of my academic colleagues and friends, with whom, I would discuss the present research, would enquire on the progress of the study. Thus it is not possible for me to mention them individually by name, but I do record my sincere gratitude to them collectively. Still there are persons with whom I have been interacting for years together informally and learnt a lot for the study. And thus it will be unbecoming of me not mention at least some of their names without lessening the significance of the other very precious friends:

Shillong: Prof. C.L. Imchen, Prof. Lanu Aeir, Late Prof. A.K. Nokinrih, Prof. P.K. Mishra, Prof. T.B. Subba, Prof. Imdad Hussain, Prof. David R. Syiemlieh, Prof. Milton Sangma, Late Prof. B. Pakem, Prof. L.S. Gassah, Late Prof. Gopal Krishna.

Nagaland: Late Prof. Kiramwati Ao, Prof. A.L. Ao, Prof. Visier Sanyo.

Sikkim and Darjeeling: Late Lal B. Basnet, Late C.D. Rai, Late Kashiraj Pradhan, Late Dr. Kumar Pradhan, Mr. P.D. Rai, Prof. Jyoti P. Tamang, Prof. Utam Lal and Dr. Charishma Lepcha, Dr. A.B. Subba, Prof. B.P. Misra, Prof. Ghanshyam Nepal, Prof. Maitryi Chaudhuri, Dr. Harka B. Chhetri, Dr. Rajendra Dhakal, Mr. Anmol Prasad.

Rajiv Gandhi Arunachal University: Naharlung, Itanagar: Prof. Sarit Choudhury, Dr. Bikash Bage, Dr. Padi Hana.

Tezpur: Prof. K. Kykhi and Prof. Robin Deka.

Aizawl: Prof. Lalmuana, Dr. Thangliana.

Silchar: Prof. Sajal Nag and Prof. Nirankar Mallick.

Agartala: Dr. Surojit Sengupta.

Guwahati: Fr. K. Jose.

Delhi: Prof. Himanshu Roy, Prof. Sanjoy Hazarika, Prof. Amarjeet Singh, Dr. K. Kokho, and Late Shakti Sinha.

And lastly from my publisher, Manohar Publishers, I admire Shri Ramesh Jain for his elephantine memory of our fifty years old proposal to publish my manuscript on Sikkim and since then waiting for me to turn up with a manuscript. I profusely thank Shri Ajay Jain and Mr. Ananya Jain, the deserving successors of Manohar Publishers & Distributors for their support. I appreciate the efforts of the staff of Manohar specially Shri Sanjay Kala to get the manuscript published expeditiously.

AWADHESH C. SINHA

PART A

Background

1

Introduction

Historical and Geographical Background of the Study

By the turn of the nineteenth century, the British Indian Empire had reached possibly its maximum limit of the great Himalayan landmass. Considered by them as the ideal limit of their Indian expansion in the north, with a view to guarding that, they had evolved an intricate strategy of brinkmanship. Known as the Great Game in the Central Asian landmass, diplomacy, espionage, chicanery, intrigue and warfare. Moreover, they had a series of external and internal buffer states around their Indian imperial possession. For example, they had carved out Iran, Afghanistan, Tibet and Thailand between their the strategy used potential imperial rivals and themselves as an external buffer state, where presence of rival powers was opposed at all cost. They drew an external boundary between their domain and the neighbouring states like Afghanistan, Nepal, Tibet and Burma. Some way or the other, they maintained a type of Munroe Doctrine with reference to the Himalaya, which was considered essential as the Himalaya is considered a natural boundary of India. However, but for occasional insistence on the principle of watershed in the higher altitudes as the dividing line between their domain, they kept the issue of boundary line invariably vague and tended to loosely control the frontier zones as an expedient device.

As theirs was the age of land army and wars were fought mainly by the standing army on the land, there was a deliberate policy not to develop these frontier regions infrastructurally. The region was deliberately left devoid of means of mass communication and transportation as a deterrent to the potential invading armies of the adversaries. The British were so enamoured by the prospect of trade with China through Tibet that they went on humouring the Chinese sensitivity at the cost of the Tibetans. Even while withdrawing from the Indian Empire, they did not hesitate to leave behind their imperial obsession with the Himalaya with reference to China:

> ... In practice, it may well prove difficult to secure a tidy solution to the future of Nepal, Sikkim and Bhutan, even to the eastern marches of Kashmir (i.e. Ladakh). This will largely depend on the future policy and fate of China and hence of Tibet. The Government of the (Indian) Union must be prepared for complications on the North-eastern Frontiers and evolve a policy to meet them. This may well have to be that of maintaining all the principalities in virtual independence of India, but as a buffer, as far as possible (as) client states. There may be greater advantages in according Sikkim a more independent status (rather) than seeking to absorb Bhutan as well as Sikkim in the Indian Union, adding the communal problem of Buddhism.... The Government (of India) will be well advised to avoid entering into fresh commitments with any one of these frontier states or seeking to redefine their status. Their importance is strategic in direct relation to China, and indirectly to Russia. Such adjustments to the relations with the (Indian) Union can fully be affected by those political and strategic considerations ... account of which, it is hoped, the treaty will take (care) rather than the political niceties, which do not help defence policy,

advised the Under Secretary, Political and Foreign Department of the British Indian Government, New Delhi to Sikkim, Bhutan, Nepal and the future government of India on 10 August 1946 (Sinha 1991: 173-4).

The Chinese People's Liberation Army (PLA) liberated Tibet in 1950. Not only that, they put some shadowy claim on the territories of India, Nepal, Bhutan in the northern Himalayan region. The frontier areas were invariably settled by a plethora of ethnic groups which the British had defined as the tribes, castes, Lamaist, Buddhist, Hindu, Muslim and the like, again as per their convenience. These areas were loosely administered, invariably by local chiefs, tribal headmen, or British administrators with police or military background. Naturally, the frontier communities and the districts were lightly taxed in the form of house tax/capital tax as a token of their loyalty to the British, as they were largely out of the ambit of the cash economy at the time of their British subjugation. So much so that but for a few horse cart tracts linking them ineffectively to the provincial capital, Shillong, most of the hill districts (of Assam) were left in splendid isolation from the people of the plains, to which they administratively belonged. Many ICS administrators and their cultural associates, the Christian missionaries, operating in the hills, actively canvassed till the 1940s that the Assam Hill tribes did not belong to India, as they were racially and culturally different from the Indian Hindus and Muslims. As such, they propounded the idea of creating a 'Crown Colony from the Chittagong Hill Tracts now in Bangladesh, the entire State of Assam and the present seven frontier states of the region to Upper Burma' under the British Empire in the early 1940s (Reid 1941; Syiemlieh 2014).

The war weary and financially bankrupt Britain was forced to withdraw in August 1947 from her Indian Empire after dividing it into two – India and Pakistan. As the Assam Hills districts and the tribesmen were kept apart from the plains, they were politically unaware of the larger developments in the other parts of India in the absence of political contacts. Moreover, many of the frontier areas were designated as partially and completely Excluded Areas, left at the mercy of the British district administrators, who were drawn from the police or army background. Various sects of foreign Christian missionaries were licensed to work among these hill districts on their evangelical programmes. But paradoxically, nationalist political parties such as the Indian National Congress and the Muslim League, etc., were not permitted to operate in the excluded and partially excluded frontier areas of Assam during the British days. And thus, these areas largely remained untouched from the ongoing struggles for democratic rights in the other parts of the country. Moreover, British India had two distinct administrative parts: directly British administered provinces and more than 560 princely states of different sizes and privileges controlled by the British Residents stationed among them.

Dissenters from the Frontiers

Traditionally, the frontiers are ecologically diverse and difficult terrain. Economically, they were often divided into hunting, collecting, pastoral and agricultural economies at the bare subsistence levels. Socially, they were divided into a number of clans, originally affiliated to or assumed to be, affliated to the tribal organizations. Besides consanguineous ties, sworn brotherhood/friendship plays a significant role in inter-tribal relationships. Hunting, raiding, swordsmanship, archery, etc., are considered to be special skills for those who claim distinction among them. Politically, frontiers have divided loyalties across the political boundaries of the nation states. Administratively, they are unstable and unsettled and thus they attracted adventurers, fortune seekers, explorers, enterpreneurs and fugitives in the past. Culturally, the frontier communities are spread across the political boundaries. Strategically, the frontiers are marginal and peripheral to the cultural core of the larger societies. If one proceeds from the cultural cores of the two adjoining societies towards the fringes, theoretically there will be a zone of mixed cultural traits high up in the ecologically difficult and undulating distant areas. This is the frontier, which is difficult to govern politically and even morally from either of the cores. In such a situation, a stable frontier is one on which equal pressures are excercised from both the neighbouring (and often opposite) cultural cores and political systems (Lattimore 1962; Shils 1961).

For India,

> the British had preferred the 'screen' of buffer states and administered tribal territories along the Inner Asian frontier. However, the effect of this policy was 'fossilizing' the structure of the frontier zone for over half a century, thus reducing the force of direct contact and the necessity of boundary making. The Inner Asian frontiers of India remained frontiers rather than boundaries. (Rao 2021: 372)

However, the centrality of the frontiers is scarcely recognized today. Moreover, frustrations among the youth, ethnic nationalism, issues of identity, self-determination, human rights, geographical isolation, the use of the armed forces by the state, cross-border terrorism and questions about governance straddles these borderlands. They have tended to be viewed as targets of the central government policy radiating from the national capitals rather than as areas that possess their own ecosystems of existence, where policy must focus on local issues that directly impact the lives of the people. Lamenting on the state of affairs there, Rao, goes on to talk about

> the concept of frontier zones which historically provided for 'an intermingling of peoples', allowing the retention of close interaction across borders between communities in terms of language, custom and religion, which has been lost. Geopolitics trumps all'. (Rao 2021: 464).

And the Indian Union has a long frontier region starting from the Karakoram ranges in the western Himalaya to all across the central Himalayan expanse up to the eastern leg of the chain of mountains from its bend to the Chittagong Hills. On the other hand, modern states have national boundaries, a thin line without width, which has to undergo the process of delimitation (allocation), definition (or description) and delineation (or mapping) and demarcation (aportionment) of the areas on the ground.

The preamble of the Indian Constitution declares, 'we the people of India, having solemnly resolved to constitute India into a sovereign, socialist, secular and democratic republic'. The objectives stated by the preamble are to secure justice, liberty, equality to all citizens and promote fraternity to maintain unity and integrity of the nation. It was a conscious decision to create a multicultural, multiethnic and pluralistic nation state in India. However, there emerged some voices of dissension from the beginning such as the Naga Hills District of Assam, which was followed by others in course of time. It is intriguing that all the four dissenters to the future Indian Union would emerge from these exclusive frontier areas, which were not part of the larger normal British administered provinces. Unlike the bulk of the leaders of India, who were engaged in freedom struggle against the British colonial rule, these dissenters claimed to belong to different ethnic, racial, religious, political and even extra territorial affiliations. For instance, Sheikh Muhammad Abdullah, a secular, socialist, and a Sunni Muslim peasant leader from north-western frontiers of the Hindu principality of Jammu & Kashmir, desired an independent Kashmir jointly to be sponsored by the Indian Union and Pakistan. Zaphu Angami Phizo, an American Baptist Christian Angami tribal leader from the easternmost frontier of the Naga Hills District, rose against the Indian Union right from August 1947 with a view to establish

'Nagaland for the Christ' not only in India, but also across the border in Burma as well. From the south-eastern frontier district of India, Mizo (formerly Lushai) Hills District in Assam, Pu Laldenga, a Presbyterian Christian, took to arms and declared independence from the Indian Union in February 1966. And lastly, Palden Thondup Namgyal, the Tibetan Buddhist Bhutia dynastic ruler of Indian Protectorate of Sikkim, opposed tooth and nail the Indian take over of his principality in 1970s from northern frontiers and did not hesitate to claim his distant Tibetan historical roots.

Why did these articulate, educated, non-Hindu and politically conscious community leaders from different regions of frontier India pose challenge to the leadership of the multicultural ethos of the Indian polity? Should their opposition be taken as symptomatic or the issues raised by them must be probed and analysed thoroughly for a robust growth of democracy in India? What were the typical or unique attribute of these individual leaders, which attracted their followers to rise against the state of India? What was the driving force/s behind them that motivated them to rise against the mighty armed forces of the Indian Union? Did they take the commitments/constitutional provisions made in favour of these territories seriously or otherwise? Moreover, has there been a consistent review of the commitments/ constitutional provisions made for the frontier regions by the appropriate authorities and on which the frontier communities been taken in confidence? Or were some other compelling reasons for them which motivated them to oppose the Indian Union as they did? Do they individually or collectively present some models of dissenters of the democratic dispensation for the future? Interestingly, while the Indian Union has been able to solve the Mizo and Sikkim 'problems' satisfactorily as of now, the older of the two among the four, the Naga and the Kashmir problems, still remain to be resolved.

Scheme of the Present Study

The present study is based on secondary data published on the regions and the pivotal leaders of the states in our study. There has been a good amount of literature available on Jammu & Kashmir, Nagaland and Sikkim but equally meagre literature on the Mizos and Mizoram.

However, there is an autobiography of Sheikh Muhammad Abdullah and a biography of Z.A. Phizo, which we have extensively used. The Sheikh himself dictated his biography, *Atishe Chinar*, which was translated from Urdu into English and subsequently published (Abdullah 2016). There are two biographical publications of Maharaja Karan Singh (Singh 1982, 1984), which work as if it is a counter check on the Sheikh's. Phizo's biography was authored by an ex-soldier and an admirer of Phizo and was published first in 2002 (Steyn 2016). So far as the other two leaders, Palden Thondup Namgyal and Pu Laldenga, are concerned, there is no full length work on either of them in English to the best of my knowledge. N.K. Rustomji's works based on his correspondence with P.T. Namgyal (Rustomji 1971, 1987) along with the author's own writings (Sinha 1975, 2008, 2019) have been used for that pupose. So far as Laldenga is concerned, there are some works published decades back, which are not traceable right now. There must be some writings in Mizo language as well, in which I have no expertise. For the purpose of uncovering the nuances of Laldenga and Phizo's personality and MNF operation of Mizo insurgency, I have used extensively Sanjoy Hazarika's and Sajal Nag's most authentic writings on the regional insurgency (Hazarika 2011, 2018 and Nag 2002). Moreover, I have been talking to the knowledgeable persons of the region, who had been known to some of these leaders.

The study is introduced in the technique of Timothy Ash's *History of the Present* (2000) in terms of the British policy addressed to the Indian demand for independence/self-rule. The main study is divided into four sections: Section A familiarizes the readers with the author's academic concerns and brief geographical and historical background of the study. Section B provides the historical, geographical, administrative, ethnic and political backgrounds of the four units of the study: Jammu & Kashmir, Naga Hills District and Lushai Hills Districts of Assam and principality of Sikkim as in 1947, when the British left India for good. Section C informs the readers on the personal backgrounds, sociocultural moorings, their political struggles and styles of functioning, and political and organizational attributes of the four main characters, who posed challenge to the Indian Union: Z.A. Phizo, Sheik M. Abdullah, U. Laldenga and Palden Thondup

Namgyal. We shall try to follow the same historical sequence of development in the four states mainly by these four pivotal characters in our presentation. Section D consists of two chapters. Chapter 11 to work out the nuances of the Indian state's strategy to accommodate the variety of demands made by the leaders, people at large and their political forums from the four states. And lastly, Chapter 12 endeavours to understand the quality of the leadership engaged in terms of collaboration, rebellion or treason with the Indian state from the frontiers and evaluates their contributions/limitations to the emergence of these four autonomous states as constituent units of Indian Federation. Why do the frontiers, or at least these four frontier regions, suspect the claimed plurality of the Indian Union and continue to see the Indian Union largly as a Hindu state, where they did not see their future safe and secure?

Lastly, the study proposes to assess and evaluate the claimed plurality and secular credentials of the Indian Union through the prism of these four distinguished dissenters from different frontier regions of the Union. Why is it so that the two oldest insurgencies, Nagaland and Kashmir, continue in some form or other all these years even after seven decades since Independence? and the other two: Mizoram and Sikkim, which arose in the 1960s and 1970s respectively, have been satisfactorily resolved? Is it not worth celebrating these achievements or are the celebrations premature? Does the study encourage the Indian establishment to mount endeavours afresh and evolve better strategies to resolve these two oldest political issues of the Indian Union? The study may emerge as a mirror in which another profile of the Indian Union may be visible.

REFERENCES

Abdullah, S.M., 2016, *The Blazing Chinar*, Gulshan, Srinagar.

Ash, Tomothy Gorton, 2000, *History of the Present: Essays, Sketches and Despatches from Europe in 1990s*, Penguin Books, London.

Dean, Riaz, 2019, *Maping the Great Game: Explorers, Spices & Maps in Nineteenth Century Asia*, Penguin Random House India, New Delhi.

Hazarika, Sanjoy, 2011, *Strangers of the Mist: Tales of War and Peace from India's Northeast*, Penguin Books, New Delhi.

———, 2018, *Strangers No More: New Narratives From India's Northeast*, Aleph, New Delhi.

Lattimore, Owen, 1962, *Studies in Frontier History: Collected Papers, 1929-58*, Oxford University Press, London.

Nag, Sajal, 2002, *Contesting Marginality: Ethnicity, Insurgency and Subnationalism in North-East India*, Manohar, New Delhi.

Rao, Nirupama, 2021, *The Fractured Himalaya: India/Tibet/China, 1949-1962*, Penguin Viking, New Delhi.

Reid, Robert, 1941, *A Note on the Future of the Present Excluded, Partially Excluded and Tribal Areas of Assam,* Assam Secretariate Press, Shillong.

Rustomji, N.K., 1971, *Enchanted Frontiers: Sikkim, Bhutan and India's North-Eastern Borderlands*, Oxford University Press, Bombay.

Rustomji, N.K., 1987, *Sikkim: A Himalayan Tragedy*, Allied Publishers, New Delhi.

Shils, Edward, 1961, 'Centre and Perephery', in *The Logic of Personal Knowledge: Essays Presented to Michael Polanyi on his 70th Birthday*, ed. Polanyi Festschrift Committee, Routledge, London.

Singh, Karan, 1982, *Heir Apparent: An Autobiography*, Oxford University Press, Delhi.

———, 1985, *Sadar-i-Riyasat: An Autobiography*, Oxford University Press, Delhi.

Sinha, A.C., 1975, *Politics of Sikkim*, Thompson Press, New Delhi.

———, 1991, *Bhutan: Ethnic Identity and National Dilemma*, Reliance Publishing Company, New Delhi.

———, 2008, *Sikkim: Feudal and Democratic*, Indus Publishing Company, New Delhi.

———, 2019, *Dawn of Democracy in the Eastern Himalayan Kingdoms*, Routledge Taylor & Francis Group, New Delhi.

Steyn, Pieter, 2016, *Zapu Phizo: Voice of the Nagas*, Routledge Taylor & Francis Group, New Delhi.

Syiemlieh, David, R., 2014, *On the Edge of Empire: Four British Plans for North East India, 1941-1947*, Sage, New Delhi.

2

Geographical and Historical Background of the Frontiers

By the turn of the nineteenth century, in the words of Lord Nathaniel Curzon, the Viceroy and Governor of India, the British Indian Empire, 'the noblest trophy of the British genius and the most splendid appendage of the Imperial Crown' (Dean 2019: 12) had reached its zenith of achievements. The British ruled over India for a total of 182 years, first through a mercantile entity, the British East India Company, for 83 years (1765-1858) and then by the Imperial Crown representatives for another 89 years (1858-1947). The first phase was known for the wanton loot of the wealth from India (Dalrymple 2019). Apart from that, the Indian natural resources and manpower were unabashedly used to build imperial assets all over the world and fight wars to safeguard the Empire elsewhere. Moreover, the Indian resources were openly used for industrialization of the British economy in the second phase. Imperialist Britain did not visualize the possibility for leaving their Indian possession in the centuries to come and for that they discovered a number of strategies. However, at last it was a bankrupt and war exhausted British Empire after the Second World War, which was forced to leave her Indian Empire in a most chaotic and disorderly manner (Reid 2019: 3).

The British Indian Empire began its journey from three port cities of Calcutta, Madras and Bombay, which were termed as three provinces (or presidencies) of Bengal, Madras and Bombay respectively. In course of time, newly acquired territories were added to them as per the British administrative convenience, turning them unwieldy. For illustration, the Presidency of Bengal included Bihar, Orissa, Bengal, Assam and even Burma for some time. Similarly, Bombay Presidency stretched from Adan in the Arabian Peninsula beyond India at one time to Kokand coast in India and the bulk of the Deccan plateau. Thus, these presidencies were not only unwieldy administratively, but they also posed serious problem of social communication, as the subjects spoke a variety of regional languages among themselves. The British ruled over them with their brute force ignoring the inconvenience caused to their subjects. Naturally, as social and political awareness increased among the subjects, demands for breaking the presidencies and turning them into linguistic states grew louder. In course of time, the Indian National Congress, which fought for independence of India, passed a resolution that when it would to come to power, it would create linguistic states by breaking the multilingual British provinces. However, a plethora of the Princely States were directly under the British Crown and when the British decided to leave India, they became notionally independent.

British Indian Ethnic Policy After 1857

The stimulus given to the British officials by the (Indian) Revolt of 1857 led to construct a theory of Indian social development based on anthropological comparative method. The British did not hasten the integration of India's movement, which was the lesson they learnt.

> There is nothing as an India; it is more of a land mass held together by the British might and it is in their (the British) interests to show India divided into regions, religions, races, languages, castes and tribes and all types of differentiations. (Owen 1973)

And for that they used anthropological techniques to display the variety of castes, tribes, religions, languages, races and social practices as discrete entities, which as if functioned like islands and did not interact among themselves. Soon enough they realized that a most viable tool in their hand would be religious division between the Hindus and Muslims, the two demographically largest communities. Incidentally, some well-meaning educated British and Indians established the Indian National Congress (INC) in 1885 in Bombay as a forum, which began raising embarrassing political demands from the British administration. Within no time, it attracted educated

Indians from various social backgrounds, which made the administration uncomfortable to handle the situation smoothly in their favour. Soon enough, they helped some landed Muslim gentry to establish the All India Muslim League (AIML) in 1905 at Dacca, which they would use as a tool to beat the increasingly populist political demands on behalf of the Congress. The Congress began as a political club of educated Indians from various ethnic, linguistic, regional and religious backgrounds. By the 1920s, it was turning into a forum of mass mobilization under the influence of Mahatma, (Great Soul) Mohandas Karamchand Gandhi, which made many urban educated leaders like M.A. Jinnah uncomfortable in the company of the rustic masses. The British watched this development with concern and evolved the strategy of divide and rule, in which they labeled the Congress as a forum of the Hindus, and prompted AIML as a counterfoil to it. Unlike populist Congress, the Muslim League was a patrician body, dominated by landed proprietors. For illustration, its long-term secretary and future prime minister of Pakistan, Liakat Ali Khan, was a big landlord and so were many other leaders, who had least interest in the betterment of the common masses. And so were most of the laders of this forum.

British Policy of Divide and Rule

In view of Walter Reid,

> many Britons found the Hindus, and the majority of the Independence movement leaders were Hindus, unappealing. No great effort was made to look into the subtleties of the Hindu religion. At a superficial level a multiplicity of gods … were to a Victorian mind almost a caricature of paganism, savagery and idolatry. The monotheistic Muslims, on the other hand, held to a religious philosophy which was much more akin to Christianity…. British civil servants tended, although there were countless exceptions, to find the Muslims easier to get on with. They seemed to be more socially welcoming as well as less arrogant. British officials knew that if they were admitted into a Hindu house for a meal, there would be a ritual of 'purification' carried out after their departure: they were regarded as unclean (beaf eaters). The Muslims were thought of as brave and intrepid warriors.

They gained points in the Second World War, when for political reasons the largely Hindu Congress party refused to cooperate, unlike the Muslims. Sixty-five per cent of the Indian Army soldiers who fought for Britain were Muslims, although they constituted only 27 per cent of the population (of the country). (Reid 2019: 15)

There were Britons like Winston Churchill who were diehard imperialists, who believed in the superiority of the British race to the black colonies. They presumed that the British had a civilizing duty and that it was neither in the interests of Britain or of the colonies that there should be transfer of political power (to them). Churchill was ambitious, aggressive, unbalanced, unprincipled, capricious, scheming and dishonest. He was so blind in self-promotion that a former British prime minister Lloyd George said of him in 1934: 'He would make a drum out of the skin of his own mother in order to sound his own praise' (Reid 2019: 100). As late as in July 1940, he told Leopold Amery, the Secretary of State (of India), that 'he would sooner give up political life at once, or rather go out into the wilderness and fight, than admit to a revolution that meant the end of the imperial crown in India'.

Prime Minister Churchill and the Viceroy Linlithgow were for doing nothing with reference to Indian independence for as long as possible. Churchill dreamed that 'we might sit on the tripos – Pakistan, Princely India and Hindus – for long on playing politics of divide and rule. When Wavell met Linlithgow in Delhi on 19 October, 1943, the later opined that in his opinion, 'Britain would have to continue responsibility for India for at least another thirty years' (Reid 2019: 185). Ishtiaq Ahmed referred that a 'secret pact' between Churchill and Jinnah already existed from 1940, when the former pledged to reward Jinnah with Pakistan in return for his support to the war efforts … from 1946 onwards, documentary evidence of Jinnah and Churchill writing to each other exists in their papers (Ahmed 2020: 415). But it is a matter of intensity. Even so-called socialist labour members of the parliament were not free from imperial virus. Leo Amery 'described the Labour ministers of the cabinet as 'Mice … incredibly feeble creatures' so far as the colonies were concened (Patrick 1997: 131). In other words, there was a consensus among the British politicians of all political persuasion that the British interests would be better served by cultivating the Indian Muslims and pandering over their demands against the Hindus, who were difficult to be subdued or turn servile.

Lord Wavell's Draft of Operation BREAKDOWN

On 1 September 1946 the Viceroy Lord Archibald P. Wavell wrote to the Secretary of State of India with the final draft of Operation BREAKDOWN with reference to Indian independence. This involved a phased withdrawal from southern India, to be followed by complete withdrawal by 31 March 1948. In other words, the Raj was to be dismantled within 18 months. Wavell said that the alternative would be a declaration that Britain would remain in India for another fifteen to twenty years. Prime Minister Clement Atlee was horrified by Wavell's proposal:

> An extraordinary plan ...(the) combined thinking of Wavell and his ICS advisors. They are going to move all the British out of India, up the line of the Ganges and put them on ships in Bombay. Winston (Churchil) would have been right to call it 'Operation Scuttle'. Out of the question. Indians would have assumed the Raj was on run. (Reid 2019: 219)

Earlier, Viceroy Lord Linlithgow and Secretary of the State Lawrence Zetland had 'decided that the Muslim League should be strengthened as to be on an equal footing with the Congress, despite the fact that in the 1936 elections the League had only 105 seats out of 489 Muslim seats and did not control a single government in any of the Muslim majority provinces. Jinnah saw that he was wanted.... Linlithgow pretty well admitted what he was up to: 'Jinnah had given me valuable help in standing against the Congress claims and I was duly grateful' (Reid 2019: 129).

It is claimed that Jawaharlal Nehru and Jinnah despised each other. No doubt, Nehru had said of Jinnah, 'You know the real reason why Jinnah left the Congress was because, about 1920, it suddenly broadened its base and began appealing to the masses.' Jinnah did not like this. Congress was no longer a party of the gentlemen. Jinnah always thought that the membership (to the Congress party) should be confined to those Indians who had passed matriculation, a standard which would have been high for any country, but for India it meant that the masses could never come in. He was a pucca snob. When the peasants began to join Congress, he was annoyed. Why? Because many of them did not speak English. They dressed in peasant clothes. It was no party for him.... (One may see Jinnah's attitude toward non-English speaking people: M.A.K. Azad, president of the Congress, spoke little English. Jinnah had said dismissively of him (to Linthithlow), 'He's like my bearer. He can understand a few words of English but can only answer "yes" or "no" (Reid 2019: 163).

Nehru said: He had no real feelings about Muslims. He wasn't really a Muslim at all. I know Muslims. I know the Koran. I have Muslim relatives and friends. Jinnah could not even recite a Muslim prayer and had certainly never read the Koran. But he was offered the leadership of the Muslim League (and) he saw the opportunity and accepted it. He had been a comparative failure as a lawyer in England, and this was a way out. (Mosley, pp. 26-7, quoted by Reid 2019: 193)

On the other hand, Jinnah described Nehru as 'an arrogant Brahmin who covers his Hindu trickiness with the veneer of Western education. When he makes promises, he always leaves a loophole, when he cannot find a loophole, he just lies' (Reid 2019: 215).

Wavell's antipathy towards the Congress has been copiously mentioned by Ishtiaq Ahmed in his book on Jinnah (Ahmed 2020: 214-459).

Wavell was looking at the role of Jinnah from a set prism in which the Congress and its leaders were the main trouble makers, with Jinnah responding to their actions. His contempt for the Congress was unmitigated indeed. The contrast between what the *Star of India* (a newspaper supportive of the Muslim League) reported about the instructions of the Secretary of the Calcutta Muslim League (to the rioters) and Jinnah's condemnation of violence is stark. At the level of high politics, Jinnah ... without mincing words said in his 29 July 1946 statement that the Muslim League was bidding goodbye to constitutional means and had even threatened civil war by famously using the metaphor of holding a pistol in his hand. Therefore, there can be no doubting that the 29 July statement on Direct Action was an ultimatum.

Jinnah had, on 31 July, refused to comment if Direct Action would be violent or not by asserting that he would not like to discuss the ethics of Direct Action. The interesting thing is that no legal proceedings were initiated against him or Suhrawardy or any other prominent Muslim League leader, whereas Gandhi, Nehru, Azad, Patel, Abdul Ghaffar Khan and others had, on several occasions in the past, been arrested for giving calls for Direct Action and civil disobedience. (Ahmed 2020: 386)

Further, Wavell's antipathy to Gandhi and the Congress was an open secret and by that token, he and other officials were sympathetic to Jinnah. (Ahmed 2020: 423).

The Cabinet Mission Plan of 16 May 1946

Regarding the princely states, it was declared that with the attainment of independence of India, whether outside or inside the British Commonwealth, British paramountcy would lapse. It would not be transferable to the new government. However, the princely states were willing to cooperate with the new developments in India. The precise form of cooperation would be decided later through negotiations.

The sections or groups would be constituted by the provinces. Group A should include the Hindu majority provinces of Madras, Bombay, the United Provinces, Bihar, the Central Provinces and Orissa. Group B would include the Muslim majority provinces of the north-west: the Punjab, the North West Frontier Province and Sind. Group C would include the Muslim-majority provinces of Bengal and Assam.

The Congress rejected the Cabinet Mission Plan for the simple reason that the central authority was weak. On the other hand, the Muslim League demanded a limited federal authority, which would be responsible only for foreign affairs, defence and communication. On 11 May 1946, Jinnah, on behalf of the Muslim League, listed the minimum conditions (10 in number) for an agreement: '7. The Union will be limited to three subjects: foreign affairs, defence and communications. Its financing will be decided by the joint meeting of the two constitution-making bodies' (Ahmed 2020: 347). There was a huge upheaval in Assam over linking it with the Muslim-majority province of Bengal. On the other hand, H.S. Suhrawardy spoke of 'Greater Bengal', which would include a portion of Bihar and the whole of Assam (Ahmed 2020: 428). Jinnah said to Lord Wavell that 'what he wanted was a nucleus Muslim territory surrounded by sufficiently additional territory to make it viable' (Ahmed 2020: 340). Jinnah insisted on 9 March 1946 that not only the whole of Bengal but Assam too, should be included in Pakistan.

Sanjay Hazarika writes how agitated the leaders of the Congress party of Assam became on inclusion of Assam with Bengal in the proposed Cabinet Mission plan (Hazarika 2011: 69-80). It was clear that for the sake of getting a united India, the Congress party was willing to let Assam go with Bengal without giving a careful consideration to its implications. A non-Muslim Assam was being unreasonably thrust upon Muslim Bengal without concern of the Assamese preference. A desperate Congress stalwart, Gopi Nath Bordolai, mounted a herculean effort to save the situation for the Assamese by courting Mahatma Gandhi at Noakhali in East Bengal. However, events moved fast and the new Viceroy, Lord Mountbatten informed the Muslim League stalwart, M.A. Jinnah, that he could not expect to get Assam on religious ground, as it was a non-Muslim state.

The Punjab premier, Sir Khizr Tiwana, confided to Cripps:

> The Muslim League had liked to keep the idea of Pakistan vague, so that every Muslim might interpret it as a sort of Utopia where his own ambitions would be satisfied. At the elections they identified it with Islam, the Koran and the Holy Prophet. At the same time it must be admitted that the Pakistan idea, in which Jinnah himself had not believed seven years ago, had now taken root among the educated classes. (Ahmed 2020: 341)

The Congress rejected the idea of interim government on 25 June 1946:

> ...Congress has aimed at establishing of a united democratic Indian Federation with a Central authority which would command respect from the nations of the world, maximum provincial autonomy and equal rights of men and women in the country. The limitations of the Central authority, as contained in the proposals, as well as the system of grouping of Provinces, such as the North West Frontier Provinces, and Assam, and some of the minorities, notably the Sikhs....The Committee are unable to accept the proposals for

formation of an interim Government as contained in the statement of June 16th. (Ahmed 2020: 360-1)

The Last British Viceroy: Lord Louis Francis Mountbatten Arrives at the Scene

Lord Mountbatten assumed the office of the Viceroy of India on 24 March 1947 amid much pomp and show. He found Gandhi a charming personality and Nehru as friendly. On the other hand, right from the start the relationship between him and Jinnah was one of mutual antipathy. He found Jinnah as cold, haughty, impregnable, dictatorial and psychopathic. With a view to guarding their defence and commercial interests, the British government was interested in keeping federal India intact in some or other form within the British Commonwealth. However, the existing administrative structure was not functioning to anybody's satisfaction. There were communal riots in various parts of the country and there was no effective mechanism to deal with the situation. The Muslim League was becoming aggressive day by day and the Congress ministers were getting frustrated, as their efforts were scuttled by their (Muslim League) adversaries. In such a situation, the Constitutional Advisor, N.B. Menon suggested an alternative plan to the Viceroy in Simla in May 1947. Two of them discussed the pros and cons of it threadbare. Once Mountbatten was convinced of its possibility of getting a consensus among the political parties, he cabled to London. The Plan was set. The new Plan envisaged a division of India into two on religious ground and they would continue to be members of the British Commonwealth. This came to be known as the Menon Plan (French 1997: 291-318; Basu 2020: 253-7). However, London was not humoured by this fast development, because they were unaware of the details and thus the implications. The Prime Minister Clement Atlee suggested

either a ministerial mission led by Sir Stafford Cripps fly out to Delhi, or Mountbatten must return to explain himself.... To his credit, Mountbatten stood firm. The Mountbattens and V.P. Menon arrived back to Delhi from Simla on 14 May (1947). With his characteristic drive and impetuosity, the Viceroy asked V.P. (Menon) to draw up a 'Heads of Agreement' draft, which would then be shown to the leaders of all major political parties (in London). He would leave for London on May 18 and would be taking V.P. with him. (Basu 2020: 256-7)

Rest was as simple as it appears. The British parliament passed the Indian Independence Act, 1947 on 18 July 1947, which stated:

As from fifteenth day of August, nineteen hundred and forty-seven, two independent Dominions shall be set up in India, to be known respectively as India and Pakistan. West Punjab, East Bengal, Sind and the Chief Commissioner's Province of Baluchistan were to be included in Pakistan. The boundaries of the East Bengal, West Punjab and Assam provinces will be decided by the Boundary Commission. The paramountcy over princely states was to cease with the transfer of power to the two dominions. They could remain independent or join either of the two dominions (Nicholas Mansergh and Penderel Moon: 1 (in London) 983: 233-49).

The Dominions Rush for the Princely States

Whether there were 561 princely states in the British India (Reid 2020: 237) or 565 (Basu 2020: 399), they were spread from Baluchistan in the west to Manipur in the east and Travancore in the south to Chitral, Hunza and Nagar in north in the Karakoram mountains. They were of different sizes in territory, population, religions, finances and other resources. Many of the rulers were known for their eccentricities and queer behaviour.

The Princes of India were a fascinating study in eccentricity. They were hedonistic, imperious and flamboyant. Some ruled the size of Germany, others lorded it over tiny specks the size of a handkerchiefs. The last decade of the Raj was halcyon in their memories. Nearly every ruler remembers armies of retainers, solid gold plates at dinner, chuckas of polo, jewels by Cartier and coffers overflowing with diamonds, rubies, emeralds and gold. They had been, for the most part, willing vassals of the British. (Basu 2020: 297)

There were five big states with precedence in that order approved by the British, which were termed by Lord Wavell out of fun: 'Hot Keeper Makes Good Breakfast' (Hyderabad, Kashmir, Mysore, Gwalior and Baroda (Reid 2020: 182). On the other hand,

Kathiawar was with 222 states within 22,000 square miles of interlaced,

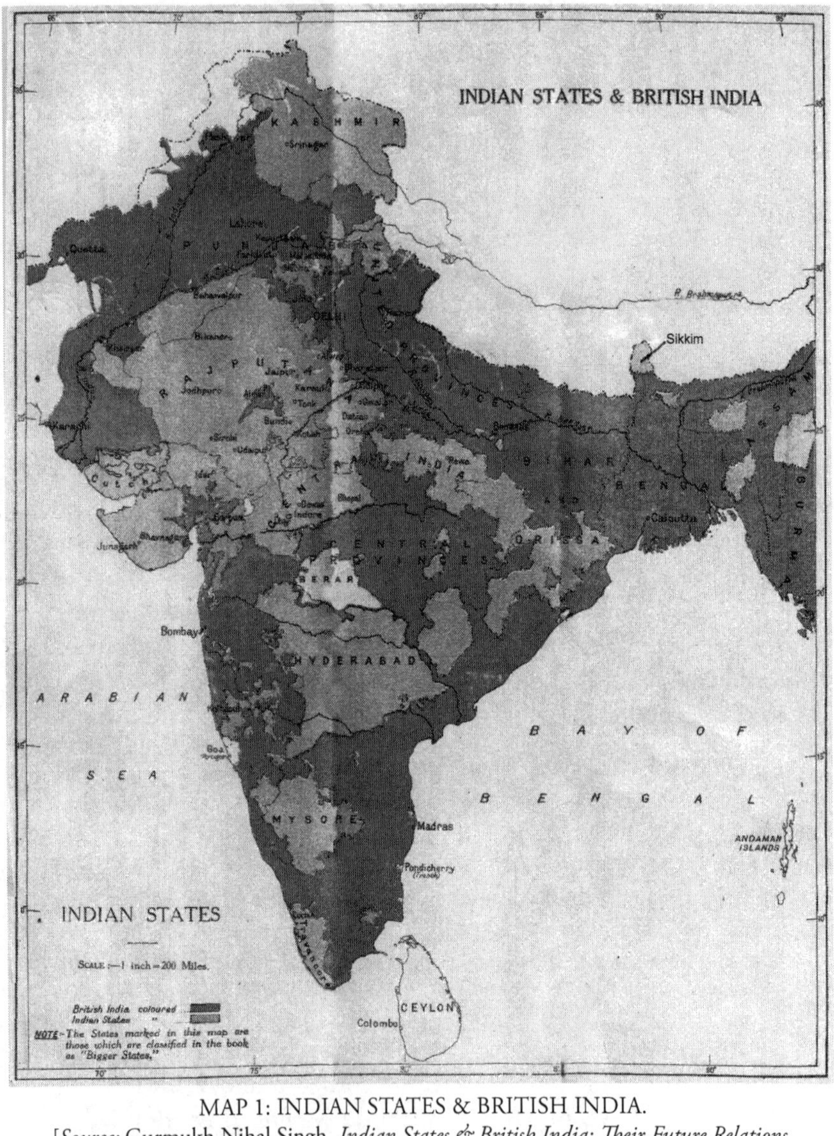

MAP 1: INDIAN STATES & BRITISH INDIA.
[*Source:* Gurmukh Nihal Singh, *Indian States & British India: Their Future Relations*, Benares: Nand Kishore & Bros., 1930, p. 381.]

interlocking land, with population of 4 million at the time of the transfer of power. As many as 46 states had an area of two or less than two square mile, even then none of them were as tiny as Vejanoness, which boasted of a territory of 0.29 square miles, a population of 206 and an annual income of five hundred rupees. But though there were so many states in Kathiawar, their financial resources were a mess. There were two states, for example – Gondal and Morvi – they had no financial revenue. (Basu 2020: 393)

Similar was the story of the princely states in Orissa, Chhattisgarh and Bundelkhand regions.

The Home Minister of the Indian Union, Sardar Vallabhbhai Patel and his Secretary of the State, V.P. Menon, insisted that the princes must sign the Instrument of Accession on three subjects: foreign affairs, defence and communication and rest of their affairs would be taken care of in course of time. There was sublime ambiguity with regard to the princely states in the British establishment at the time of their departure from India. The Congress party had decided at one point to abolish the princely states by the final stage of the freedom struggle. Thus, the princes were naturally apprehensive of their future in the Congress ruled India. The Congress did not seek accessesion of princely states located outside Indian Territory. K.S. Khurshid, the private secretary of Jinnah, writes: '…On the question of princely states, he felt Mr. Jinnah, being the clever tactician that he was, was playing for some higher stakes, but obviously he did not succeed' (Ahmed 2020: 584-5).

But Jinnah was totally unscrupulous about enticing the princely states into his gambit. He tried to entice non-Muslim rulers from the Hindu or Sikh majority states such as Jodhpur, Jaisalmer, Patiala and Nabha to join his Muslim homeland. Ultimately, Pakistan could manage to integrate the Muslim majority states of Bhawalpur, Khairpur, Kalat, and Chitral, Dir, Swat, Amb, Hunza and Nagar in the Karakoram mountains. The last six among the above were parts of Jammu & Kashmir till then. Two Muslim rulers of Hyderabad and Junagarh with predominantly Hindu subjects and surrounded by the Indian territories were unsuccessfully encouraged by Pakistan in joining her. Moreover, thousands of tribal raiders, trained and led by armed and demobilized Pakistani soldiers, invaded the state of Jammu & Kashmir, which sought support from India against the raiders in

1947, leading to its merger with India on 26 October 1947. Writes Sheikh Muhammad Abdullah:

> The Maharaja's accession (of Kashmir to the India) covered external affairs, communications and defence. Mountbatten as Governor General of India approved the accession but added to it the much celebrated caveat.... My Government desires that as soon as peace is restored in Kashmir and the state gets rid of the aggressors, the issue of accession shall be resolved after the people's will is taken into consideration. (Abdullah 2020: 292)

Similarly, on 5 December 1950, the Maharaja of Sikkim and Harishwar Dayal, the Indian Political Officer, Sikkim and Bhutan signed the Indo-Sikkim Treaty of 1950 at Gangtok, which stipulated Sikkim to be an Indian Protectorate and the Government of India would be responsible for its defence, external relations and communication. At the end, India successfully integrated as many as about 550 odd princely states in the Indian Union, which was in itself not a mean achievement.

Steps Adopted by the Indian Union to Consolidate the Country

British India was divided into two in 1947: India and Pakistan. This division was based on religious affiliation of the British subjects leading to violent migration of uprooted people from one part of British India to another in the country. On top of that, the country was yet to recover from the devastation caused during the Second World War, in which the British had unilaterally dragged India as a party. There was still rationing of the essential commodities in the country such as salt, sugar, cloth, cereals and kerosene oil. Moreover, the resources, in terms of men and material, were divided between the two countries. Creation of East Pakistan had also cut-off the province of Assam from the rest of the country in terms of road and railways communication, which needed time to be restored urgently. Furthermore, the princely states, scattered through the length and breadth of the country, where common people were agitating for merging with the Indian Union, needed to be integrated into the Indian Union.

In such a situation, the India Union took a pragmatic step.

Essentially, the States needed to be safe. India needed to secure their acceptance on these three subjects alone. External affairs, so that no State could act inimically to the interests of India; communications, which were necessary to maintain the economic lifeline of the country. However, [the] key was defence. This clause covered not only external aggression but internal unrest [as well]. Any potentially dangerous internal situation could merit an intervention on the part of the Union, should it see fit to do so. This was a useful clause, which was tweaked into integration process (of the Princely States), most notably in the case of Kashmir, Junagadh and Hyderabad ... Patel (Minister of State, Home and Deputy Prime Minister) himself had reservations about how 565 States could be persuaded to sign on the dotted line within such a tight deadline (of two months). V.P. (Menon, Secretary, and Ministry of States) however, took it as a challenge (which) he couldn't resist. I told Sardar that the shortness of time itself would work to our advantage. (Basu 2020: 293-4)

Location of Kashmir in the north-western corner of British India was advantageous to Pakistan. Normally, the Kashmiris would travel out from the valley via Punjab, which was controlled by Pakistan after 1947. Pakistan was determined to take Kashmir at any cost, but the Hindu ruler of the state could not make up his mind to join any one of the two on time. Egged by the Pakistani leadership and clandestine support from the still functioning British administrators, the Mahamud tribes from North West Frontier Province mounted Operation Gulmarg on 22 October 1947 by arson, loot, rape and devastation of the public properties and they reached Baramullah, close to Srinagar, the capital of Kashmir. The panicky Maharaja requested the Government of India for armed assistance against the invaders, which was reached only when he signed the Instrument of Agreement on 27 October 1947. Indian air and land forces mounted counter-attacks and the raiders' onward march was stopped. India went to the United Nations Organization under Article 35 of the Charter of the UNO against Pakistan for mounting an attack on Kashmir. And since then, the matter is still hanging on fire in the UNO.

The Muslim rulers of Junagadh and Hyderabad wanted to join Pakistan, but both states had majority of their subjects who belonged to the Hindu faith and they were also surrounded by the Hindu majority areas of the Indian Union. From India's point of view, these steps (by the two Muslim ruled states) were seen as dangerous, as they set the bad precedence for other states. So India launched Operation Polo against Hyderabad on 9 September 1948 and within a week the story of Hyderabad was complete with its merger in India. In course of time, States Reorganization Commission (SRC) would recommend in 1956 to break Hyderabad into three on the linguistic ground and merged them into Andhra, Karnataka and Maharashtra provinces respectively.

On the other hand, the Nawab of Junagadh had not only joined Pakistan, but also made arrangements by the end of October 1948 to fly away with all his assets, which he would carry. In the words of a historian,

> ...the Nawab decided that the time to abandon his principality had arrived. For a man who had spent so much of his last days as a dithering ruler, he moved with remarkable speed to protect his personal interests. A special plane was chartered, on to which was loaded the entire cash assets of the State, all the shares and securities of the Treasury, his favourite dogs, his favourite Begums and their children. As the plane prepared to take off, one of the Begums realized that in her hurry to catch the flight, she had forgotten her baby at the palace. She was summarily ordered off the plane. Her 'devoted' husband deposited her on the runaway, and told her to fend for herself and their child as best as she could. The plane took off for Karachi, leaving the hapless Begum on the tarmac. (Basu 2020: 337-8)

After that, the Government of India promptly clamped down on lawlessness and restored financial discipline by disposing off kennel of the dogs, which cost rupees 16,000 a month at the time. At last, India closed the chapter on Junagadh on 20 February 1949, when it was merged to form a new State of Saurashtra.

There was another problem faced by the new Republic of India.

> It was natural for (J.L.) Nehru and (Sardar Vallabhbhai) Patel to be concerned with communist activities in different parts of the country, particularly in what was then Hyderabad state and the provinces of Madras and Bengal. The Communists, taking a cue from Moscow, had rejected the independence of India as being a sham and denounced Gandhi and Nehru vituperatively. The new country racked by the horrors of Partition was now confronted by the threat of communist-led insurrections of the type that were being

witnessed in large parts of South East Asia, including neighbouring Burma. (Ramesh 2019: 342)

There were many problems for the new state of the Indian Union. And the leaders of new India were aware of many of them and they took many corrective measures. However,

> While a sense of unity, spatially, culturally or in religious terms, may have contributed to our understanding of India as it exists today, modern Indian ethos rests on more than a unified historical consciousness, however one sided, faulty or misplaced that may be. Bipin Chandra and Mridula Mukherjee, historians of modern India, 'have repeatedly drawn our attention to the vision of the Indian national movement, articulated by so many great women and men in different tongues and emphasizing specific elements more than others, but all very clear that equality, dignity, freedom of expression and diversity were to be the pivot on which the idea of India rested. The struggle for independence also opened up avenues for disavowal of pre-existing ideas and assimilation of new ones, including those related to women rights and the abolition of caste discrimination. The colonial context in the configuring of modern borders cannot be understated, and the new India was as much of the citizen in Nagaland or Mizoram, absent in hegemonic historical imaginations, as of Kashmir or Gujarat.' (Mahalakshmi 2020: 99)

So far as the territorial unity of the country was concerned, India inherited former British provinces as integral parts of the Republic. However, so far the princely states, big and small in territories, were concerned, they had signed the Instrument of Accesion to begin with only on three items: foreign affairs, defence and communitication. It was implied that they had already surrendered their paramountcy to the Indian Union, which India had inherited from the Britain. And once they had signed the terms of treaty with the Indian Union, many of them, especially smaller ones, were merged with adjoining provinces or constituted into a larger state such as Rajasthan. At last, the story of the princely states came to an end with the acceptance of the reports of the States Reorganization Commission (SRC), which had recommended merger of most of the smaller princely states in the adjoining states on the principle of linguistic affinity. The territorially largest Princely State of Hyderabad was broken into three parts on the linguistic ground and merged with adjoining Andhra, Maharashtra and Karnataka states on the recommendation of the SRC.

This issue of joining the Indian Union ONLY on three subjects of foreign relations, communication and defence will keep on recurring in the coming pages, as the nature of merger (either complete or limited to the three items) itself would be debated and interpreted differently. So far as the federal government was concerned, its main objective after 1947 was to tie the princely states within the Indian Union by the earliest. Its extent, modality and other details were left to convenience in the future. In reality, the Instrument of Accesession was in a way buying of time for the princes as well as the Indian Union in the surcharged environment of 1947. But two frontier states, Jammu & Kashmir and Sikkim, viewed it in course of time as the final commitment to them from the Indian Union. The Indian Union decided to clear this confusion in case of Kashmir in 1953 by arresting the Premier S.M. Abdullah and taking other administrative steps. Similarly, the Government of India took steps in 1975 to merge Sikkim into the Indian Union by abolishing Namgyal's dynastic rule in the principality. The frontier state of Assam came in discussion frequently earlier in this book. Two of her frontier districts, the Naga Hills and the Lushai (Mizo) Hills, raised the flags of revolt against the Indian Union, which caused enough political problems for the Union. We shall be dealing with in the next sections four locales from where dissenters hailed, and try to understand the circumstances in which they emerged and the consequences thereof the administration and the citizens. It is to be noted that the preamble of the Indian Constitution of India adopted on 26 January 1949 ensures equality of all citizens irrespective of cultural, ethnic, linguistic, political, racial, religious, and regional background.

REFERENCES

Ahmed, Ishtiaq, 2020, *Jinnah: His Successes, Failures and Role in History*, Penguin Random House India, New Delhi.

Basu, Narayani, 2020, *V.P. Menon: The Unsung Architect of Modern India*, Simon & Schuster, New Delhi.

Dalrymple, William, 2019, *The Anarchy: The East India Company, Corporate Violence, and the Pillage of an Empire*, Bloomsburry, New Delhi.

Dean, Riaz, 2019, *Mapping the Great Game: Explorers, Spies & Maps in Ninteenth Century Asia*, Penguin Random House India, New Delhi.

French, Patrick, 1997, *Liberty or Death: India's Journey to Independence and Division*, Penguin Books, New Delhi.

Hazarika, Sanjoy, 2011, *Strangers of the Mist: Tales of War and Peace from India's Norheast*, 2nd edn., Penguin Random House India, New Delhi.

Mahalakshmi, R., 2020, 'India in Historical Imagination' *Frontline*, 9 October 1999.

Nicholas, Mansergh and Penderel Moon, eds., 1983, *Transfer of Power*, vol. XII, Her Majesty's Stationery Office, London.

Owen, R., 1973, 'Imperial Policy and Theories of Social Change: Alfred Lyall in India', in *Anthropology and Colonial Encounter,* ed. Talat Asad and Ethaca Press, London, pp. 223-44.

Ramesh, Jairam, 2019, *A Chequered Briliance: The Many Lives of V.K. Krishna Menon*, Penguin Viking, New Delhi.

Reid, Walter, 2019, *Keeping the Jewel in the Crown: The British Betrayal of India*, Penguin Random.

PART B

Locale

3

Naga Hills District in the Province of Assam

The eastern-hill ranges or the Indo-Burmese ranges of the Himalaya start from the Dihing-Lohit knot between Siang and Buri-Dihing rivers and radiates westwards from there. From there Namkin mountains forms the boundary between Burma and Tibet (People's Republic of China) in the east. The southern ranges known as the Patkoi hills (Tai: the resting place for the Ahom invaders on the way to the Brahmaputra Valley in 1228) forms the boundary between India and Burma, and on which Saramati (12,500 ft), the highest peak, is located in Nagaland. One of its western upshots is Barail range, which enters Naga hills at its south-east corner and ultimately divides the state into two halves of north-eastern and south-western. The drainage system in the Naga hills is from east to west and north-east to south-west and, ultimately, various rivers such as Dikhu, Janji, Disoi and Dhansiri, join the Barak River in the district of Cachar. This region has one of the highest precipitations in the world and most of the rivers discharge their water ultimately into the River Brahmaputra. The Indian state of Nagaland is located on the Indo-Burmese borders and its modern history starts roughly from about 200 years back with the Burmese-Ahom conflict. Ahoms referred to the denizens of their south-eastern hills as Nogalok and possibly they had some limited and at times intimate interaction. For example, it is claimed that the fugitive Ahom prince, Godapani, was protected by Ao Nagas against the invading Burmese king.

MAP 2: NOTIONAL MAP OF NAGA HILLS
(*Source:* https://nagalandgk.com/history-7-formation-of-naga-hills/)

Indigenous Nagas, Their Culture and Economy and the British Intrusion

Perhaps the indigenous people of the land did not use a common term either for the people or their land. Thus the terms referring to them currently were given by the outsiders, for whom they were ferocious strangers. It was the land of people, who used to live in thatched huts on the hilltops or high on the hill slopes with a view to avoiding malaria fever from down below. Their demographic size was small; they were basically hunters of the wild games and lived on collected bovine's trotters, roots and fruits from the jungles. At times they fished in the nearby water bodies. They were aware of wet paddy cultivation, but their major economic activity was associated with the slash-and-burn type of rotational cultivation on hill slopes. They were organized on kin bands; under their village elders (*gaonburas*); chiefs, rulers such as the Konyaks or Semas. Angamis in the west were led by their clan elders and warriors. Aos in the middle were nearly democratic without a chief to begin with. The Nagas were surrounded by the Ahom kingdom in the north, Dimasa in the south-west and Mietei kings in the south-east. The Nagas were such ferocious warriors that none of these neighbouring kingdoms could subjugate them. Their hilltop villages were heavily guarded by youth bands located right at the imposing village gates in their youth dormitories.

The Western presence appeared in the region in the year 1838 in two forms: first, the American Baptist missionaries landed in Dibrugarh to open a mission station at Jaypore to convert the local people. But soon they had to close it for a more favourable location of Jorahat. Second, the Assam Company was founded in London and Calcutta to begin tea plantation in the region with a nursery at Chhabua and experimental plantation at Jaypore in the district of Lakhimpore with local resources. The second enterprise turned out to be one of the most successful British enterprises in the world, which is still going strong after nearly 200 years. Tea plantation began as a labour-intensive enterprise, which required inexpensive and assured labour-force for the success of the industry. However, the region was depopulated after the Burmese incursion. The indigenous economy of the region was based on the extraction of the forest produce largely through communally organized labour force. The individual economic efforts in terms of earning wages and transaction through money were yet to emerge in the region (Sinha 1993: 89).

In such a situation, the earliest tea planters such as Charles Bruce thought of recruiting the Singhpho Chief on monthly basis to collect tea leaves from the jungle of tea plants. Subsequently, an Ahom dignitary, Maniram Dewan, was employed to help recruit plain tribes. Some Mon Nagas were contracted on inducement to large white shells, cowries, lead and tin-made armlets and glass tumblers to work on plantations. In certain cases, the tribesmen were induced to work on payment of rum. On one occasion, 60 Nagas offered to work on the plantation and demanded a buffalo as their combined remuneration. In spite of these inducements, the planters failed to recruit sufficient number of dependable local labour. The Naga labourers were not only seasonal, but the same set of labour was not ready to work on the plantation for consecutive seasons. Consequently, they required coaching time and again in the delicate process of tea plucking. Historian of the tea plantations in Assam, H.A. Antrobus recorded the human aspect of this encounter:

> ... the Singhphos, who only worked under their own chiefs and would brook no control as to whether they would work or not ... had no inclination to work for any one so long as they had enough rice and opium for their immediate need. (Antrobus 1957: 375)

Eastern Himalayan and Patkoi foothills were covered with dense evergreen rain forests, where plenty of wildlife and variety of fish were available. These jungles were also notorious for malarial pests, which worked as a deterrent to the permanent human settlement. However, these areas were the hunting grounds for wild games of the sturdy young men descending from the hilltops. They would fish in the various water bodies available around. These areas provided the hillmen usual meeting grounds with various ethnic communities in their sorties, especially during the winter months. Not only that, there were locations, especially on river junctions, where weekly *haat*s were held, in which the hillmen would exchange their hill produce with that of salt, cotton threads, iron bars, trinkets, etc. So by tradition, many of the hill communities claimed certain portions of the foothills as theirs.

In the days gone by, the hillmen would descend chasing some games to the foothills; if they would miss the game, they would fish in the waterbody in the foothills and return with the catch. If no game was available, they would catch someone's domestic animals instead of returning empty handed. Not infrequently, they would catch some sundry individual, if resisted, slash some body parts or drag the unfortunate creature to their hilltop abode. Incidentally, this vast area right from Patkoi hills to Darjeeling hills in the Himalayan foothills in the north and all through the Barail ranges up to Hill Tipperah on the southern bank of the Brahmaputra River was ideal for growth of tea plants. And thus most of the tea plantations were located in the British provinces of Assam and Bengal and not in the hill districts, as they were deliberately laid down on the lands outside the Inner Line for the hill districts drawn in 1873 by the administration. And that was the beginning of the territorial disputes between Assam with all the 'hill states' in the region: Meghalaya, Arunachal, Nagaland and Mizoram.

As soon as tea bushes were discovered, there was a mad rush for appropriate locations on the site. Finally, the Governor-General Lord William Bentinck appointed in 1832 Captain Jenkins, the Commissioner of Assam, to report on the resources of Assam. Captain Jenkins appeared to be in a hurry and he filed his report on 22 July 1932 recommending 'a scheme of colonization by the Europeans on the ignorant and demoralized state of native inhabitants'. Furthermore, Jenkins report advocated a scheme of speedy colonization by a class of European planters to invest their capital in cash crops. As the war ravaged local population did not have means to invest in land, he recommended their replacement with that of the European colonizers. For that matter Jenkins wrote,

> To obtain the full advantages that could accrue from the European settlers, it appears to me that the grants (of the Land) must be altogether freehold, subject to no other condition than that of a fixed and an unalterable rate of rent and absolutely unencumbered, with any stipulations in regard to ryots and sub-tenants.

These recommendations were incorporated in the Wasteland Rules of 6 March 1838. Naturally, in an unsettled and depopulated province of Assam, there was little competition for the white planters from the local population, who were endowed with courage, endurance, fortitude and state patronage.

The so-called wasteland was offered to the colonizers on a 45-year lease basis on the condition that the one-fourth of the allotted plot must be cleared within five years. Otherwise, the lease was to lapse. No applicant with less than 100 acres of land lease at a time and a capital at the rate of Rs. 3 per acre was entertained. One-fourth of the leased land was to be held revenue-free in perpetuity. For the rest of the grant, no revenue was to be paid for the initial 5 to 20 years depending on the type of wasteland. All these resulted into a situation in which:

> The wastelands settlement policy tempted the planters to grab more land than what was required or what they could manage. This was because such lands provided them with much more resources than what land as a factor of production ordinarily denotes. They contained necessary housing materials including, in many cases, even valuable timber. Being transferable under the 1854 Rules, such lands could later be sold with unearned profit. Above all, labourers could also be settled as tenants on the surplus lands of the plantations like so many serfs tied to the soil. It was an additional bait to allure land hungry tribal peasants from famine stricken areas outside Assam.... (The planters) were the biggest landlords in the countryside they dominated, but they paid the lowest average rates per acres of holdings. Not only did they employ wage workers, but also tenant cultivators on their lands, so that in peak season the latter could provide them with casual labour. The planters usurped the grazing fields and encroached upon the jhum rights of the tribal shifting cultivators. They often disrupted inter-village communications by fencing in portions of existing public roads and denying rights of way to the villagers. There were cases where cultivators' lands not regularly settled, were sold as waste lands to tea companies over the heads of their occupants (Guha 1988: 14-15).

The entire plantation paraphernalia was a strange intrusion in the local indigenous economy for the profit of the investors in the industry seated in distant metropolis of Calcutta and London.

Naga Hills and Communities thereof

Soon after conquering Assam from the Burmese, the British began to move to still unchartered frontiers in the east towards Burma. Thus, it were the British who discovered 'Nagas' and the 'Naga Hill District' in the last quarter of the nineteenth century out of a variety of communities inhabiting various hills, woods and rivers slopes on left bank of river Brahmaputra. The communities were invariably settled on the hilltops or higher slopes as a defence mechanism against their warring adversaries and for avoiding malarial insects causing fever from the low lying areas. They were engaged in slash-and-burn type of rotational cultivation (*jhumming*), hunting games in the woods and collecting roots and fruits from the forests. They were known to enslave strangers, enemies, and war-captives. They were alleged to chop off heads of strangers, enemies and anybody unknown to them. They were ferocious warriors, who used to live in well-fortified villages guarded by the young and alert sentries all twenty-four hours. Warfare was considered to be a normal regular activity and most of the settlements were in conflict with each other. They guarded their territorial limits jealously. However, they often went to the foothill fairs and *haat*s (markets) for exchanging their forest produce with salt, cotton thread and iron implements such as spears, *dao* (a crucade bigger knife) or the like.

Historian Visier Sanyo claims that Angami Nagas lived in the fortified villages, which were like Greek city states. He also refers to a common ancestral village, Khezhkenoma (Hazarika 2011: 92), from where Angami, Chakesang, Sema, Lotha and other tribes migrated to western Nagaland. It may be another illustration of myth keeping in mind the political exigency. On the other hand, there is enough evidence that there was very little contact among the various Nagas before the arrival of the British. Verrier Elwin refers to a story of seven Nagas of various communities travelling together to the plains to visit a *haat* (Elwin 1961). They stopped at stream side and tried to converse among themselves. To begin with, they asked one another what had they got in their bags for lunch, but none of them understood the replies. At this, they profusely laughed at themselves and then they opened their bags. An lo and behold! All of them had roasted rice and green chillies with them for the travelling lunch, which they then shared with one another. And possibly that is how their *lingua franca* Nagamese (pidgin Assamia mixed with terms from various Naga languages) developed, which continues to be the means of communicatation among them and the outsiders.

Nineteenth century was the age when the European Imperial powers propagated a pseudo-scientific racial theory of the Whiteman's superiority. And conversely, the rest of the world was termed as barbarians. The worst form of nomenclature they accorded to the distant small communities who lived in the hills, mountains and jungles is that they were savage, primitive and naked hunters. The colonial scholars of the time would isolate some physical features or cultural traits, invariably out of context, as the unique attribute of a community, or a stage of development, and that would come to be accepted as the scientific knowledge. For illustration, some stray kinky hair among a few of the Angamis linked them to distant Igorot of Luzon in the Philippines. Not only that, some of the Nagas and other communities of Assam were linked to Malaysia, Indonesia, Micronesia, Madagascar, or even to New Zealand. Dr John H. Hutton, ICS, who was trained in anthropology and was the author of two monographs on two important Naga communities and had married a Naga girl (Steyn 2010: 49), played a critical role in it. He was associated with the Nagas in general and Angamis in particular for about a quarter of a century since 1912. It was he who propagated alleged similarities of between the Nagas people of the Pacific region and ignored their centuries-old contact with the Assamese in the adjoining plains. In fact, there was a motive behind the enterprise to show that the Nagas and rest of the tribal communities in the hills were dissimilar to the Assamese and the rest of the Indians.

Creation of the Naga Club and Coupland Plan for the Crown Colony

Dr Hutton, the Deputy Commissioner of the Naga Hills, was asked in 1915 to recruit coolies from among the Nagas, who would constitute the Naga Coolie Corps to be sent to France to assist the Allied forces in the First World War. When these coolies, about 2,000 of them, returned to Kohima in 1918, Hutton took them under his wings and planted the idea of a Naga Club among them. Many of the village headmen were roped in as the founding members of the Club. However, in the absence of political education and experience, 'the

Club had (the) limited purpose or aims of representing Naga interests (?) to the government' (Hazaika 2018: 49, 383) without permission of the Deputy Commissioner. Nobody knew the functionaries, programmes and activities and even material support system of the club for a decade. Thus for the next ten years, the club was possibly dysfunctional and was hardly in the news. Look at Z.A. Phizo's claim while still in the primary school,

> He established a solid relationship with the medico-evangelist (Dr Sidney Rivenburg of the American Baptist Church, Kohima).... Within three years, while still a student, he had become a one-man band running the Kohima Naga Club, which aimed to forge a common Naga social awareness, by combining the duties of a secretary, treasurer, maintenance man and gardener all rolled into one. (Steyn 2010: 42)

What type of club was it, which was run by a primary school boy? And this was the club, which would petition to the Indian Statuary Commission in 1929? The Naga Club was with the all-powerful Deputy Commissioner, J.H. Hutton all through and even in 1945. It was revived by another Deputy Commissioner, Charles R. Pawsey, when another batch of Naga coolies came back from Europe from their war duties.

Anybody may take the credit for activating the forum and drafting the memorandum (see Phizo's alleged role, Steyn 2010: 49-50), but again, it was the same J.H. Hutton, who was instrumental in getting a memorandum presented to the Simon Commission on 10 January 1929 at Kohima.

> At that time there were few Nagas who could write in English, but District Commissioner Hutton was determined that a memorandum as such should be submitted. Twenty Nagas signed the memorandum, among them were a range of government employees who were mostly interpreters (*dobhashis*) and teachers as well as a doctor, an overseer, and a clerk. (Hazarika 2018: 50)

Moreover, the signatories 'claim(ed) to represent all those tribes to which we (they) belong: Angamis, Kukis, Semas, Lothas, and Rengmas' (Steyn 2010: 174). Names of the twenty signatories were arranged in four columns of five each. After that, for the next fifteen years, the Naga Club remained dormant. It was revived only after the end of the Second World War, when another contingent of Naga coolies returned from Europe.

The last British Deputy Commissioner of Naga Hills, Charles Ridley Pawsey (1938-48), inspired some of the more exposed Nagas to turn the Naga Club into the Naga Hills District Tribal Council (NHDTC) in April 1945. Pawsey's intention was to take the help of the forum for the reconstruction of the district after the devastation during the Second World War, which was fought in the district, but it did not work to his satisfaction.

He tried again the following year with more success. With active participation of Kevichusa, the most influential (Angami) Naga government official of the day, the Naga National Council (NNC) was formed with aims and objectives of the NHDTC, eschewing politics in favour of social projects. Mayang Nocha, a teacher was its first president. Two months later, a young intellectual of ideological conviction, Theyiechuthia Sakhrie, became secretary of the council (Steyn 2010: 69-70).

Thus, there was a sequence of developments: ICS anthropologist administrators and their racial prejudice, establishment of Coolie Corps, Naga Club, Crown Colony, and ultimately Naga National Council (NNC).

Sir Robert N. Reid (1883-1964) joined the ICS in 1907 and worked in Bengal for the next three decades, when he was appointed as the Governor of Assam in 1937. J.H. Hutton was the Chief Secretary of the Province and the Governor's Secretary was another ICS, J.P. Mills, who had begun his career in Naga Hills District along with Hutton. These two experts on Naga Hills worked on the mental make-up of Governor Robert Reid. Hutton showed how Nagas and the frontier tribes like them neither racially, historically, culturally, nor linguistically had any affinity with the people of the plains of Assam. Moreover, the administration of the Excluded Districts such as the Naga Hills, was also on a different plane than that of districts in the Brahmaputra Valley. Hutton considered that the true solution to their administration was the gradual creation of self-governing communities, semi-independent in nature, for whose external relations the Governor of Assam would be alone responsible. Reid was greatly influenced by Hutton, as his 22-page Report refers to J.H. Hutton about a dozen times. The Report also contains at least four long quotations running into several paragraphs from Hutton's writings. Similarly, Reid took help from the writings of J.P. Mills for drafting his Report. Thus, these two scholar-bureaucrats took upon themselves to champion the cause of the Excluded Hill Districts such as Naga Hills, the Lushai Hills and the unadministered Frontier Areas in the North East and East as distinct from India and Burma. And it was they who provided fodder for Governor Robert Reid's fanciful idea of the Crown Colony and Reginald Coupland's Coupland Plan for the North Eastern Frontier of India and the Burmese Hills.

These two scholar-administrators wrote the first authentic monographs on the various Naga tribes: Angami and Sema (Hutton), Lhota Nagas, Ao and Rengma (Mills), which were published some hundred years back. However, these classic monographs still provide the first authentic pre-Christian social base and any discussion on the Nagas remains inconclusive without reference to them. Incidentally, both of them were re-employed in two leading departments of anthropology in universities, Cambridge (Hutton) and London (Mills) approximately for about a dozen of years each after their superannuation. While it was Hutton who provided critical stimulus to Sir Robert Reid for writing, *A Note on the Future of the Present Excluded, Partially Excluded and Tribal Areas of Assam* (November 1941), pleading for a Crown Colony in Assam Hills, Mills authored *A Note on the Future of the Hill Tribes of Assam and the Adjoining Hills in a Self-governing India* (October 1945). Hutton canvassed his ideas on the Frontier tribes; he wrote:

(1) on March 17, 1928 (at page 111-22 of the Assam Government's Memoranda prepared for the Indian Statuary (Simon) Commission);
(2) on July 6, 1930 (at 31-34, notes in Assam Secretariat Proceedings, Political (Reformed) A, December 30, Nos. 1-3);
(3) on September 18, 1935 (at pages 7-9 notes in Assam Secretariat Proceedings, Political A, December 1936, Nos. 1-30); and
(4) 'Problems of Reconstruction in the Assam Hills', Presidential Address at the Royal Anthropological Institute of Great Britain and Ireland, 1945.

Hutton's colleague, N.E. Parry, ICS, who had worked for many years in the Excluded Lushai Hills district and also in the Partially

Excluded Garo Hills district, offered two alternatives for the future administrative set-up of these frontier districts. He suggested (i) creation of a Hill Division under a Commissioner directly under the Governor of Assam or (ii) a North-East Frontier Province to comprise backward regions of Burma and Assam under a Chief Commissioner. Ultimately, the proposal would include Chittagong Hills of Bengal, Tripura Princely State, Lushai Hills, Manipur Princely State, Naga Hills, Balipara, Lakhimpur and Sadiya Frontier Tracts, Khasi Hills, Garo Hills of Assam and Chin Hills and the hill districts of Burma. The author of the Report happily accepted Mills' suggestion to propose Imphal as the capital of the Crown Colony, as it had an airport unlike Shillong in the Khasi Hills. It is said that only 50 copies of the Report were printed in October 1941, and a copy of the proposal was sent to the Governor-General of India, Lord Wavell. Wavell gave a copy of the Report to the Secretary of State of India, Lord L.S. Amery in London, who enthusiastically shared his copy with a young political scientist, Reginald Coupland. Coupland enlarged it and added further details of a possible British Crown Colony in the Indo-Burmese Frontiers in the event of British withdrawing from India and Burma. He pleaded in his publication, *The Future of India*, for the amalgamation of the tribal areas of Burma and India into a British Colony separate from India and Burma. In this way, Reid's private and confidential report turned out to be a public document known as the Coupland Plan, which was publicly debated as if it was an official document.

The proposal for the creation of a Crown Colony and suggestion of the Coupland Plan in the hill districts of India and Burma was almost ignored by major political parties in India. Some of the active tribal leaders of the affected region out-rightly rejected the proposal. The issue of amalgamating the hill districts of Burma and India was considered in a meeting of the Committee on the Scheduled Areas on 5-11 December 1942.

> A vote was taken whether the Scheduled Areas of Burma should be amalgamated in whole or part with similar areas outside Burma to form a North East Frontier Agency. Four (out of five) members voted that the amalgamation should not be resorted to.... The Chairman of the Commission of Scheduled Areas of Burma, H.J. Mitchell, had prepared a long confidential note on the subject which may have been read by other members.... Mitchell

concluded his note by saying that the proposal for amalgamation of the Scheduled Areas of India and Burma into an agency administered from the Whitehall should be dropped. (Syiemlieh 2014: 11)

Sir Andrew G. Clow (1890-1957), successor to Sir Robert Reid as the Governor (1942-7) of Assam, demolished the arguments advanced for the sake of creating the Crown Colony point by point. He wrote on the role of the two scholar-administrators and the context in which they worked in the hill districts of Assam:

> Even so, service in the pre-war Assam, which was more backward and isolated than most Indian provinces, was a handicap which only the most vigorous officers entirely overcame. And the officers who spent long periods in the hills tended to deteriorate. The man who is dealing year in and year out with primitive peoples, and seldom has to pit his brain against other educated minds or face the currents of a wider world, and who does not lose 'edge' is exceptional. The result, even when the physical vigour is maintained, appears in a settling into mental grooves and, in some cases, the loss of a sense of proportion. (Clow, Andrew G. in Syiemlieh 2014: 205).

Interestingly, Andrew Claw found his Advisor to the Tribal Affairs, J.P. Mills, 'more regressive' between the two anthropologists (Syiemlieh 2014: 194). But it looks as if the Governor's office left behind some understanding among the Deputy Commissioners of the Excluded Areas that their districts should be provisionally associated for a period of ten years with the future Government of India. And that is why Sir Andrew Claw's successor, Sir Akbar Hydari, included that clause in the Agreement with the Nagas. In the same way, possibly at the instance of the Deputy Commissioner of the Lushai Hills district, the (Mizo) tribal leaders wished to align with India provisionally for a period of ten years in 1947.

Christianity and the Naga World

There is a deep rooted Western view that the history of the Third World really begins from the time when they were 'discovered' and integrated into the history of Western expansion and progress. It all began in 1493, hardly a year after Christopher Columbus' discovery of the New World (America), when Pope Alexander VI divided the

New World between Spain and Portugal and termed the conquest of foreign territories as the sacred extension of 'God's Kingdom on Earth'. Thus, from the very beginning the conquest of the distant lands by the Western imperialistic powers had been associated with a strongly developed sense of Christian Mission. Since then, the colonial authorities and the missionaries have worked more or less in overlapping areas. Both were conscious of representing and disseminating Christian culture: mission and civilization went hand in hand (Witvliet 1985).

In the same tradition, the early British administrators believed that the conversion to Christianity and spread of Western education through the missionaries might lead to 'civilizing' the 'heathen' and 'pacification' of certain tribes. Captain Francis Jenkins, the Governor-General's Agent and Chief Commissioner of Assam in the 1830s, was one such a person, who was enthusiastic to contribute his money for settling the missionaries in the newly conquered province of Assam in the 1840s. Charles Bruce, the pioneer tea planter, persuaded Jenkins to invite American Baptist Missionaries working among the Shan tribes of Burma to Sadiya in upper Assam. The missionaries did come to Sadiya, and then they shifted to Sibsagar which was closer to the Naga Hills (Barpujari 1985: 2).

Rev. Bro. Edward Winter Clark, a trained missionary from Rochester Theological Seminary, along with his wife, Mary, Clark reached Sibsagar in June 1869 to take charge of the mission there and the printing press along with it. The couple was confronted with disquieting climatic conditions of the region and absence of good response to missionary activities in the plantations. The Clarks got busy in looking for a way out and took initiative to create new possibilities. Among other things, the Clarks encouraged an Assamese evangelist, Godhula, to visit an Ao Naga village, Haimong, for exploring the possibility of evangelization of this area. Godhula returned with nine young Aos, who were baptized on 11 December 1872. As against the apathy at Sibsagar from among the tea plantation labourers, as many as two dozen Aos were converted to Christianity within six months as part of the Sibsagar Church (Downs 1971: 65). Incidentally, the Ao region uptil then did not form an administrative part of the British province of Assam. And thus, missionary activities among the Aos were entirely the private initiative of the Clark couple.

The Clarks then moved to the Ao Naga Hills in 1873 at Molong and then to village Impur in the year 1876, almost in the heart of the Ao community, from where E.W. Clark would retire to the USA in 1911. For his initiative in moving to the Ao Hills, Rev. Clark came to be known as the inventor of the 'Naga Field' for evangelization. He produced textbooks in Ao on theological and biblical themes in Roman script for the first generation of Ao students attending the schools. He wrote the first Ao-Naga Dictionary, a pioneering work, by which he standardized the Ao dialect into a language. Rev. Clark was credited to have started the first Ao Baptist Association, the precursor of ABAM in 1897 at village Molong. The first subject on the programme of association meeting was the prayer. Then,

> other topics such as evangelization, the Holy Spirit, Christian benevolence, should the Nagas bury their dead? Should all Christians learn to read? By what changes in food, housing, sanitation, and clothing shall Christians better their mode of living (compared to non-Christian Aos)? (Clark 1978: 143)

Longkumer, an Ao missionary, reviews the growth of the Ao Baptist Church and divides the hundred year of its history into three phases: (i) establishment of the first church in Nagaland, (ii) expansion of the churches, 1897 to 1926, (iii) expansion of the churches, 1927 to 1972 (Longkumer 1988: 15-25). The Ao Baptist Association organized its centenary (1872-1972) as a year-long festival and tried to take stock of the messianic movement. From 24 in 1872 to 368 in 1900; then 8973 in 1926; 16,680 in 1950 and finally 58,757 Christians out of 59,859 Aos in 1971 (Philip 1983: 78). In this way, almost the entire Ao community had turned Christian within a hundred years. We shall see below how the newly adopted Baptist Naga Christianity turned out to be a critical factor in the ethno-political consolidation of Aos along with other Nagas.

To begin with, the British Colonial administration could not provide any security to Rev. Clark, when the missionary moved to Molong village close to Sibsagar. On the other hand, the government 'pacification forces' did not hesitate to take help from the missionaries in their efforts. In fact, the missionaries pleaded for the extension of the British rule to the Naga Hills in the interest of their evangelical activities, as they considered the British Empire to be a Christian government favourable to them (Clark 1978: 126-7). Two ICS offers, J.H. Hutton and J.P. Miles, were of the view that the role of the Baptist missionaries among the tribes in general and Nagas in particular had been injurious and disruptive to their culture (Hutton 1921; Miles 1973). Though the missionaries felt that their strategy of charity, literacy and primary health programmes turned the tribes into good Christians, in the eyes of the British administrators and many other observers, these were possibly the inducements to conversion to Christianity. The converted tribals might turn to be loyal to the administration, but they could as well be defiant, if not rebels.

W. Chubanungba Ao wrote the memoirs of his centenarian father who had taken part as a porter in Abor Expedition in 1911 and the First World War 1917 in North Africa and Europe and who had seen how animist Aos got converted to Christianity:

> The saab (the Whiteman, here it was Sub-Divisional Officer, Mokokchung, Naga Hills District in the first decade of twentieth century, Jack Francis Needham) was delighted to be with us and even participated in the folk dances. The British always respected and honoured our cultural festivals. When the Saab came to visit us, the gaunbura would wait outside the village-gate to receive him. We showed him the respect that his official status deserved and welcomed him warmly. He was always courteous and cheerful and spoke meaningful words and made relevant points only. He would hand out *jorep* (cigar) to us and even pick up a few morsels from a plate of food. They had no taboo in eating pork, beef or other meat like us. They were warriors like us; we fought with spears and daws and they fought with guns. (Ao 2017: 21-2)

W.C. Ao records that his father-in-law, W. Senkalemba, who was a Dobhashi in the Sub-Divisional court from 1920 to 1960 and had been a member of the Coolie Corps to Europe, assessed the role of missionaries and the British administration in the Naga hills:

> Though the functional roles of the American Missionaries and the English Administration were of different natures, they conferred and shared ideas with the singular purpose of ushering in some positive changes in our society. One of the most enduring contributions would be the introduction of formal education and the retention of our own language. (Ao 2017a: 42-3)

All these paved the way for conversion to Christianity. There was a change in attitude as well. Look at what Havildar W. Ao advised his school-going son, W.C. Ao:

> Of course, no one can compel you to become a Christian; it would all be up to you. Later on, if you happen to discover that their belief has a positive influence on you and want to follow it, we would not stop you from becoming a Christian. We do not regard Christianity as an inedible or poisoned fruit. You will be able to judge for yourself. (Ao 2017: 70)

Unlike the Ao situation, the American Baptist missionary, C.D. King from Ukhrul (among the Tankhul Nagas from the adjoining Manipur princely state) moved to the Angami Nagas field at Kohima in 1885. Again, unlike the Ao field, where the missionaries moved from the plains of Assam in Sibsagar to an Ao village in the hills on the fringe, they came to Kohima, the district headquarters in the heart of the Angami tribe. The missionaries were the forerunners to the British administration among the Aos, which was established in 1890 with Mokokchung as the sub-divisional headquarters. Among the Angamis, the case was the exact opposite; the British had already reached the foothills at Chumekedima in 1872 and then to the district headquarters at Kohima in 1878, and only then, the American Baptist missionaries moved to Kohima after seven years. The missionaries would settle down in the Mission compound at Kohima, closeby to the Deputy Commissioner's compound, as if in the shadow of the British administration. Physical proximity to the administrative headquarters possibly gave the impression to the nearby tribal folks that conversion to Christianity was also part of the administration, which was seen by the Angamis as an intrusion. Naturally, the progress of evangelical activities was slow to the extent that within the first 15 years, there were only four converts at the Kohima station.

Incidentally, Angamis' conversion to Christianity picked up momentum by the beginning of the twentieth century. Almost all the Angamis, like the Aos, were Christians and within the next five decades other Naga communities from the eastern part of Naga Hills did not lag behind in converting themselves to Christianity. With the exception of some small communities far away on the Burmese frontiers, the entire Nagaland had turned to Christianity. They are very proud to be Christians. But the question is what type of Christianity was it? What was the texture of Naga Christianity? What made it so attractive that the tribal folk turned to Christianity within a few decades? And what happened to their indigenous faith, their world view, and nuances of their cultural heritage, ancestor worship, kinship ties, their myths and indigenous folk ethos? On the other hand, construction of the subject in the evangelical mould requires the internalization of a set of values, an ineffable manner of seeing and being. While the colonial process often entitled material disposition, the critical part of subjection of native peoples lay in the subtle colonization by the missionaries of the indigenous modes of perception and practices.

Elizabeth Colson reports from Tonga Valley, Zambia on the impact of Christianity on the indigenous faith. The hymns, prayers and the order of service were treated almost as though they were magical formulae which would bring about the desired result, the control of European knowledge. Equating the Bible with the source of truth, was the source of European power and wealth. This belief convinced the new converted Christians that those who learned to read could acquire knowledge and power which the Europeans possessed! The power and position of the European was for taking; the Bible was a means to an end (Colson 1970). The Naga scenario post-conversion to Christianity vis-à-vis their indigenous worldview, cultural ethos, ancestor worship, kinship, clan and tribal solidarity and the new package of individuality, self-promotion, objectivity and search for truth demand dispassionate analysis and clarity (Sinha 1994: 88).

The British Moves to the Naga Hills

Khonoma historian, Visier Sanyo, who earned his Master's and PhD degrees from North Eastern Hill University, Shillong in early 1980s and taught history, claims that Angamis were not typical tribes like others in the neibourhood. Angami villages were something like Greek city states of ancient times. An Angami village has its own territory of fertile fields for wet paddy cultivation; hill-slopes for slash-and-burn type of rotational cultivation (locally known as *jhum* cultivation) and forested hillocks for hunting and collecting fruits and roots. They too had satellite and dependant villages around who provided them support system in the hours of need. They too had friendly and enemy villages from among the neighbourhood. They were organized in the warrior guilds manner. Similarly, every Angami village had its defence walls, watch towers with sentries, and imposing entrance gates with motifs engraved, painted or erected in the form of wooden or stone slabs. Both friends and enemies were appropriately welcome to enter the village through these gates. In one way, these villages were self-sufficient in themselves as per their simple needs and they could barter their products against the articles of defence and adornment. Similarly, games, sports, songs, tales, riddles and colourful folk dances were organized and for that, the young folk were duly trained by the village experts.

It is said that a British officer, Lieutenant Vincent, captured Mezoma, a neighbouring village of Khonoma in November 1849. He tried to repeat the same performance with that at Khonoma, which was heroically opposed by Angami warriors to the extent that the intruders had to withdraw from the battle. But it was a contest in which both the parties appreciated one another's capabilities. The British forces were led by Major Henry, who was supported by Lieutenants Campbell, Vincent and Bivar and a complement of medical staff. Khonoma's warriors led by Pehlu fought bravely on the day, but against the unknown artillery attacks their traditional armaments were no match to the occasion. The defenders had suffered heavily, and a large chunk of village defence embankment was demolished and the empty village was captured by the British forces.

An ex-army officer describes the aftermath of Khonoma's tribulations:

> By secret routes that night, the women, children and old people, laden with *jhapas*, left Khonoma to make their way up the cliff-like slopes and dark chasms of the Barail range. There they hid in dank caves, while Khonoma fell to bombardment of the British guns. The slaughter of the very old and of livestock left behind was as horrific as senseless.... Pelhu and most of his surviving warriors extricated themselves by the same secret paths, little more than game tracks, used by earlier escapees, aided by a great pall of smoke blanketing the forest, as proud Khonoma crumbled into flame.... (However)

the essence that was Khonoma, the will of its people, had not been broken. The village had been destroyed, its population scattered, its cultivations ruined; but no power on earth could shake its resolve to be free. A new bitterness would enter its soul, a gnawing bitterness, which like a smouldering fire straddling the years would ignite to hatred from time to time, setting more killing, even greater suffering. (Steyn 2010: 17)

For the next 15 years, the British, as if, left the Angami Nagas to themselves. However, the Lieutenant-Governor of Bengal, Sir Cecil Beadon, got 'convinced that a policy of masterly inactivity in dealing with a savage tract lying in the middle of our settled districts is no policy at all, but a specious synonym for neglect of duty'. He ordered the Chief Commissioner of Assam to 'enter boldly on the work of civilizing the hill man'. Lieutenant John Gregory, an officer known for his tact and patience, was sent to establish an outpost in the Naga Hills. He moved fast and selected Chumukedima, a village in the foothills in the Angami hills, for an administrative outpost. The adjoining villages were left to their headmen to try petty crimes themselves as per their traditions and a house tax of Rs. 2 per annum was imposed. The scattered tribesmen of Khonoma were permitted to return and build their village. Very soon, John Butler was appointed as the Political Agent at Chumukedima in 1872. While leading a survey party to the Lhota area, he was ambushed and killed in December 1875. After three years, the headquarters of the Naga Hills Agency was shifted to the heart of the Naga Hills at Kohima in 1878, which was occupied by Henry Damant as the Political Agent.

On 13 October 1879, Damant left Kohima accompanied by a body of armed escorts for Khonoma to investigate the murder of a policeman escorting a mail-runner on his way to Chumekedima. He spent the night at village Jotsoma on the way. Before he could proceed on his mission to Khonoma, a *dobhashi* had warned him to be careful and take precaution, as the Khonoma people were well prepared to give him a befitting reply for his moves. It is said that the officer stubbornly brushed off the advice and went ahead to the village gate. A single shot from a Khonoma warrior struck on the head of Damant, which instantly killed him on 14 October 1879. Having seen their leader struck down, the accompanying escorts ran away for the safety in a disorderly way, which turned out to be easy target for the Khonoma warriors waiting for opportunity. In all, 33 of the escort party were killed and 19 were seriously injured. At the end, Damant's orderly made back to Kohima and broke the story of the debacle.

The District Superintendent of Police, Kohima, S.J. Crawley, asked for urgent reinforcement from Wokha, Imphal and Nowgong, as he was expecting a counterattack from Khonoma. The response from all three British administrative centres was prompt and a massive army with appropriate armaments was assembled to take action and teach the Angamis a lesson. Steyn records:

> The place (Khonoma) was by nature strong, had fortified with immense labour and skill, and was deemed by the Nagas (as) impregnable. The (British) assault lasted all the day and at nightfall only the lower portion of the village had been captured after the severest fighting ever known in these hills. In the night, the Nagas evacuated the upper works, and on the following day the British forces occupied the position, having lost in the assault two British and ten native officers wounded, and forty men of the rank and file killed and wounded. (Steyn 2010: 26)

The Khonoma warriors were able to inflict casualty on at least 25 per cent of the attackers. However, Khonoma and Jotsoma villages were razed to the ground by the victorious British forces. The British were determined to inflict such wounds on the Angamis that they would think afresh before undertaking another adventure against them. As the Khonoma warriors had done in the past, they abandoned their village stealthily and joined their women, children and old and wounded persons take shelter in the nearby woods and hillocks. Undoubtedly, the British decisively broke the claimed supremacy of the Khonoma veterans. At the same time, the events of 1879 left serious prejudice against the British in the minds of the Khonoma warriors. Moreover, bitterness, distrust, and insecurity, which bedevilled the veterans, turned into a long lasting distrust in 'others' at large. However, the British administration realized that it would be magnanimous on their part to make a move for reconciliation with the Khonoma. Emissaries were sent and feelers came back with the reactions from the Khonoma camps. At last, the villagers were informed that the new Chief Commissioner of Assam, Sir Steuart Bayley, had modified the imperial policy regarding punishment. A conclave was held on 27 March 1880 and an oral understanding was reached for the mutual trust and respect for each other. Even then the Nagas did not rush to the village site immediately from their secured hideout. Meanwhile they got engaged in agricultural activities in their spare time. Nature responded favourably and there was a bumper crop next year. Reluctantly, slowly, they returned to the village site and got busy in building their houses one by one in 1881. And at least for the next seven decades, Khonoma was one of the most prosperous Angami villages in the Naga Hills district of Assam.

There were three important issues from the British point of view which led to clash of interests in the Naga Hills district leading to clash with the tribesmen. First, to begin with the British demand for coolies during the armed operation in and around Naga Hills led to resentment among the tribesmen, because tribesmen considered it demeaning to carry load of others for payment. The problem with the British was that they needed coolies to carry head loads in the roadless mountainous Naga country. Second, the issue of keeping captive domestic slaves by the tribes' men was another problem which caused conflict with the British administration. While the practice of keeping domestic slaves out of war was considered natural by the Nagas, efforts of the British administration to abolish it as a crime against humanity was not appreciated by the Nagas. Third, an ancient institution of head-hunting as a relic of old practice of warfare, was considered as an article of displaying bravery among many of the Naga communities. So much so that the practice of head-hunting got reduced to a cultural practice among some of the tribes to chop off parts of the body such as ears or the like. The British effort to stop head-hunting was considered as interference in their age-old cultural practice.

Denis Fitzpatrick, the Chief Commissioner of Assam, recorded on 15 November 1887:

> Now it seems to be admitted by all who have from time to time considered the question, that it is our (British) destiny, if not our duty, to bring these wild tribes more and more under control, and there can be no doubt that in time the tract in question, and a great deal more besides, will come to be included in our ordinary fully administered districts. (Reid 1983: 114)

Thus, east of the Lhota tribal areas, the region inhabited by the Aos and Semas was surveyed. A 'site situated midway between three large villages: Ungma (600 houses), Khenza (300 houses) and Mokokchung (300 houses), none more distant than two and a half miles, and consequent facilities for procuring supplies and coolie labour', was recommended for establishing the sub-divisional headquarters by the Chief Commissioner of Assam to the Government of India. At long last, it was decided to establish another sub-division in the Naga Hills district, Mokokchung on 28 January 1890. It was also decided that in case of extension of the administration eastwards towards Burma, the unit would be tribe in question, and not the physical landmarks like rivers or hillocks to be occupied as effective British administrative limit.

The rest of the British history of Naga Hills district will be remembered for a set of developments. First, coolies were recruited from the Ao tribe for the Abor Hill Expedition, 1911. Second, 2,000 coolies were recruited for Naga Corps to be sent to France in 1917 during the First World War from Sema (1 000), Lhota (400), Rengma, Chang and Aos (200 each) and another 810 coolies were hired in January 1918 from the various Naga tribes for the same objective. Third, the administration inspired various headmen of some important villages, and some Dobhasis to organize a Naga Club in 1918 to work as a pressure group for Nagas. Fourth, the British bureaucrats saw to it that the Naga Club met the members of the Simon Commission in January 1929. Fifth, Naga Hills district like other hill districts of Assam was termed as the Excluded Area within the province of Assam in 1935. This was disenchantment for the Nagas for the simple reason that this development was against the hope created by the British that a different dispensation would be created for the Excluded Districts in case India became independent. Sixth, the Second World War was fought briefly in Naga Hills and adjoining Manipur princely state and the Japanese were soundly beaten. And last, the Naga Club turned Naga National Council, claimed (?) to have telegrammed to the Government of India that the Naga Hills district had declared its independence on 14 August 1947.

Indian Union, Naga National Council (NNC) and the Naga Insurgency

The Founder-Secretary of NNC, Theyiechuthia Sakhrie, had sent a memorandum to Jawaharlal Nehru, the President of the Indian National Congress: (a) The Council stands for solidarity of Naga tribes, including those in the un-administered areas, (b) The Council strongly protests against the grouping of Assam with Bengal, (c) The Naga Hills should be constitutionally included in autonomous Assam, in free India, with local autonomy and due safeguards of interests of the Nagas. (d) the Naga tribes should have a separate electorate (Steyn 2010: 70). In response to that Nehru had replied that:

> It is obvious that the Naga territory in Eastern Assam is much too small to stand by itself politically and economically. It lies between two huge countries, India and China, and part of it consists of rather backward people who require considerable help. When India is independent, as it is bound to be soon, it will not be possible for the British government to hold on to Naga territory or any part of it. They would be isolated between India and China. Inevitably, therefore, this Naga territory must form part of India and of Assam with which it has developed such close association. (Hazarika 2018: 53)

Sir Andrew Claw, the last British Governor of Assam, handed over charge of the administration to his successor, Sir Akbar Hydari, in May 1947. Sir Hydari realized the gravity of the turmoil among the Nagas and signed a comprehensive nine-point agreement with the Naga leaders on 9 June 1947 at Shillong. However, the last clause turned out to be most controversial, which stated: 'after ten years of the agreement's implementation, the Naga National Council will be asked whether they require the above agreement to be extended for a further period, or a new agreement regarding the future of the Naga people arrived at'. This last provision of the agreement turned to be vague: a section of the Nagas interpreted that after 10 years they would have a right to self-determination. The Government of India meant that the agreement may be extended or negotiated, but the issue of self-determination was ruled out.

A group of Nagas paid a visit to Delhi to apprise the Indian National leaders of their pints of view, but could not meet either

Nehru or Patel in those eventful days. However, they managed to meet Mahatma Gandhi at Bhangi Colony in Delhi and acquainted him of their points of view of Naga Hills vis-à-vis Indian Union. They tried to convince Gandhi that Indian Union intended to forcefully take over Naga Hills. Gandhi disapproved the idea of forceful integration of Naga Hills to India and allegedly agreed to oppose it himself (Zinyu 1979: 21; Steyn 2010: 73-4). After meeting Mahatma Gandhi in Delhi in July 1947, some of the Nagas like Zapu Phizo announced that they would declare their independence on 14 August, a day before India became formally independent. Thus a section of the NNC went ahead and declared independence of Naga Hills District on 14 August 1947. They claimed to have sent telegrams informing New Delhi and United Nations Organizations, which were aborted by an alert district administration.

Hazarika records, referring to W.G. Archer's note, that

> the Naga Flag was raised at the Kevichusa residence, but (it) was taken down by (Deputy Commissioner, C.R.) Pawsey and that Mrs. Kevichusa was 'in hysterics'; one note says that there were twelve efforts by the 'Kevichusa group' to send telegrams announcing Nagaland's freedom but Pawsey intercepted all of them and ensured that no telegrams were sent. (Hazarika 2011: 52)

There is another version of the same incidence. It was to streamline the materials and cash that Pawsey

> facilitated the formation of NHDTC in April, 1945, and whose mandate it became to unite Naga tribes to effectuate reconstruction (after the devastation of the war). Less than a year later, the council had rechristened itself as the NNC, and became the platform for debates on Nagas' political future. Initially the debate was between those who envisaged a genuine Naga autonomy within Assam and India and those who insisted that only an independent 'government of the Nagas, for the Nagas, by the Nagas' (Kevichusa) would ensure Nagas' welfare. (Wouters: 2018: 19).

This led to a division within NNC, and a split of a group calling themselves the 'People's Independent League', of which Z.A. Phizo was a member. By then, a new Naga leader was emerging on the political horizon of Naga Hills. It was Zapu Phizo. He elbowed out the moderates from the NNC and placed his followers among the office bearers. In him, the Nagas had found their spokesman and he championed their cause ceaselessly, fearlessly and even fanatically. Moreover, though religion, Christianity was mentioned earlier also in the public debate, but it was Phizo, who introduced Christianity as a factor of differentiation between Indians as Hindus and Nagas as Christians. On the other hand, T. Sakherie, the Secretary of the NNC, was a cool, level-headed, competent and articulate personality. However, the destiny of the Nagas began to shift fast under the emotive and theological spell of Phizo. Slowly and steadily, he was consolidating his hold, influence and his network of supporters.

NNC and Murder of the Political Dissenters

India announced its Federal Constitution on 26 January 1950. As per it, Assam was one of the States of Indian Union and Naga Hills district was a scheduled district within the state. Moreover, the Constitution stipulated the formation of autonomous District Councils to be formed of the scheduled tribal representatives to govern the district as per traditional customary laws, which were guaranteed by the Indian parliament. NNC opposed it and passed a three-point resolution: (1) No Naga should join the Assam Legislative Assembly or the Indian parliament representing the Nagas. (2) Anything that is autonomous in character will not be accepted by the Nagas. (3) The aspiration and inspiration of the Nagas is to fight for freedom through peace and goodwill, not through bloodshed. The Nagas are strongly determined to fight constitutionally for the liberation of their motherland, Nagaland.

Phizo was elected as the President, the fourth and the last one till 1990, of the Naga National Council on 11 December 1950. He did not waste any time in political niceties and decided for 'non-cooperation and civil disobedience' with the Government of Assam and the Government of India. The first General Election to the State Assembly of Assam and the National Parliament in 1952 were boycotted by the Nagas. Instead of that, NNC announced the formation of the Sovereign Republic of Nagaland. T. Sakhrie, the founder secretary of NNC and politically more mature operator, warned his uncle, Phizo, that the Nagas were not prepared for a confrontation with the Government of India. In the emotionally surcharged politics of the day, he felt alienated from the political forum, which he had built some five years back. Their differences came in the open and frequently they began to debate in public, which Phizo took as a challenge to his leadership. Rest I shall quote historian of war and peace in the region:

> At a critical meeting in Khonoma, Phizo confronted Sakhrie and attacked him bitterly, 'You do not deserve to live', he roared....The first prominent moderate among the Naga national leaders was seized when he went to meet his lover at a village near Kohima. Sakhrie was tortured brutally and then killed (on 18 January 1956). But till the end, Phizo denied any role in the plot leading to Sakherie's death. (Hazarika 2011: 99)

After Sakhrie's death, the Government of India took a serious view of the Naga affairs and Prime Minister Nehru sent army to the Naga Hills to crush the simmering revolt.

Phizo took his NNC with himself to East Pakistan in 1957. From there he went to Karachi and tried to work out the cause of Naga independence from abroad. However, inside Naga Hills, things were changing fast. While Government of India had mounted massive military crackdown under AFSPA (Armed Forces Special Power Act) with a view to control insurgency, NNC too was engaged in counter-attacks on loyal and dissenting Nagas to their points of view. In either ways, the Nagas suffered untold misery. While NNC continued to defy the Government of India, a group of educated Nagas, in and outside the government, got together to organise Naga Peoples Convention (NPC) largely under the leadership Imkongliba Ao, an unattached medical practitioner. An appeal was made to the government of Assam in Shillong to cease wanton destruction of the villages, unleash cruelty and wanton brutality towards women and children. But nothing came out of its first effort. There were two more conventions held in 1958 and 1959: slowly more and more notable Nagas moved to the NPC: Shilo Ao, R. Chiten Jamir, Hokise Sema, Jasokie, Akum Imkong and other. They asked for a State of Nagaland in the Indian Union consisting of all the Naga inhabited areas. However, the main mover of the NPC, Imkongliba, was assassinated by a young man in Mokokchung in the middle of 1960. After T. Sakhrie's assassination, this was the second high profile murder of another notable Naga person, who made the move for peaceful resolution with the Indian Union.

1950s had been one of the darkest phases of Nagas' history. NNC organized boycott of the first general election. The Government of India ignored it as a factional response to the Indian democracy. For the Government of India, Nagas's independence was a small issue compared to similar claims by Hyderabad, Travancore, Jamnagar and Kashmir. NNC organized a plebiscite on the issue of Nagas' independence and claimed that 99.9 per cent Nagas opted for independence. Like their declaring independence on 14 August 1947, this was another unverified incidence on which NNC writes its history. Prime Minister Nehru and Premier Thakin Unu of Burma met at Kohima in 1953 for signing a boundary pact between the two countries, which ended in a fiasco because of the bureaucratic lapse. NNC had already decided to boycott all the administrative functionaries and had mounted a non-cooperation with the government. The Government of India sent armed forces to control insurgency, which was retaliated by NNC. At last, a desperate Government of India enacted the Armed Forces Special Power Act (AFSPA). Once the armed forces began operating under the shadow of the ACT, it led to untold miseries to the Naga civilians. It was one of the darkest phases of the Nagas' and Indian history.

Creation of Nagaland as a State in the Indian Union

After prolonged lobbying, intense discussion and stoppage of regrouping of the villages for security reasons, demands of the NPC to create a state of Nagaland with elected legislature, a cabinet of ministers, and other amenities were conceded by the Government of India in 1963. Thus, an Indian State of Nagaland was created and it was inaugurated by the President of India, S Radhakrishanan on 1 December 1963 and he said on the occasion:

> Friends, I have great pleasure in inaugurating the new state of Nagaland. It takes an honoured place today as the 16th state of Indian Union ... our attempts to secure you the fullest freedom to manage your own affairs have culminated in the creation of Nagaland State. The rule of law and government by the consent of the governed are the essence of democracy. Government

must be the custodian of the general welfare of its people and not of any special interest. The government must capture the hearts and minds of the people. The administrators must exercise the human, healing touch in the relations with the people and should not deprive the Nagas of their innocent joys, their songs, dances, their feasts and festivals which are not repugnant to our moral sense....On this auspicious day I make an appeal to all Naga people: let all past rancour and misunderstandings be forgotten and let a new chapter of progress, prosperity and goodwill be written on the page which opens today. I once again say that a bright future awaits the brave people of Nagaland. (Wouters 2018: 126-7)

The State of Nagaland went on for its first election to the Legislative Assembly in February 1964 and a cabinet led by Shilo Ao was sworn in. Since then, there have been regular elections for the State Legislative Assembly and the lone seat from Nagaland to the lower house of the Indian Parliament. S.C. Jamir has been one such Naga politicians, who held position of the chief minister for many terms and had been an active leader of the Indian National Congress. In course of time he would be the Governor of Maharashtra, Goa and Orissa. Defying the insurgents' dictates, he had the 'audacity' to raise the question:

Did we (the Nagas) have an independent political existence immediately before the British rule or even during the British days? Were we really an independent nation? And Jamir's answers: The stark inescapable truth is that neither did we have a definite and unified political structure nor did we exist as a nation. We were actually a group of heterogeneous, primitive and diverse tribes living in far-flung villages that had very little in common and negligible contacts with each other.... In these circumstances, the question of 'Naga nation' did not arise.... Naga undergrounds immediately condemned S.C. Jamir as a reactionary and a traitor, and planned yet another ambush on his life (he had already survived several such attempts. (Wouters 2018: 73)

However, NNC straightaway rejected the statehood of Nagaland and termed the Nagas, who took part in the electoral process, as traitors. Moreover, NNC mounted its subversive activities all the more to display its strength at the grassroot level. Twenty-four curfews were clamped and the armed forces were called in to remove the hurdles from the routine functioning of the state government. In the process, ordinary citizens suffered untold miseries and lived their lives in hardship. Moved by the plight of the common people, some public men took the initiative to form a Nagaland Peace Mission. The Government of India agreed to provide all possible amenities within its control and the Baptist Church in Nagaland wholeheartedly supported the move. The Peace Mission consisted of the Gandhian Jayaprakash Narayan, Bimla Prasad Chaliha, the chief minister of Assam and a controversial English missionary, Reverend Michael Scott, Phizo's patron from the United Kingdom. There was a huge expectation from the Mission and that did some good work to restore normalcy to an extent through its calling for truce between the two parties. However, Michael Scott contacted some foreign governments and United Nations to internationalize the Naga issue on behalf of the Peace Mission. Both the other members of the Peace Mission, Jayaprakash Narayan and B.P. Chaliha, decided to dissociate themselves from the Mission and this noble move came to an end to much regret.

Shillong Accord, Diminishing Role of Phizo in NNC and Emergence of NSCN

After a decade or so, another move was made after taking some of the notable Naga public men in confidence. This time the Baptist Church of Nagaland was very much associated with the move. This time, it was Lallan Prasad Singh (L.P. Singh) ICS, the Governor of Assam and Nagaland, who took the challenge and opened the negotiation with NNC to find the solution from the political stalemate. There were four rounds of talks between the functionaries of the Government of India and half a dozen of the representatives of the Underground Organizations. At last, a three-point accord was signed on 11 November 1975 at the Raj Bhawan, Shillong. While the Governor L.P. Singh signed it on behalf of the Government of India, I. Temjen, S. Dahru, Z. Ramyo, M. Assa and Keviyally initialled it on behalf of the representatives of the underground organizations. The three-point accord consisted of:

(1) The representatives of the underground organizations conveyed their decisions, on their own, to accept, without condition, the Constitution of India.

(2) It was agreed that the arms, now underground, would be brought out and deposited at an appointed place. Details of giving effect to this agreement will be worked out between them and representatives of the government, security forces and the members of the Liaison Committee.
(3) It was agreed that the representatives of the underground organizations should have reasonable time to formulate other issues for discussion for final settlement (Steyn 2010: 211-12).

Pieter Steyn informs that Phizo's brother, Keviyally, one of the signatories of the Accord, was keeping the details and the course of talk informed to his brother in self-exile. Thus, Phizo was in the know of the details of the discussions and the outcome thereof. However, he believed in the known formula: 'Heads I win and tail you lose'. Once the armed wing of the NNC led by Isak Swu and Thuengaling Muivah opposed the Accord publicly, he tried to convince the dissenters that he was not a party to the Accord. But that the opposite party had done their homework thoroughly and they refused to buy Phizo's innocence. Thus, an irreparable gulf between the two factions of the NNC was created leading to the formation of National Socialist Council of Nagaland (NSCN) in 1978 as the dominant force among the Naga insurgents. Phizo continued to claim to be the sole arbitrator of the fate of the Nagas and the president of his faction of NNC and kept on making feeble noises from his British hideout. On the other hand, the Government of India went ahead as if it had solved the problem of Naga insurgency by signing the Shillong Accord.

Phizo maintained that those of the Nagas who signed the Shillong Accord had no mandate from the NNC. However, he met prime minister of India, Morarji Desai at his residence on 14 June 1978 and pleaded for the case of Naga independence. Morarji Desai was blunt enough to tell him that there was no problem of Naga independence so far as India was concerned. And the Naga rebels would be killed by the Indian forces (Zynyu 1979: 48-53; Hazarika 2011: 90-1; Steyn 2010: 186-9). Phizo kept on issuing statements from his English home, but it was not taken seriously. In the last quarter of twentieth century, it was NSCN, which was calling the shots in the affairs of Nagaland. The Government of India and the NSCN got engaged in peace talks in 1993 and after six years of negotiation, a ceasefire was agreed upon between the two parties in 1997. Almost after two decades of the ceasefire, a 'Preamble to the Agreement' between the two parties was signed on 3 August 2015, as a gesture to respect the wishes of ailing Isak Swu, who shortly expired. Since then, both the parties are engaged in negotiating a final accord. NNC is almost a dead letter in Nagaland right now. NSCN itself is divided in four factions and the commoners are groaning under the heavy burden of extortion and continued armed violence.

Two sides, the NSCN and the Government of India, continued talking for nearly three decades; cease fire agreement continued to be maintained for the last two decades, and in spite of having an agreed preamble, no agreement has been reached. But as it is said there is a devil in the details: shared sovereignty, separate flags and integration of the Naga inhabited areas from other states and even Burma in to Nagaland are the sticking points (Hazarika 2018: 75-81). Meanwhile an ominous development has been happening in the eastern part of the state of Nagaland. An apex body of Chang, Konyak, Sangtam, Phom, Yimchunger and Khiamniungan tribes from four eastern districts of Mon, Tuensang, Longleng and Kiphire had met in 2011 and formed the Eastern Naga People's Organization (ENPO) for demanding separate state of Frontier Nagaland:

> Of the eleven districts of Nagaland, these four backward districts have almost half of the state's population. But despite that, they continue to remain extremely underdeveloped. Our demand for the creation of Frontier Nagaland is based on historical facts. This is something like going back to the earlier arrangement when the entire area was under the erstwhile Tuensang Frontier Division of NEFA.

The proponents of the Frontier State like the NNC in old times some seven decades back, used the local church leaders to propagate their views and pray for the creation of Frontier Nagaland as the state of their dreams (Woulters 2018: 206-10). The popular imagination has also altered the image of insurgents' cadre with the changing time. Thus, the Naga scenario has turned out to be a local joke:

> Those who achieve distinction in the examinations become top scientists. Those who pass in Second Division become bureaucrats and rule over the

scientists. Those who get Third Division turn into politicians and rule over the scientists and bureaucrats. Finally, those who fail their examinations or are school drop-outs join the underground and rule over the scientists, bureaucrats and politicians. (Wouters 2018: 114) with possibly their unlicensed arms.

REFERENCES

Antrobus, H.A., 1957, *A Histry of Assam Company: 1838-1953*, T. and A. Constable, Edinburgh.

Ao, W. Chubanungba, 2017, *Havildar Watigangshi Ao Longkhum off the Coast of Tunis*, Galaxy Book Centre, Shillong.

Ao, W. Chubanungba, 2017a, *Wabong Senkalemba BEM: An Account of His Life*, Galaxy Book Centre, Shillong.

Barpujari, H.K., 1986, *The American Missionaries and North East India: 1836-1900*, Spectrum Publications, Guwahati.

Clark, Mary M., 1978, *A Corner in India*, Christian Literature Centre, Guwahati (Reprint).

Colson, Elizabeth, 1970, 'Converts and Traditions: The Impact of Chrstianity on Valley Tonga Religion', *Southern Journal of Anthropology*, pp. 149-51.

Crone, G.R., 1969, *Background to Political Geography*, Pitman Paper Back, London.

Downs, Frederick S, 1971, *Mighty Works of God: A Brief History of the Council of Baptist Churches in North East India – The Mission Perios: 1836-1950*, Christian Literature Centre, Guwahati.

Elwin, Verrier, 1961, *Nagaland*, Oxford University Press, Bombay.

Guha, A., 1988, *Planter Raj to Swaraj*, 2nd edn., Peoples Publishing House, New Delhi.

Hazarika, Sanjoy, 2011, *Stangers of the Mist: Tales of War and Peace in Northeast India*, 2nd edn., Penguin Random House India, New Delhi.

_____, 2018, *Strangers No More: New Narratives from India's Northeast*, Aleph, New Delhi

Hutton, J.H., 1921, *The Angami Nagas*, Macmillan, London.

_____, 1921, *The Sema Nagas*, Macmillan, London.

Longkumer, N., 1988, *The Growth of Baptist Churches among the Aos of Nagaland*, Changtongya Baptist Church, Changtongya.

Miles, J.P., 1922, *The Lhota Nagas*, 2nd edn., Oxford University Press, Bombay.

Philip, P.T., 1983, *The Growth of Baptist Churches in Nagaland*, 2nd edn., Christian Literature Centre, Guwahati.

Reid, Robert, 1983, *History of the Frontier Areas Bordering on Assam from 1883-1941*, Eastern Publishing House, Delhi.

Sinha, A.C., 1993, *Beyond the Trees, Tigers and Tribes: Historical Sociology of the Eastern Himalayan Forests*, Har Anand Publications, New Delhi.

———, 1994, 'The American Baptist Mission among the Nagas', in *North-Eastern Frontier of India: Structural Imperatives and Aspects of Change*, ed. A.C. Sinha, Indus Publishing Company, New Delhi, pp. 69-89.

Steyn, Pieter, 2010, *Zapu Phizo: Voice of the Nagas*, Routledge Taylor & Francis Group, New Delhi.

Syiemlieh, David, 2014 (?), *On the Edge of the Empire*, Sage, New Delhi.

Witvliet, Theo, 1985, *A Place in the Sun: An Introduction to Liberation Theology in the Third World*, Orbis Books, New York.

Woulters, J.J.P., 2018, *In the Shadow of Naga Insurgency: Tribes, State, and Violence in Northeast India*, Oxford University Press, Delhi.

Zinyu, Mhiesizokho, 1979, *Phizo and the Naga Problem*, Nagaland Times Press, Dimapur.

4

The Princely State of Jammu & Kashmir

Maharaja Ranjit Singh (1776-1839), king of Lahore, had conquered Kashmir in 1819 after vanquishing the Afghans. He died in 1839 leaving behind a number of wives, concubines and a brood of children, but there was no one strong enough to manage his political legacy, the strong Sikh army. Ranjit Singh used to pay his soldiers in cash as their salary, which remained in arrear because of the factional fights and administrative negligence. Most of the Sikh princes were killed in the succession wars fought in the early 1840s and at last, a boy, Dalip Singh, son of a scheming concubine of the ex-king, succeeded as the king to control the strong Sikh army. In the process, abandoning sagacious old policy of the Ranjit Singh, the Sikhs invaded the British Indian territories across the river Sutlej in the east, only to be soundly beaten back.

The British were as if waiting in the wings not only to grab the fertile Punjab plains, but also to vanquish the last Indian resistance in the form of Khalsa kingdom of the Sikhs at Lahore to their Indian Empire for all times to come. Punjab was annexed in 1846 by Lord Dalhousie to the British Indian Empire and 11 year old prince Dalip was disinherited and taken to England. Dilip would get converted to Christianity, only to reconvert to Sikhism later and would purchase a property of 17, 000 acre farmland in England. He would even dream of reclaiming his patrimony back in Punjab, only to be rebuffed by the British. Naturally, the British found the Sikh treasury empty to begin with and they looked around some source to recover the heavy war indemnity of 500,000 pounds imposed on the defeated Punjab.

MAP 3: NOTIONAL MAP OF THE PRINCELY STATE OF JAMMU & KASHMIR
(*Source:* https://upload.wikimedia.org/wikipedia/commons/8/8f/Kashmir_region._LOC_2003626427.jpg, Public Domain, https://commons.wikimedia.org/w/index.php?curid=116804120)

A courtier of Raja Ranjit Singh, Gulab Singh Dogra from Jammu, paid the above amount and he was declared the ruler of Jammu & Kashmir in 1846 as per the terms of the Treaty of Amritsar (Kwarteng 2012). In course of time, Mahatma (Mohandas Karamchand) Gandhi would rightly term the text of the treaty as 'the sale deed' of Kashmir.

Raja Ranjit Singh had extended his kingdom all around from Punjab to Sindh, Baluchistan, across the Suleiman ranges to Afghanistan, the Karakoram ranges, Valley of Kashmir and Jammu. He sent one of his bravest and senior Generals, Zorawar Singh, to conquer Tibet, who was unfortunately frozen to death along with his forces in a ruthless Himalayan snow blizzard. The Raja was ahead of his time among the Indian rulers in making cash payment as the salary to his soldiers instead of letting them loot the defeated kingdoms. This practice of cash payment attracted a number of young men to join his army from far and wide. For example, prior to the British conjecture of Gorkha martial race as a mark of brave soldiers, Gorkhas would address their brave soldiers as Lahure (those who had returned from Lahore after serving in the Sikh army) equivalent to bravery and experience in wars.

British Sell Kashmir to Establish a Satellite Dogra Ruling Dynasty

Coming back to Kashmir and its new ruler, Maharaja Gulab Singh (b.1792, r. 1846-57) had purchased Kashmir for Rs. 75,00,000 and an annual token tribute of 'one horse, 12 goats (six male and six female), and six pairs of shawls to the British East India Company'(Kwarteng 2012: 90). He could act as the buffer between the British and the Russian empire advancing from the Central Asia, managing favourably in the ongoing 'great game of Central Asia'. He was known as a difficult man who had no formal education, but he could shoot and wield the sword, and was known to be a savage, but a courteous man. He was shrewd enough to know that the British were the most powerful force in the India of his time. He adopted a policy of sycophancy, stark flattery and double dealing with British functionaries such as the Governor-General Lord Dalhousie, a diehard imperialist, who understood that Gulab Singh's attachment to the British crown was purely of self interest.

He was a rich man and among all his possessions, the fertile Valley of Kashmir was his prime possession, which he ruthlessly oppressed. Kwasi Kwarteng notes:

> The Maharaja has taken everything (from Kashmir) into his own hands, and that is, with the exception of five or six shawl merchants, the only trader in Cashmere. Taxes were exorbitant; from every 100 acres' worth of grain cultivated, Gulab Singh takes 90; leaving 10 to the cultivator … upon shawls and every other article of manufactured goods he takes half of its sale price. The result of all this greed was that the people lived in the 'most abject poverty'. (Kwarteng 2011: 94)

The king adopted a three-prong strategy as a mechanism of survival to deal with the suspicious British colonial regime. His first strategy was of courting the British with sycophancy, buffoonery and outright double speak, which the British understood but could do nothing about. His second strategy was to man all the administrative and military posts as a monopoly of the Dogra Hindus from Jammu to which he belonged. In course of time that got translated into a ruthless Hindu raj imposed on the largely Muslim subjects. Slowly and slowly, the king turned more and more to the Hindu holy men and seers even in his routine affairs which affected the administration. And third, he evolved a policy of holding the densely populated Muslim Kashmir Valley under extreme economic distress through excessive taxation and administrative exploitation. The Dogra state had a tendency to make every product of the valley as a state property. It is said that even the prostitutes were taxed in Kashmir. The diabetic Maharaja died in 1857 and was succeeded by his son, Ranbir Singh, who continued the policies evolved by his father more ruthlessly. Similarly, the third ruler, Pratap Singh, who had succeeded his father in 1885, proceeded in the footsteps of his father rather more vigorously.

Pratap Singh (b. 1850, r. 1885-1925), who had the longest period as the ruler of the dynasty, was a strange man, to say the least. He was something like a 'story book Indian prince, vacillating and oppressive, bedecked in silk pyjamas, pearls and a diamond-encrusted turban'. He was eccentric, a nuisance and an opium addict, who was a devout and excessively orthodox Hindu. So much so, that he had kept a dozen of cows tethered in the garden outside his bedroom window so that he could be sure to see the holy creatures when he would wake up each morning. However, he did not like his younger brother, Amar Singh, but as he was issueless, ultimately Amar Singh's son, his nephew, Hari Singh (b.1995, r. 1925-48, d. 1961), succeeded him as the Maharaja. And effectively, with Maharaja Hari Singh's removal in 1948, the Dogra dynastic rule in Kashmir came to an end.

Kwasi Kwarteng found Hari Singh as a 'bullying, vain and pompous man'. Though educated at Mayo Prince College, Ajmer, he was vindictive, proud and status conscious. Moreover, his uncle, King Pratap Singh, kept him virtually under house-arrest as a lonely friendless soul, when the prince came back home from college. Finally, he became the Maharaja of Kashmir in 1925, at the age of 30. A huge majority of his subjects were Muslims, but the Maharaja was oblivious of the ongoing developments in British India.

> While most Kashmiris were Muslims, the Maharaja was a Hindu. His court, ministers and senior administrators were preponderantly non-Muslims and its senior officers even more so. Almost a quarter of his subjects were non-Muslims, and these included the Maharaja's own community, the Dogras of Jammu. (Whitehead 2007: 98)

Like his uncle Pratap Singh, he was getting more and more closer to the Hindu ascetics, who predicted that he would be a Hindu king (of sovereign Kashmir). Thus, the Maharaja lived in delusion that he would be an independent king of Kashmir. So much so that he 'had already "at a great cost" prepared a crown of diamonds and emeralds for his coronation as the ruler of this new kingdom' (Kuwarteng 2012: 121).

By then things had gone out of control. Way back in 1931, a firebrand preacher from North-West Frontier Province, Abdul Qadeer, had given a provocative speech instigating his largely Muslim audience to attack the ruthless Maharaja's palace and destroy it brick by brick. The preacher was arrested and naturally put on trial, but on the day of trial, 6 July 1931, a huge crowd assembled and stones were pelted on the police, who responded by opening fire. In the process, 21 demonstrators were killed. The emotionally charged demonstrators denounced the Hindu Maharaja's rule. And that was the time the All India Muslim League, claiming to represent all the Muslims of India, had raised the demand for a separate homeland for the Muslims – Pakistan. Till today this day of the police firing is marked martyr's day in Pakistan and Kashmir. The ruler, in spite of the cacophony of the political agitation, was 'much happier in (horse) racing than administering the state' (Singh 1982: 31).

Emergence of Sheikh Muhammad Abdullah

By then, unlike illiterate preachers, an educated Kashmiri, Sheikh Muhammad Abdullah (1905-82), who had come back home in 1930 after getting his MSc degree from Aligarh Muslim University had emerged as the spokesman of the toiling and struggling Muslim masses. He began organizing the toiling poor masses for the redressal of their multifarious demands. But the Maharaja had nothing to do with him and went on in his old ways. During this period, S.M. Abdullah emerged as the voice of Muslim opinion. Once installed in Srinagar as a teacher, he threw himself headlong into politics and within no time he was recognized as the voice of the oppressed Muslims. However, he, with his scientific, rationalist background, was a committed nationalist even before he was a Muslim. Like many of the leaders of colonial independence struggle, he was attracted by the twin goal of socialism and secularism. The All Jammu & Kashmir Muslim Conference in Kashmir led by Abdullah, had organized non-violent agitations against the Maharaja's partisan attitude towards his Muslim subjects. But Maharaja Hari Singh had taken a fancy for an independent kingdom. With a view to reason with him, Lord Mountbatten, the Governor-General of India, travelled to Srinagar and reasoned with him that he could not be independent as 'his country was land-locked, over-sized and under-populated'. If you do not decide quickly, 'you will be the tug-of-war between them (India and Pakistan). You will end up being a battlefield. That is what will happen. You will lose your throne and your life too, if you are not careful'. And after waiting for days, Mountbatten left Srinagar for Delhi, as the Maharaja was unable to meet him because he was 'suffering from a stomach upset' (Kwarteng 2012: 123).

Maharaja Hari Singh, notified his son, Karan Singh, that he had a strange tendency not to 'trust anyone for any length of time' (Singh 1983: 12). In his heart, he never believed that the British would actually leave India. Indecisive by nature, he merely played for time.

> To be fair to him, the situation he faced was a complex one, and there was no easy option. If he acceded to Pakistan, a large chunk of his people, including his entire Dogra base, would have been outraged. If he had acceded to India, he risked alienating a large section of his Muslim subjects. Independence could perhaps have been an attractive proposition, but to carry that off would have required careful preparation and prolonged negotiations with the parties concerned as well as tremendous political and diplomatic ability. Mountbatten, in fact, had come to persuade my father to make up his mind well before 15 August, (1947) and had brought an assurance from the Indian leaders that they would not take objection to his deciding in whatever he thought fit, even if it was accession to Pakistan.... A typical feudal reaction to a difficult situation is to avoid facing it, and my father was particularly prone to this ..., Mountbatten, as has been recorded by his aide Campbell-Johnson, saw through the deception without any difficulty and returned to Delhi. Thus, the last real chance of working out a viable political settlement was lost. (Singh 1983: 48)

Pakistan Invades Kashmir, 24 October 1947

V.P. Menon, secretary to the deputy prime minister and minister of state, Government of India, Sardar Vallabhbhai Patel, was asked to rush to Srinagar, the capital of Kashmir, to assess the situation. When he reached Srinagar, he wrote, 'It was, really speaking, a dead city. There was no one at the airport. I went to the State guest house, even there, apart from one or two peons, there was nobody there. I had no armed guard, nothing'. He goes on: 'I asked him (Maharaja Hari Singh) to ascertain from his chief officer how long the city would hold out. He said it would hold out for the next 48 hours. I said, 'If that is the case, then we will fight to the last ditch'. This tenuous assurance did nothing to soothe V.P.'s own fears. 'I had to get the Maharaja and his family out of Srinagar'. If the raiders entered as soon as they were predicted to, V.P. had no doubt about the fate that would befall Hari Singh and his family. He managed to persuade the Maharaja that there was only one recourse left to him: flight' (Basu 2020: 370).

A large-scale invasion of tribesmen from North-West Frontier Province happened on Kashmir on 24 October 1947. The next evening while the Maharaja was entertaining 200 guests in his palace, suddenly all the lights went out. The blackout was caused by the invading Pakistani tribesmen, who had burnt the powerhouse.

The following night, the Maharaja's servants began to empty his strongboxes of pearls, emeralds and diamonds. The Maharaja himself frantically searched his palace … for his two Purdey shotguns. Once these had been found, they packed in his car. Now, accompanied by his friend Victor Rosenthal, a Russian Jewish jeweller and financier, Hari Singh was driven away, never to return to his palace in Srinagar. The palace itself would be sold in 1954 to the Oberoi Hotel chain by Hari Singh's son, Karan. (Kwarteng 2012: 127).

Meanwhile, the so-called Pathan tribal volunteers, aided and abeted by the Government of Pakistan, had mounted a most violent attack on Baramulla, a district town only 30 miles away from Srinagar, the capital, and resorted to loot, arson, rape and all types of atrocities on settlements and installations. So much so, that even the Convent of the Franciscan Missionaries was attacked; nuns, doctors on duty, patients on the beds were killed, and women raped most brutally. The report says that in Kashmir the outrage committed by the raiders perpetrated against the Muslims and the Hindus alike for both religions met the fate alike and they collected a rich booty. It appears that after the excessive arson and violence the Maharaja was coerced to accede to the Indian Union. The first plane from New Delhi touched down at Srinagar at around 9 a.m. in the morning on 27 October 1947. Jinnah ordered Pakistan's army into Kashmir with a full-scale military mobilization. This could only mean full-scale war.

As soon as the Defence Committee meeting was over, V.P. flew back to Jammu on 27 October 1947. When he arrived at the palace, he found the garden within the palace walls strewn with valuables. Hari Singh, exhausted and terrified, had gone to sleep. 'The Maharaja was ready to accede at once. Having written to the Viceroy (a letter acknowledged by the Viceroy on 27 October) that he was handing over responsibilities to Sheikh Abdullah and Mahajan, and he requested for immediate assistance to Kashmir'. More crucially, V.P. records, 'he also signed the Instrument of Accession'. From there, it was a matter of quick decision to and move troops into the palace. V.P. writes that he was back in Delhi on the evening of 26 (?) October, with Kashmir, literally, in his bag. He was met by Sardar Patel at Safdarjung Airport, and from there, both men went straight into yet another Defence Council meeting. In the early hours of 27 October 1947, 'over a hundred civilian aircrafts and RAF planes were mobilized to fly troops, equipment and supplies to Srinagar' (Basu 2020: 373).

> The order to mobilize was made through General Francis Mudie to Pakistan's acting Commander-in-Chief, General Douglas Gracey in Rawalpindi. He refused to obey insisting first of all on consulting the Supreme Headquarters in Delhi.... At 1 at night General Gracey phoned his supreme commander, Field Marshal Auchinleck in Delhi and acquainted him of this dramatic turn of events. If pursued, the deployment meant of Pakistan troops in this manner would have entailed the issue of 'stand down' order, the withdrawal of all British officers from the Pakistan and Indian armies, which, given Pakistan's acute shortage of senior officers, the staff officers in particular, would have been very substantial blow.

Next morning, Auchinleck flew to Pakistan to meet Jinnah for what was certain to be a difficult and enormously sensitive meeting ... Auchinleck cabled a 'top secret' account of this talk to London later that day:

> Met Jinnah, who is in Lahore and discuss situation at length. I pointed out incalculable consequences of military violation of what is now territory of Indian Union in consequence of Kashmir's sudden accession....
>
> Jinnah withdrew the orders but is very angry and disturbed by what he considers to be sharp practice by India in securing Kashmir's accession. (Whitehead 2007: 120)

Even after that, the Maharaja had not learnt anything about living his life honourably in the changing circumstances.

> Thanks to his pomposity and tactlessness, he was antagonizing the Indians, who were, after all, supporting his throne with their army.... The Maharaja was fixated on small things; he did not get the big picture: 'when there is an obvious possibility of his losing everything he still wants to hold on to relatively simple things.' To secular-minded modern Indian nationalists, the maharaja had shown absolutely no leadership. He had not led 'his people in the hours of crisis', but had 'left in the night for Jammu' where his winter

palace was situated. He had left, moreover, 'in a caravan of cars carrying his family, his jewels', as well as 'costly furniture and carpets from his palace'. This had been a ignominious betrayal. The Pakistanis were implacably hostile to the Maharaja, because he had signed his state to India. The Indians had grown weary of his vanity, his grand airs and his greed, as he kept complaining and asking for money.(Kwarteng 2012: 135).

While the negotiation between Delhi and Jammu was on, the Maharaja had asked his prime minister, Mehar Chand Mahajan, to go and set up by proclamation, an Emergency Administration headed by Sheikh Muhammad Abdullah. However, away from what was going on the war front between the Pak raiders and the Indian retaliatory forces, 'the old bitterness between the Dogras and the Kashmiris had surfaced again with the dramatic reversal of their roles after a century of Dogra rule ... (the King) was jealous of his authority and prestige as Maharaja, and deeply resented the manner in which Jawaharlal had made him handing over power to Sheikh Abdullah a virtual condition for extending military aid to save the State from Pakistani occupation'. Further, writes Dr. Karan Singh,

This marked for me the beginning of a deep conflict between loyalty to my father who, I realized, represented a system and mode of thought rapidly becoming obsolete in free India, and regard for Jawaharlal Nehru, who was my political guru and whom I greatly admired. (Singh 1983: 77-8).

The Issue did not die there. Even Karan Singh in spite of what he wrote above, takes pains to explain further on the issue:

Apart from the merits of these and other disputes, the basic fact was that my father and Sheikh Abdullah represented two political cultures so dissimilar and desparate that the possibility of any compromise was virtually non-existent. My father belonged to the feudal order and, with all his intelligence and ability, was not able to accept the new dispensation and swallow the populist policies of Sheikh Abdullah. The Sheikh, on the other hand, while a charismatic leader and a superb orator in Kashmiri, was imbued with a bitterly anti-Dogra and anti-monarchical attitude. His socio-economic policy spelt out several years earlier in a pamphlet entitled, 'Naya Kashmir' was based on egalitarian and socialistic thinking in which the ruler, at best, would be a powerless figurehead. (Singh 1983: 85)

Maharaja Hari Singh Abdicates

In spite of Lord Mountbatten's advice to the Maharaja to decide the future of Kashmir after taking the view of his restive subjects, the Maharaja kept on dreaming of independence. When he decided to merge his state with India, it was too late to avoid the arson and violence resorted to by the Pakistani elements. For Pakistan, its existence without Kashmir was incomplete (as per their formulation, 'k' in PAKISTAN represents Kashmir along with other Muslim-majority states in the British India). So in their way of thinking, they must have 'Kashmir' by fair or foul means. Seeing no easy way out of the tangle, Governor-General Lord Mountbatten advised the Government of India to take the issue to the United Nations Organization (UNO) for a fair redressal of the dispute. The UNO debated the issue and sent its military observers to oversee the cease-fire between the two countries and asked for a plebiscite after withdrawal of armed forces of both the countries. And there, instead of identifying the aggressor and taking action against the arson and violence thereof, the Kashmir issue turned out to be an article of power play between the two blocs of the countries: the Western Bloc and the Soviet Bloc.

Nye, the British High Commissioner in India, informed Noel Baker, (the Secretary of State for Commonwealth) on 5 November 1949:

> In confidential conversation today General (Sir Roy) Bucher (Commander-in-Chief) told me that before Nehru left for the United Kingdom he asked Commander-in-Chief to prepare a military appreciation to show the possibility of Indian forces being able to clear Kashmir of Pakistan troops and tribesmen by offensive military action. The result of this appreciation, which had been communicated to Sardar Patel, is that *it will not, repeat not be possible for Indian forces successfully to clear Kashmir either during winter or later when the weather improves.* In the opinion of the Commander-in-Chief, while certain minor offensives may successfully be undertaken, from a broader point of view they are confronted with a military statement. I think it follows from this that the possibility of war between the two dominions breaking out as a result of successful military operations in Kashmir penetrating into Pakistan, is improbable.

The Commander-in-Chief informed Sardar Patel that the only effective military steps which could be taken to deal with the Pakistan troops in Kashmir was by attacking their bases in Pakistan itself, a course which would lead to unrestricted warfare with all its dire consequences and one which could not therefore be contemplated. With this view Sardar Patel agreed. (Noorani 2019)

There is a feeling among some Service officers, as well as a section of the civilian population that India should not have accepted the ceasefire or any Ceasefire Line, and should have pressed on to liberate the rest of the territories of J&K state. The enemy had in December 1948 dispatched two infantry divisions of the regular Pakistan Army, and one infantry division of so-called 'Azad Kashmir army' fighting in (the) theatre. These comprised 14 infantry brigades, 23 infantry battalions of Pakistan Army and 40 infantry battalions of 'Azad Kashmir', besides 19,000 scouts and irregulars. Against this, the Indian Army had in J&K only two infantry divisions, comprising 12 infantry brigades, a total of 50 infantry battalions of regular army and the Indian State Forces, plus 12 battalions of the J&K Militia and 2 battalions of the East Punjab Militia.

Even if the above statement of comparative strength is taken as approximately correct, it is clear that Indian forces were certainly outnumbered by the enemy in J&K, and only superior valour and skill, and perhaps firepower, together with the invaluable help from the tiny Air Force, enabled the Indian Army to maintain its superiority on the battlefield. There can be no doubt, however, that any major offensive required more than troops in J&K....

Indian forces, however, therefore, had to operate in J&K under a definite and a severe handicap. *The enemy could not be decisively beaten by local action within the boundaries of J&K.* For a decisive victory, it was necessary to bring Pakistan in the battle on the broad plains of Punjab itself; the battle of J&K, in the last analysis, had to be fought and won at Lahore and Sialkot, as events brought home in 1965. So, if the whole of the J&K had to be liberated from the enemy, a general war against Pakistan was necessary. There can be hardly any doubt that Pakistan could be decisively defeated in a general war in 1948-49, although both the Indian and the Pakistan armies were in the throes of partition and reorganization then. (Quoted by A.G. Noorani from *History of Operations in Jammu and Kashmir 1947-48* by S.N. Prasad and Dharam Pal, published in 1987 by the History Division of the Ministry of Defence in his 'The Atlas and the Army Chief', *Frontline*, 14 February 2020, p. 105.

When ceasefire was affected, the Ceasefire Line was drawn up at Karachi in 1949 and the Line of Control was drawn up at Shuchetgarh in 1972.

To repeat, in 1947, Sheikh Mohammad Abdullah was the most reputed leader in the Kashmir Valley (not so much in other regions).

> In Kashmir, Abdullah had found the Muslim Leagues's Pakistan idea insufficiently accommodating of Kashmiri distinctiveness with Muslim commonality. The Congress', especially Jawaharlal Nehru's, sympathy and indirect support for the popular movement against Maharaja Hari Singh led by Sheikh Abdullah was manifest. But it turned out that Abdullah was too much of an autonomist for either the League's or the Congress's tastes. He had stood with Delhi as the invading tribes from Pakistan were repelled in the 1947; in Indian eyes this was a definite Kashmiri rejection of the Pakistan option. However, at no point had Abdullah conceded the Maharaja's accession to be anything but provisional, the final outcome to be decided by a plebiscite, which had been promised by Louis Mountbatten and confirmed by Nehru following the accession. The Delhi Agreement he signed with Nehru in July 1952 ratifies Kashmir's autonomy and restricted the Indian Union's jurisdiction to the same limited terms as those in the Instrument of Accession. (Rai 2019: 26)

There are some ex-soldiers and politicians who claimed that India was capable of driving away the Pakistani raiders and armed forces from Kashmir in 1948. There are two points to be kept in mind. First, there is a difference of perspective of the fighting soldiers, howsoever brave they might be, and a commander, who had to have a larger perspective not of the battlefield alone, but also the overall logistics of uninterrupted support system. In this context, hind side expertise would not do.

> If it were not Nehru's pledge, Kashmir would not have come to India. It is a part of India only because he backed out of his pledges. He was no idealist but a ruthless hardliner on Kashmir as well as the boundary. India has reaped and still reaps the fruits of Nehru's breach of faith, while Kashmiris refused to reconcile themselves to their fate. That is root of 'the Kashmir problem'. There are some 30-odd pledges on plebiscite by Nehru from 1947 to 1953. Patel concurred publicly. (Noorani 2019: 108).

Then five instances of pledge were mentioned. The Secretary of State and Sardar Patel's right hand man, V.P. Menon gives his opinion,

When you send in an army, there will always be ancillary questions.... The responsibility here was ours: we saw to it that Kashmir was defended, but we made a condition that the will of the people must be ascertained. If the answer had been no, we would have packed our bags and come home. But if the answer had been yes, well, that is the expression of the people in a constitutional manner. The thing is, we would not have done this without accession. Look at it like this, Maharaja or no Maharaja, you think anyone who would have laid their hands on Kashmir would have let it go like that? (Basu 2020: 384-5)

Maharaja Hari Singh was advised in 1949 by the Indian Home Minister, Sardar Patel, to abdicate in favour of his son, Karan Singh, which made him 'shocked' and 'bewildered'. However, the Indian establishment had enough of his antiques and he was advised to leave Kashmir in the hands of the Crown Prince, Karan Singh, and retired in Bombay. At the end, he expired on 26 April 1961 of diabetics at the age of 65. India claimed Kashmir to be an integral part of its Union. So much so, that India let Kashmir have its own constitution and government. The State Assembly of Kashmir decided to join the Indian Union with certain reservations. Their uncrowned popular leader, Sheikh Muhammad Abdullah, opted for India and went to the UNO to plead the Indian case. However, apart from 1948, Pakistan attacked Kashmir in 1965, 1971 and 1999 on its Kargil sector. Both the countries claimed every time that the other side as aggressor and it appears that the world opinion had enough of Kashmir dispute hanging on fire ever since 1948.

The Government of India abrogated on 5 August 2019 Article 370 of the Indian constitution, granting certain special rights to Jammu & Kashmir and divided the composite Kashmir into Jammu & Kashmir and Ladakh and turned them as union territories to be ruled directly by the Indian Federal government. Meanwhile, insurgency is on and there is a heavy presence of armed forces in Kashmir to take care of that. Most of the people's leaders including the son and grandson of Sheikh Abdullah, who happened to be the former chief ministers of the state and former members of the Indian parliament, have been put behind the bars and common citizens lead a life of great deprivation because of armed operations under military and their life in incessant curfews.

REFERENCES

Basu, Narayani, 2020, *V.P. Menon: The Unsung Architect of Modern India*, Simon & Schuster, New Delhi.

Kwarteng, Kwasi, 2012, *Ghosts of the Empire: Britain's Legacies in the Modern World*, Bloomsbury, London.

Noorani, A.G., 2020, 'The Atlas and the Army Chief', *Frontline*, 14 February, pp. 104-6.

_____, 2019, 'Secrets Held in Archives, Books Review: Towards a Cease Fire in Kashmir, British Official Reports from South Asia, 18 September-31 December 1948', Selected and Edited by Lionel Carter, Manohar, *Frontline*, 26 April, pp. 105-9.

Rai, Mridu, 2004, *Hindu Rulers, Muslim Subjects: Islam, Rights, and the History of Kashmir*, Permanent Black, Delhi.

Rai, Mridu, 2019, 'History of Betrayals', *Frontline*, 30 August, pp. 25-7.

Singh, Karan, 1982, *Heir Apparent*, Oxford University Press, Delhi.

_____, 1985, *Sadar-i-Riyasat: An Autobiography*, Oxford University Press, Delhi.

Whitehead, Andrew, 2007, *A Mission in Kashmir*, Penguin, New Delhi.

5

Lushai, No Mizo Hills District of Assam

The triangular land south of the district of Cachar in Assam lying between Koladyne River in the west, an imaginary line drawn from east to west through Darlung peak in the south and the Manipur River in the east, was known as the Lushai Hills district in the province of British Assam. The old British Lushai Hills district was renamed Mizo Hills district on the demand of the Mizos in 1954. Its modern history starts roughly from 1890 onwards, when the local chiefs mounted raids on the British tea plantations in Cachar and Chittagong Hills and Hill Tipperah districts in Bengal. The residents of the region were variously known as Kookis, Lushais, Pois, Shendus, Chins, etc., who were organized under their clan chiefs popularly known as 'Lal'. However, there was no tradition of one strong chief who commanded allegiance of other chiefs or if not all, most the members of the community. The land had a rugged irregular topography, which was in the rain shadow of the Chittagong Hills. There was a relative lack of dense forest with good timber, though the region was covered with thick bushes of dry bamboo forests. With a view to assert their relative superiority, the clan chiefs used to mount head hunting expeditions far and wide, invariably on the adjoining plains in the north in Cachar and west in Hill Tipperah district. John Edgar, the Chief Secretary of Bengal, suggested on 3 August 1888:

> ... apart from the danger to our tea gardens, it is almost certain that if no punishment is inflicted on account of successful raids of the past years, the offending villages will be emboldened to make more extensive attacks on all parts of the frontier next year or year after. It seems clear, therefore, that punitive measures are imperatively called for.... Of one thing I am absolutely

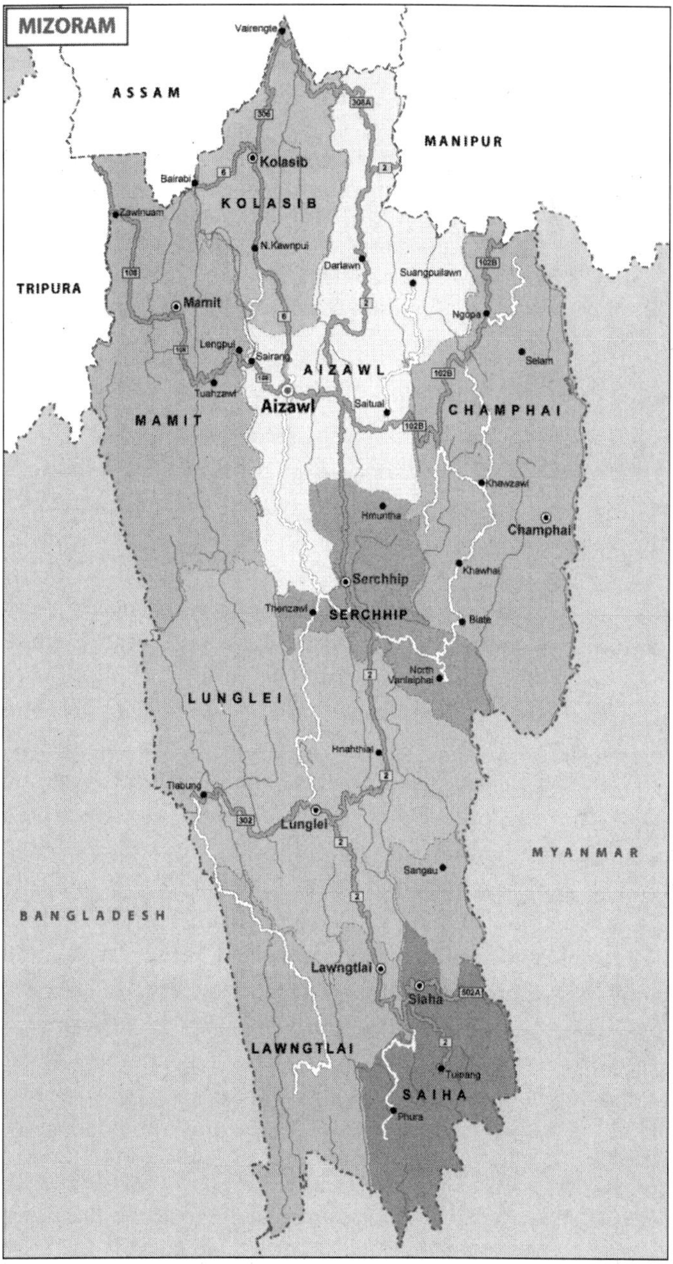

MAP 4: NOTIONAL MAP OF LUSHAI MIZO HILLS

(*Source:* https://www.mapsofindia.com/maps/mizoram/)

convinced. Any plan for dealing with these hill men should be worked in concert by the Governments of Bengal, Assam and Burma. (The region) is now surrounded on all sides by our settled districts...we cannot permit the continuance in our midst of groups of head-hunting savages without responsible chiefs, without organization, and not amenable to political control, who yet from their geographical position are enable to commit outrages with practical impunity upon our territory on all sides of them. (Reid 1983: 3-6)

The British Move to the Lushai Hills

In 1889, an expedition to Lushais, or the Shendoos, was organized to punish clan chiefs who had been raiding the hills of the Chittagong Hills district. Colonel F.V.W. Tregear of the 9th Bengal Infantry was to command the operation in which 1,150 armed men were included from the Madras Pioneers, Bengal Infantry and the Gurkha Rifles. When they reached Saipuia village, the chief readily agreed to support the visitors' demands. They established an administrative centre in March 1889 on a hillock at a height of 3,500 ft, which came to be known as Fort Lungleh and which was linked with a road to Demagiri in the Chittagong Hill district. A durbar of the chiefs was held on 3 April 1889, in which three important offending chiefs participated and agreed not to offend the British subjects. The expedition was disbanded after establishing a Frontier Police Station at Fort Lungleh with a British officer and a body of 212 men of the Frontier Police.

A more ambitious Chin-Lushai Expedition 1889-90 was organized to avenge the killing of Lieutenant Stewart and release of the captives taken in 1883, thus permanently bringing the Lushais under British control. This was the expedition jointly organized by three provinces: Bengal, Assam and Burma. The Chittagong Column, based at Demagiri, was once more led by Colonel Tregear and the Surma Valley Battalion of the Military Police was under the command of W.W. Daly, a police officer.

The general plan was that a Chittagong Column should move via Lungleh to Haka, meeting a Burma Column coming from Gangaw via Yokwa, a column from the former force to go north to punish the raiders on the Chengry Valley and Pakum Rani....The objectives of (the) Expedition will be, firstly, to punitively visit certain tribes that have raided and committed depredations in the British territory, and have declined to make amends or to come to terms; secondly, to subjugate tribes as yet neutral, but now, by force of circumstances brought within the sphere of the British dominion; thirdly, to explore and open out as much as can be done in the time, as yet only partly known, (the) country between Burma and Chittagong; and, lastly, if the necessity arises, to establish semi-permanent posts in the regions visited so as to ensure complete pacification and recognition of the British power. (Reid 1983: 10)

Daly left his base camp at Jhalnachera in Cachar on 18 January 1890, reached Changsil on 24 January and joined hands with Colonel Skinner's column on the 11 February at Ajail. On 30 January, 58 of Lengpunga's captives were brought to Changsil, to be followed by 5 more on the next day, while the last remaining captive, a young girl about 8 years old, was brought in good deal later on 9 February. In this way, the recovery of the Chengry Valley captives, one of the most important objectives of the expedition, was completely and expeditiously attained without bloodshed. On 4 February, 1890, Daly reached Ajail Range and built a stockade on a site, which he described as 'a good one for a permanent post', and which eventually became the site of the headquarters of the Lushai Hills district and subsequently, the capital of the State of Mizoram, to be created in 1987. He proceeded some 16 miles south of Aijal to Lengpunga's village near Tacchip on 8 February, and interviewed the suspect chief, but could not arrest him, as he had come to the meet on the good word of the political Jamadar, Chib Charan. The whole operation was completed in March, 1890.

Creation of North and South Lushai Hills Districts

These operations led to the creation of two districts: North Lushai Hills district at Aijal (spelt subsequently in Mizo as Aizawl) in the Province of Assam and South Lushai Hills district at Lungleh in the Province of Bengal under the charge of the two superintendents respectively. Captain H.R. Browne, the personal assistant to the Chief Commissioner of Assam was appointed as the Superintendent of the North Lushai Hills district and was asked to take over charge at the earliest. The Western Lushai chiefs were restive and were determined neither to pay revenue nor to supply labour and objected to the punishment awarded to Lengpunga, their former clan chief. They ambushed to death Captain Browne on 9 September 1890 on his way from Aijal to Changsil. Besides the Captain, his three bodyguards were also killed. Another attack was mounted by the Lushais on the same day on another party consisting of sepoys and coolies, in which 11 persons were killed. Retaliatory expeditions were mounted immediately to confront the violence and they were completed successfully fast enough considering the rugged topography of the Lushai Hills.

The Chief Commissioner of Assam transferred R.B. McCabe, ICS, the Deputy Commissioner of Lakhimpur to North Lushai Hills district as the Superintendent to take over charge of North Lushai Hills immediately. Having taken charge, McCabe identified five chiefs as the ring leaders: Khalkam, Lengkhunga, Sailenpui, Thanruma and Thangula. He reported to the Chief Commissioner on 19 January 1891:

> Khalkam was the leading spirit in the rising, and I consider that his deportation will have a good effect on the Lushai chiefs generally. Lengpunga has a bad record and the punishment inflicted on him last year does not seem to have proved an effective deterrent. He openly disregarded the orders of the government, rebuilt his villages, and threatened Lenkhai Mantri, who had made himself popular with the Political Officer. During the present outbreak he has undoubtedly been one of the most subtle, though not prominent, opponents, and his presence in these hills would always prove a source of danger to us. Thangula Raja is Khalkam's stepbrother and his right-hand man in the attacks on Ajail and Changsil. After careful delibration, I have come to the conclusion that the deportation of Khalkam, Lengpunga, and Thangula will prove of salutary effect, and facilitate the administration of the Lushai Tribes. (Reid 1983: 19)

The British Government of India concurred with the above recommendations. Khalkam, Lengpunga and Thangula were detained for ten years each. Two former chiefs, Sailenpui and Thanruma, hanged themselves in Hazaribagh jail in the following September of 1892. The Superintendent of the district reported: 'the complete pacification of the North Lushai villages west of Sonai River'. The administration noted the presence of two Presbyterian missionaries, Messrs Lorrain and Savidge, from 1893 and their role in introducing education leading to the creation of a positive atmosphere in the conflict-prone hills. However, it was at times felt that the administrative arrangement of the Lushais in three districts led to various chiefs demanding tributes from the weaker chiefs from the other districts without the knowledge of the authorities. This situation created enough administrative irritations in the sensitive un-administered area. Moreover, the higher authorities were aware of this anomaly right in 1892 itself. A 'Conference on Chin-Lushai chiefs' was held at Calcutta on 29 January 1892 among the Lt. Governor of Bengal, Commander-in-Chief, Madras, Chief Commissioner of Burma, Chief Commissioner of Assam, Foreign Secretary, Government of India, and top army officers of the Government of India. It was noted that the northern Lushais are under the Chief Commissioner of Assam, the southern Lushais are under the Bengal government and Chins are under the Chief Commissioner of Burma. This tripartite division of authority was open to objections and the Conference was asked to suggest remedial recommendations.

Establishment of Lushai Hills District in the Province of Assam

The Conference made the following final recommendations:

> The majority of the Conference are of the opinion that the whole tract of the country known as the Chin-Lushai Hills should be brought under one administrative head ... the new administration should be subordinate to the Chief Commissioner of Assam ... and the transfer of the southern Lushais from Bengal to Assam should be made as early as possible.... The Northern Arakan hills tracts should be transferred from Burma to Assam. (Reid 1983: 38-9).

On 1 April 1898 the new district of the Lushai Hills was created in the Province of Assam with Major John Shakespear as the first Superintendent. Shakespear introduced the circle system of administration by dividing the whole district into 18 Circles: 12 in Aijal subdivision and 6 in Lungleh subdivision. He also introduced a system of Land Settlement, in which each chief and his people would move about in an area of the district. An interpreter each was appointed in the Circles as the channel of information between the Sub-divisional Officer and the chiefs and their people. Sir Robert Reid informs that the Circle system of administration in the district worked satisfactorily for the next 40 years at least.

In September 1915, the District Superintendent along with two agricultural inspectors and some of the chiefs visited Kohima in the Naga Hills district, with a view to understand the practice of terrace cultivation of rice. Subsequently, one Angami each was employed at Aijal and Lungleh for instructing on the practice of terrace cultivation of rice in the district. Prior to that in the year 1910-11, *mautam*, flowering of the bamboos-producing seeds, which led to multiplication of rats feeding on those seeds, who ate every vegetation subsequently, leading to starvation in the district. The government distributed Rs. 5,85,000 as relief measure to the villagers.

During the First World War, Lushai Hills district sent 2,000 men to the Labour Corps in Europe at the instance of the administration. As in the case of 1910-11, another wave of *mautam* visited the district in the year 1925-6 causing great anxiety among the Lushais. The Superintendent of the District, N.E. Parry, instituted a rat killing campaign among the residents of the district to control the rat menace. The Lushai Hills district was placed as a 'Backward tract' as per the stipulation of Montagu Chemsford reforms in 1919. In the year 1936, the Lushai Hills district was declared as an 'Excluded Area' from the general administration of the province of Assam as per the Constitution Act of 1935. In the year 1937-8, a religious revivalist movement was launched, in which many of the Lushais became hysterical to the extent that the administration had to intervene to restrain them.

Simon Commission, Crown Colony, and End of the British Rule

John H. Hutton, ICS had roped in N.E. Parry, ICS, the Superintendent of the Lushai Hills district, to prepare a report on the Lushai Hills Backward Tract pleading for keeping it away from the future constitutional consideration for India. In 1929, this Report was submitted to the Indian Statutory Commission headed by John Simon, popularly known in India as the Simon Commission. And those pleas made by the two ICS officers provided the plank on which Sir Robert Reid built up his arguments for a proposal for creating a Crown Colony under the British Empire for the backward tracts of Assam and Burma, away from the Indian provinces. Writes a historian of the region:

> The impression of the Governor (Sir Robert Reid) was formed in part after a second visit he made to Aizawl in December 1940, where he got the sense that the Mizo 'the most alert and quick witted of the hill tribes and a race that takes keen interest in the outside world', were uncomfortable being labelled as 'Excluded' or 'Backward' and could not tolerate the idea of being swamped by the Indians. Reid saw a way out of this situation by reviving the idea of (Dr. J.H.) Hutton had given to the Indian Statuary Commission in 1928 of a North East Province or Agency embracing the entire hill fringe from the Lakher land in the south of the Lushai hills in a crescent shape to the hills of the present day Arunachal Pradesh. (Syiemlieh 2014: 8)

The Mizos of the Lushai Hills, despite the stand they would take later on their union with Burma, voiced their disapproval and turned down the proposal of the Crown Colony for their district through their forum, the Mizo Union.

> The party favoured autonomous status for the Lushai Hills within the province of Assam. The Mizos, who had just begun a movement to abolish Lalship (Chieftainship) realized that any call for Mizo independence as well as continued British administration would only perpetuate that institution (Chieftainship). (Chaube 1999: 175)

Philip Francis Adams, ICS, whose last role for a few months was that of Advisor to the Governor of Assam in 1947, wrote 'Some Notes on a Policy for the Hill Tribes of Assam', which was published on 5 August 1947, ten days before India's Independence (Syiemlieh 2014: 228-52). Adams suggested that the Lushai Chiefs' positions were being diminished and that the chiefs were trying to get government support to maintain their privileges while decreasing their obligations. A suggestion was made that the government should make constitutional provision for the chiefs' position by giving recognition to the village elders, and that instead of chiefs being recognized as village authority, they should be the chiefs in the village council.

Independence of Burma in 1948 and better bargaining position granted to the hill tribes thereof encouraged some of the Indian frontier tribesmen to look for incorporation into Burma. There were a number of opinions for the people of the former Lushai Hills. Some of them thought of an independent state; other wished to remain in India as the Mizo Union had expressed, even if only for ten years; while others hoped that the Lushai Hills could be tagged with the Chin Hills of Burma (Chaube 1999: 161-3). The Mizos were quite content to be under the British rule but had to consider their future in the event of the British withdrawal from India. Many of their leaders wrote to the powers that were in Britain in a last ditch attempt to express their concern for being left to look after their own destiny. The Secretary of the Lushai Chiefs Council wanted to opt for Burma and so did Lalbiakthanga, the President of the United Mizo Freedom Organisation (UMFO). It is difficult to believe that 'when the country became independent, the Mizo people joined most heavily the big family of diverse people which constitutes the great Indian nation' (Thanga 1978: 166).

It is worth keeping in mind that as they did elsewhere, the British administration under Major A. Shakespear had empowered the Lushai chiefs by granting them Circles, a distinct territorial area, with the right to move their villagers within. In course of time, the chiefs' families would get subdivided and stronger sons would opt to move out of the original household and settle in their own villages. There were 'interpreters' between the chiefs and the office of the administrative head of the district, the Superintendent. These chiefs lorded over the commoners, whose lives were miserable as they had to provide numerous unpaid services to them. Thus by 1940s there was a clear polarization among the Lushais: the chiefs supported by the administration in their Council were in favour of joining the Chin chiefs in Burma; the commoners, who formed their forum, the Lushai Commoners' Union on 6 April 1946, opted for joining Assam. Like C.R. Pawsey in the Naga Hills district, first it was Major A. MacDonald and later L.L. Peters in Lushai Hills district, who put the idea that hill districts should join the Indian Union provisionally for a period of ten years and then try to 'find their place under the sun'. In a politically uncertain environment prevalent at the time, naturally the proposition appealed to the Lushai Commoners' Union, which would change itself to be known as the Mizo Union in 1947 (Hazarika 2018: 91). Gopinath Bordolai, the Premier of Assam, visited Aizawl on behalf of the Constituent Assembly of India in April 1947 with a view to understanding the views of the Mizos on the constitutional provision for the district. And thus, the provision of the Sixth Schedule of the Indian Constitution was enshrined for the district and the Mizo community at large along with the other similar regions of Assam.

Lushais Turned into Mizos and Creation of the Mizo Hills District

In the confused situation of north-east India soon after the Second World War, which was fought at the doorstep of the Lushai Hills, and subsequently, all powerful British rulers of the region left India in 1947. To illustrate, for instance, for the Lushais, there was talk of Zoro or Zomi, or Mizo as the imagined land of the Zomia community. James Scott would ultimately write on the imagined ancestral land of the Zomias (Scott 2009). As it was believed that the term, 'Lushai', referred to one particular clan only, there was a consensus to adopt Mizo as the appropriate term for the community. Thus, nomenclatures of the community and the district were changed to Mizo and Mizo Hills district respectively in 1954, at the instance of the Mizo Union which controlled the Lushai Hills District Council. Since then, the term 'Lushai' almost ceased to be used in common practice. Though the district was administratively part of Assam State in the Indian Union, there was little evidence of infrastructural development. The district was one of the most isolated and ignored corner of the country surrounded by undeveloped Burmese or hostile East Pakistani territories from three sides. There was a tenuous road link with the rest of Assam through a meandering riding tract, which ran through most of the hillocks in the district. It was at most a thin cart tract on which running of both ways vehicular traffic was difficult to imagine. The Mizo Union tried to associate itself with the All Parties Hill Leaders Conference (APHLC), taking shape as an apex organization of the hill communities of Assam against the plains people of the valley, but it could not work. On the other hand, the ruling Congress party of Assam desired the Mizo Union to merge itself with the Congress, but the Mizo Union was determined to maintain its individual identity as an organized political forum of the district. The State of Assam itself was cut-off infrastructurally from the rest of India after the creation of East Pakistan and it took massive efforts for the Government of India to restore road and rail links between the state and the rest of the country. However, it appears that far away Mizo Hills district did not figure anywhere either on the State of Assam or the Union government's list of infrastructural initiatives for the first 15 years after Independence. And this apathy towards the district led further to Mizo isolation from the rest of India still more.

Mautam, Mizo National Front (MNF) and Operation Jericho

There were enough indication that another bout of *mautam* would visit the district in 1959, as it had happened in the past.

> Mizo leaders appealed to the Assam Government in 1959 for help: the condition of the people was desperate, they said, the crops had been destroyed, food stocks devastated, there was starvation because with the loss of crops, they had no cash to buy even the bare minimum for survival. Famine stalked the land. Exasperated by the Assam government's failure to rush assistance in time, the Mizos formed a few famine-fighting squads. The most prominent of these groups was the Mizo Famine Front (MFF), launched by a young bank clerk named Laldenga. Laldenga was a man who took part in regular political discussions in Aizawl, which functioned as the capital of the district. He too dreamed of a strong and vibrant nation for his people, who had been lightly administered by the British in the nineteenth century and until independence. But ... Laldenga kept his dreams to himself until he saw his chance in the famine. (Hazarika 2011: 111-12).

The Mizos suffered for about two years because of *mautam* coupled with apathy of the state government of Assam. That was the time, insurgency started in the Naga Hills district and a group of Nagas were engaged in talking with the Government of India for creating a State of Nagaland in 1962-3. The Indian Union suffered a crushing defeat on her northern borders at the hands of the People's Republic of China in 1962; the charismatic Prime Minister Jawaharlal Nehru died in May 1964; his successor Lal Bahadur Shastri, fought a war with Pakistan in Kashmir in 1965. But his life was cut short as he died of heart failure at Tashkent on 10 January 1966. The Indian Union now had a new Prime Minister Indira Gandhi. And that was the time, Laldenga and his outfit, the Mizo National Front (MNF), no more Mizo Famine Relief Front, chose to launch Operation Jericho on 18 February 1966. It appears that the Government of Assam was taken aback at the ferocity of the MNF operations. As there was no preparation in advance to counteract the rebellion, MNF guerrillas overran the district headquarters within no time: Deputy Commissioner's Office, the Treasury, the radio station, and the police lines all fell in the hands of the rebels without resistance. The worst thing was to happen when all the high ranking district level officers (nine in number) were gunned down while holding a meeting in an apparently secured locale at Aizawl. A twenty thousand strong and well-trained MNF army took complete control of the district within no time.

Taking advantage of the rugged forested topography of the region and its adjoining districts of Burma and East Pakistan, the MNF cadres easily slipped off across the borders for safety. They used these locales for armed training under the ex-Assam Rifle soldiers as well, who were persuaded to join the insurgents' rank. They slipped off to East Pakistan for procuring arms and training in sabotage of the State's strategic installations. They got limited supply of arms from Pakistan. A small band of the MNF cadre managed to reach even the People's Republic of China (PRC), but they could procure only limited arms and ammunitions. According to Bertil Lintner: 'China's only interest in the Mizo rebellion was that it needed a fifth column in India. It was part of the Great Game that was being played out in north-eastern India's border land, and nothing more' (Quoted by Hazarika 2018: 96).

If Naga insurgency was inaugurated in the Naga Hills district of Assam by the federal government's lack of concern for the distant, obscure and small tribal communities on the Burmese borders, Mizo insurgency was in a way reared by the state government of Assam callously. The MNF did not hide its intents right from 1959, but the state government not only ignored it, rather it was busy encouraging it to settle its score with the Mizo Union, which controlled the District Council. So much so that Laldenga was intercepted on the Indo-East Pakistan border by the security forces for his clandestine contacts with Pakistan for arranging arms for the rebellion. But the state government let him loose on his promise of future good conduct. The State Intelligence branch was aware of Laldenga's intentions long before Operation Jericho, but the state administration did precisely nothing to nip the impending rebellion in the bud. For example, MNF was busy recruiting youths in its ranks not within the district alone, they were enlisting them from far away Guwahati, Shillong and wherever the Mizo youth were. There is no evidence to suggest that effective steps were taken to frustrate them in their recruitment drive. It appears that the state government presumed that the MNF would emerge as an effective forum to arrest the hold of the Mizo Union in the district and that would work as proxy to the ruling Congress party in Assam.

Look at the irony of fate. Sanjoy Hazarika, historian of the regional insurgency, records:

> Chhunga, (the Head of the Mizo Hills District Council), was kind but a firm man. He had seen the uprising coming and made a desperate, last ditch effort to calm and prevent the horrors which were to be visited on his people. He reached out to his greatest foe, the man behind the MNF. A few days before Christmas, 1965, two months before the MNF seized most of the district, Chhunga and another Mizo Union leader went to see Laldenga. The MNF boss, who had demanded independence from India, was uncertain. 'Even if we decide to change our plan, our boys will kill us'. To which Chhunga responded: 'If Zoram (Mizoram) can be saved ... by the death of Laldenga and Chhunga, we should both be ready to make the sacrifice.
>
> Laldenga was not prepared to make that sacrifice. The peace mission failed and the war erupted. Yet, although an MNF marksman once had Chhunga in his sights, he did not pull the trigger. The explanation was simple: 'I did not have a reason to shoot him; he was doing what he thought was right for the people and the country'...Chhunga later became Chief Minister of Mizoram when it was upgraded from a district to a union territory. However, others were not that lucky. More than 200 members of the Mizo Union and their associates were to die at the hands of the MNF fighters in the long drawn out conflict. (Hazarika 2018: 93-4)

Counter-Insurgency Steps of the Government

The Deputy Commissioner of the district, T.S. Gill and left over civilian officers took shelter in the Assam Rifles camp, the only area under Indian control in those chaotic days. The MNF leadership had visualized its physical control of the entire Mizo Hills at least for eight months so that the leadership could canvass support for its recognition by international capitals. The Government of India was determined not to let Mizo Hills turn into another Nagaland for a long drawn insurgency. Leadership in armed forces reasoned with the political leadership that even 100 or 200 guerrillas could effectively pin down a large number of army in a difficult terrain such as Nagaland and Mizo Hills. So a three-point alternative strategy to combat the MNF guerrillas had to be evolved:

First, in a roadless locale of poor logistics, fighter jets of the Indian Air Force were commissioned on 1 March 1966 and they strafed the towns and big villages indiscriminately. It was a ruthless exercise to pound the civilian population irrespective of their political loyalties.

Second, a policy decision was taken to re-group the villages on the roadsides under the strict watch of the armed forces. Initially, it was proposed to create 18 Progressive Protected Villages (PPV) along Vairengte-Aijal and Aijal-Lungleh Road out of 106 villages with a population of 50,000. The idea was to starve the insurgents by denying them access to food, which they could force from the villagers and deny them to seek shelter in the settlements.

Third, villagers were forced to move out with whatever they could carry to the PPV sites at a short notice by destroying their living structures along with all immoveable property in their villages with a view to deny the rebels to seek shelter there.

These were really very inhuman and unpleasant tasks for the already depleted civil administration to implement. And implement they did within a short span of time. Ultimately, two-thirds of the entire Mizo population of the district were shifted to the Protected Progressive Villages under the guards of the armed forces. These hurriedly created settlements were at times wrongly located; they could not be provided with the basic amenities on time such as water, sanitation, food, other consumer goods, clothes and what not. On top of that, the armed security guards themselves were exposed to the risk of being easy targets of an individual insurgent hidden in the difficult terrain. In many cases, desperate MNF cadres moved on the fringes of the district to small communities such as Chakmas, Chins, Lais, etc., and harassed them to the extent that many of them were uprooted for good from their habitat and moved to any place they could find security. In short, it was huge tragedy for the innocent rural people, who did not understand the politics of either insurgency and/or security. The issue was raised on the floor of the State Assembly and the chief minister cut a real sorry figure of himself to defend the indefensive acts of the eastablishment, while the opposition termed it as 'concentration camps'.

Laldenga Slips off to East Pakistan and the Crackdown on the Bengalis by Pakistan

Laldenga had slipped off to East Pakistan again, where his cadre were provided with shelter, money, training in arms and some arms and ammunitions. At that time, the Indian leadership was determined to act fast and decisively to crush the rebellion without caring for world opinion. The district was handed over to the armed forces, who were given a free hand to operate as per their book of rules. The insurgents in spite of their initial success were now on the run. Slowly, it was becoming clear that Laldenga had no vision for an independent Mizoram and no nation bothered to respond to the MNF's appeal for international recognition. The military dictator of Pakistan, Ayub Khan, was by then removed from his post after an armed uprising by another military dictator, General Yahya Khan. There was a popular upsurge in favour of democracy in East Pakistan. Elections were ordered and Sheikh Mujibur Rahman's political forum, the Awami League, won the maximum number of seats in the newly elected parliament in Pakistan. However, the power to be in that country refused to honour the electoral verdict and put the popular East Pakistani leader, Mujibur Rahman in jail. Naturally east Pakistan rose in rebellion; Pakistan imposed martial law and its administrator, General Tikka Khan, who came to be known as the Butcher of (East) Bengal, inflicted the most inhuman torture on the East Pakistani masses. A large number of Bengalis were massacred; women were subjected to the most inhuman atrocities; properties were looted, burnt, destroyed and any type of real or imagined opposition to Pakistani designs were ruthlessly suppressed.

Minority Hindus and tribes were special targets of the military operation. In such a situation, millions of East Pakistanis: Bengali Muslims, Hindus, tribals and others were forced to flee from their home and took shelter in neighbouring India. India appealed for international support for the huge number of refugees, to the extent of ten million, who had crossed over to India with a view to saving their lives, but it got a limited response from the international community. Desperate Bengalis formed their own guerrilla force, the Mukti Bahini, and waged a relentless war of liberation against the butchering Pakistanis. With a view to weakening Indian support to the Bengalis in East Pakistan, Pakistan attacked India in December 1971 and India retaliated by declaring war on Pakistan. In the absence of support from the East Pakistanis, Pakistan was losing the war on all fronts in its eastern wing. At last, a 73,000 strong Pakistani army, led by Gen. Niazi, surrendered before the Indian Commander, Gen. Jagajit Singh Aurora and Commander of the Mukti Bahini, the East Pakistani, now Bangladeshi Liberation Army. Pakistan was forced to set free the captive Bangladeshi leader Sheikh Mujibur Rahman. In this chaotic situation, a new nation, Bangladesh, came into being in 1972.

It is instructive to recall that fed up with the atrocities committed by the Pakistani armed forces and its Urdu-speaking supporters, the Bengali East Pakistanis had formed their own liberation army, the Mukti Bahini, and tried to oppose the atrocities inflicted on the unarmed masses by the Pakistani army. Once the Pak forces surrendered to the victors, there was nobody responsible enough in Pakistan to take care of the MNF rebels and they were simply advised to slip off by the familiar Arakan forests in Burma. Before they made their armed surrender to the Indian forces, the rulers of Pakistan managed to reach the Mizo rebels safely to Karachi, where they were provided with modest shelter and some cash for their maintenance. By then, it was clear to Laldenga that his game of insurgency was over. With the loss of East Pakistan and creation of Bangladesh they had become a liability to their Pakistani benefactors. Naturally, a defeated and demoralized Pakistan had little reason and capacity to support Laldenga's adventure and host the rebels comfortably. However, it appears a greedy Laldenga asked his Pakistani hosts to fund running his government and armed operation against the Indians. Pakistani intelligence agency, ISI, was nobody's fool; in fact, they were shocked at Laldenga's audacity. Their response was predictable:

> Give us the name of the person and the town where he is located, in Rangoon, or Bangkok or anywhere and we will transfer the funds to him directly. Laldenga was insistent that the money should be given to him, as MNF president. He could have been more prudent: after all, it was a time when Pakistan had just been through the worst experience of its short life and was reeling from the humiliation of defeat, surrender and vivisection. (Hazarika 2020: 115)

Laldenga Negotiates and becomes the State Chief Minister of Mizoram

The North-Eastern States Reorganization Act, 1971, created three new states of Manipur, Meghalaya and Tripura and two Union Territories of Mizoram and Arunachal Pradesh with the stipulation of upgrading them to statehood. In this way, the Government of India had taken steps to resolve the Mizo unrest within the ambit of the Indian constitution to the maximum possible limit of statehood. As we have noted earlier, by the middle of the 1970s Pakistan and the MNF/Laldenga had enough of one another and both were looking for a way out of their predicament. At last, Pakistan issued a passport to Laldenga on the name of one Peter Lee of Chinese descent in 1973 and he reached Geneva, where the Indian intelligence agency, RAW, got in touch with him. Once he was on his own, Laldenga wrote a letter to Prime Minister Indira Gandhi offering to call off all the operations against the Indian security forces by the MNF insurgents and asking for a 'reciprocal action' from the security forces. He also indicated through his letter to the prime minister his willingness to work under the ambit of the Indian constitution. At last, Laldenga arrived in New Delhi in January 1976 and remained a state guest for about ten years till the Mizoram Accord was hammered.

In spite of the above development, the armed wing of the MNF was unwilling to accept the above stipulation and lay down their arms. The negotiation between the two sides continued at a slow speed. Meanwhile, the political scenario in New Delhi went a sea change in 1977: Indira Gandhi and her political party, the All India Indian National Congress, lost the general election; a politically confused combination of former Congressmen, a variety of socialists and the Bharatiya Jana Sangh, precursor of Bharatiya Janata Party, got together to form a government under an authoritarian Morarji Desai as the prime minister and a new political party, the Janata Party, was born. Chaudhuri Charan Singh, the deputy prime minister and the home minister, got Laldenga briefly arrested for non-compliance of the understanding with the government. For a little while, he was sent to London. But things changed in New Delhi soon and Janata Party fell apart like a house of cards. Morarji Desai lost power; his deputy, Chaudhuri Charan Singh, took over as the new prime minister; but his government resigned without ever facing the Indian parliament.

Another general election was held in India and Indira Gandhi got elected with a thumping majority and she formed the government. Laldenga was brought back from London and details of the terms of agreement were sorted out. There were still two problems: one each on both the sides, the government and the MNF. While a vocal section of the rebels were reluctant to accept the terms of negotiation, the popularly and democratically elected chief minister of the Union Territory of Mizoram and the president of the Mizo National Conference, Brigadier Thenphunga Sailo, was insistent that Laldenga should face the electorate. In fact, he refused to resign to facilitate Laldenga without a popular contest as a policy. And Mrs Gandhi honoured his sentiments and let him complete his term in the office as the chief minister. But another big tragedy occurred in India, as Prime Minister Indira Gandhi was assassinated by her bodyguards on 31 October 1984.

Once more there was a new prime minister, a new general election and new threads of negotiation were to be picked up afresh. This time, the new prime minister, Rajiv Gandhi, was determined to close the chapter of insurgency in Mizoram. At last, Laldenga on behalf of the MNF, R.D. Pradhan, Home Secretary, Government of India and

Lalkhama, Chief Secretary of the Union Territory of Mizoram, signed the Mizoram Accord on 30 June 1986 in New Delhi and the Congress Chief Minister Lalthanthaula was persuaded to resign from the post and Laldenga was sworn in as the new chief minister and his former rebel colleagues were rehabilitated. Laldenga was elected as the first chief minister of State of Mizoram in 1987 when the new state was inaugurated, but he did not prove to be an effective administrator. Very soon there were defections from his ranks and he could not complete his full term of five years in the office. He expired on 7 July 1990 from lung cancer in London. He was accorded a befitting state funeral and he was buried at a commanding location in the heart of Aizawl town at the Treasury Square. Since then Mizoram has been one of the states where there has been regular elections after every five years and two political parties, the Congress and the MNF, have been competing for the office. It is a credit to the Mizos that Mizoram is one of the most peaceful states in the north-east region of the Indian Union today, which had belaboured India two decades back.

REFERENCES

Chaube, S.K., 1999, *Hill Politics in Northeast India*, Orient Longman, New Delhi.

Hazarika, Sanjoy, 2011, *Strangers of the Mist: Tales of War and Peace from India's Northeast*, Penguin, New Delhi.

_____, 2018, *Strangers No More: New Narratives from Northest India*, Aleph, New Delhi.

Reid, Sir Robert, 1983, *History of the Frontier Areas Bordering on Assam: 1883-1941*, Astern Publishing House, Delhi.

Syiemlieh, David R., 2014, *On the Edge of Empire: Four British Plans for North East India, 1941-1947*, Sage, New Delhi.

Scott, James C., 2009, *The Art of Not Being Governed: An Anarchist History of Upland Southeast Asia*, Yale University Press, New Haven and London.

Thanga, L.B., 1978, *The Mizos*, United Publishers, Guwahati.

6

The Indian Protectorate of Sikkim

It is claimed that Guru Rimpoche (Padmasambhava) had set apart Sikkim (*Denjong*: land of rice) from the mundane world and created it as 'a hidden blessed land' (*sbas yul*). This theocratic model of state draws upon the Tibetan idea of invitation of a king to rule and the Indic model of Dharamraja (the Chho + rgyal) and Chakravartin (whose wheel of reign moves in all the four directions). Interestingly, kingship in the Tibetan tradition was seen as contractual between the king and the ministers and not as sought after prize; rather it has to be seen as a burden shouldered at the request of others in order to benefit 'poor subjects'. It has to be seen as a social contract between the king and his subjects, failure on the part of the king could result in regicide or rebellion. In the words of Soul Mullard,

> The appearance of these themes in 17th century sources have to be understood as legitimatizing agents of the newly formed state and monarchy and not as a reflection of political reality; as the political reality of formation in 17th century Sikkim, however, was far complex and was brought about, not by religious invitations to the first Sikkimese Chos-rgyal, but by conquest, alliance formation, and the subjugation of the population under the figure of the Chos-rgyal. The reason they appear in later historical narratives is to characterize the formation of the Sikkimese State as the fruition of divine prophecy. (Mullard 2011: 27)

Creation Myth of Dynastic Rule and State Formation in Sikkim

The official history of the former ruling family of Sikkim, the Namgyals, runs as follows. A prince, who happened to be a descendant of king

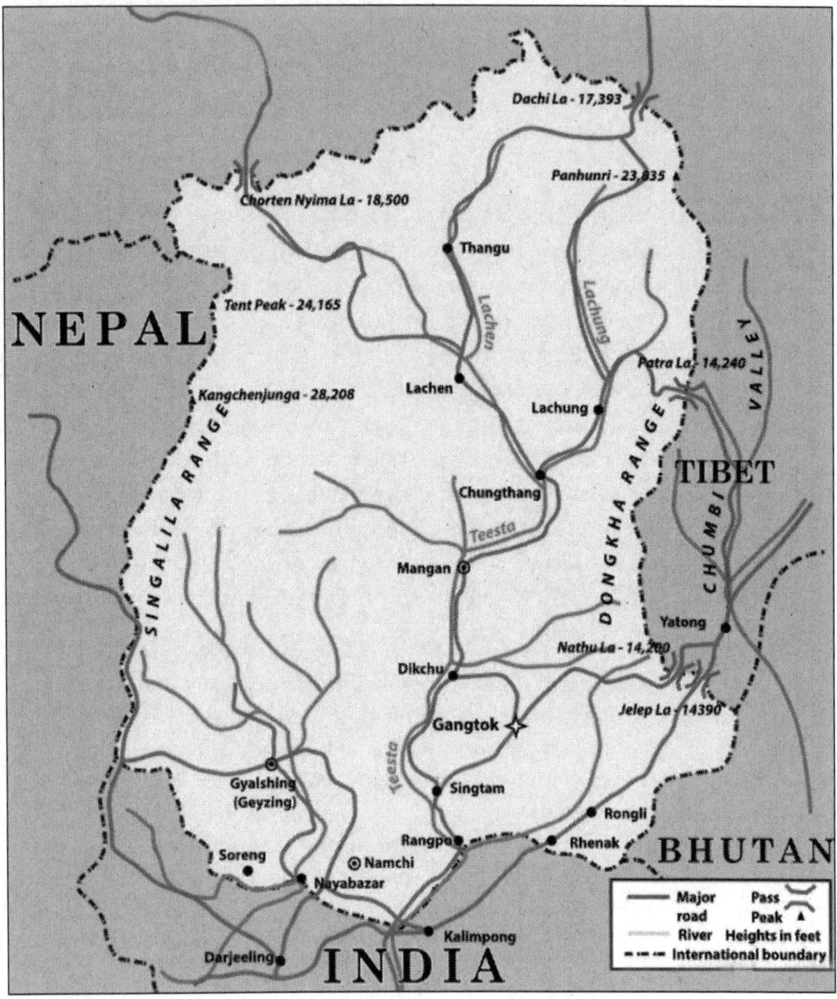

MAP 5: NOTIONAL MAP OF SIKKIM
(*Source:* https://en.m.wikipedia.org/wiki/File:Sikkim_area_map.svg)

Indrabodhi of Himachal Pradesh in India, is known to have founded the Mynak Kingdom towards the ninth century of Christian era (in eastern Tibet). Twenty-five generations later, in the first half of the fifteenth century, a scion of the Mynak house went on pilgrimage westwards with his five sons to Sakya, his *guru*, who was building his abode. Many persons failed to erect a pillar, which one of his sons was able to erect alone, earning the title of Khaye-Bumsa (one with strength of ten thousand persons). So pleased was the hierarch that he offered his daughter in marriage to Khaye Bumsa, who happily got settled in the nearby Chumbi Valley, which later became the nucleus of the later kingdom of Sikkim (Unknown 1963:1). It is claimed that the issueless Khaye Bumsa contracted blood brotherhood with the regional powerful Lepcha chief, Thokengtek, which proved profitable for the immigrants, as one of his descendants, Phuntsog, a peasant patriarch from Gangtok, was consecrated as the first Bhotia king of Denjong in course of time.

It is claimed that three Nyingmapa Lama missionaries travelled from three directions to the Himalayan region in search of a holy land to establish their respective kingdoms in the aftermath of the Geylugpa supremacy in Tibet. They debated among themselves on the respective merits of their individual claims to Denjong. Lhatsun Chhenpo Namge is credited to have said,

> In the prophecy of the Guru Rimpoche it is written that four noble brothers shall meet in Sikkim to arrange for its government. We are three of those (who have) come from the north, west and south. Towards the east, it is written, there is at this epoch a man named Phuntsog, a descendant of the brave ancestors of Kham in Eastern Tibet. According, therefore, to prophecy of the Guru, we should invite him.

Two messengers were then despatched to search for this man, Phuntsog. Going towards the extreme east, near Gangtok, they met a man churning milk and asked him his name. He, without replying, invited them to sit down and gave them milk to drink. After they were refreshed, he said (that) his name was Phuntsog. He was then conducted to the Lamas, who crowned him by placing a holy water vase on his head and anointed him with water, and exhorted him to rule the country religiously, giving him Lhatsun's own surname of Namgye (Namgyal) and the title of the Chho-rgyal, or religious king' (Patterson 1963: 25) at a place Yoksom, in western Sikkim.

Since then, Lhatsun Namkha Jigme turned out to be the guardian saint of the new regime. It is claimed again that the newly appointed king selected twelve of his Bhotia elders (or soldiers?) as his kalongs, councillors or advisors and another bunch of twelve Lepcha chiefs as dZongpens (regional administrators) and they were advised to intermarry among themselves laying the foundation of the Sikkimese aristocracy, Kazihood in course of time. It is also claimed that the borders of the state was extended from Dibdala (?) in the north to Naxalbari and Titalia in the south, and Walung and then following the course of River Arun in the west to Thangla in the north-east. However, in spite of the best scheming of the Bhotia grandiose, there appears to be armed clashes and violence on the occasion. Possibly from the Lepchas, the ninth descendant of Phuntsog Namgyal, Thutub Namgyal and his consort, Dolma recorded thus:

> So he (Phuntsog Namgyal) started forth with (from Gangtok) with his entire retinue of followers, officers and household establishment ... as the party happened to be riding on ponies and some of the retainers had matchlock guns, which they went on firing along the road, the simple natives, who had never seen a pony nor firearms, said to the others: 'the entire party rode on huge hogs, and some of them bore sticks, which when pointed towards you, produced great sound. (Namgyal 1908)

It is difficult to believe that they were just celebratory or ceremonial displays. Possibly, there were either violent opposition or some latent opposition was forestalled with display of mounted armed forces from Lepchas and Limbu communities.

Phuntsog's ancestor, Khaye Bumsa, had already contracted ritual brotherhood. Incidentally, the pre-Namgyal Sikkim was inhabited by Rong (Lepcha) and Tshong (Yakhthumba, Limbus). The ninth Namgyal ruler Thutub and his consort wrote:

> Hearing that in the interior of Sikkim, there was a great Lepcha patriarch and wizard, called The-Kong-Tek, who was reputed to be the incarnation of the Guru Rimpoche, he (Khaye Bumsa) after due consultations with his

lamas and divinations, all of which promised success, resolved to pay a visit to the great Lepcha wizard, and started with 16 followers, carrying various kinds of silk, etc. ...they came upon The-Kong-Tek and his wife, Nyo-Kong Ngol, who were clearing a patch of jungle for the purpose of cultivation. Gyad (Khaye) dBum asked them where The-Kong-Tek and Nyo-Kong-Ngol lived, not being aware that they were the identical persons. Both said they do (did) not know. On asking again, the couple said, 'Let your party stay here, while we go to find them'. So saying, they went away and did not return. After waiting (for) some time, the party saw that they had been given the slip, now they tracked them to the bamboo house. Entering inside they discovered the old gentleman on a raised throne of bamboo. He had washed off the dust and ashes, which had covered his face during his work of clearing jungles. He had donned on his feather cap and his garland of teeth and claws of wild beast, interspersed with various cowries and shells. He sat with a dignified mien, while his wife was busily engaged in getting food and drink ready. When the strangers entered, a wide bamboo mat was spread on the ground, where they sat and instantly were served with tea (?) and wine. Khaye Bumsa, seeing that this was The-Kong-Tek, offered him presents, which he had brought for him, asked for the boon of a son, which the wizard promised him. This was at Ringchom. And sure enough as soon as they returned to Chumbi, in the proper time, Jomo Guru showed the sign of conception, and later birth of a son, which event was followed by two more issues. He thought that in the time to go to celebrate the thanksgiving by puja, of local deities of Sikkim. So they came down via Cho-la and arrived at the cave.... There they were met by The-Kong-Tek and Nye-Kong-Ngol, who had come up bringing various fruits from Sikkim, upon the same errant, viz. to see Khaye dBumsa and to celebrate the thanksgiving by a puja.... As eternal friendship was made between Khaye Bumsa and The-Kong-Tek, they agreed by this that all the males should be considered to be related to the sons and all the females of the daughters. The friendship was cemented by a ceremony at which several animals, both domestic and wild, were sacrificed and all the local deities were invoked to bear witness to this solemn contract of friendship binding the Lepchas and Bhutias in an inseparable bond. They sat together on the raw hides of the animals, entwined the entails around their persons, and put their feet together in a vessel filled with blood, thus, smearing the blood troth to each other. The invoking all the local spirits, asked them to stand witness to this solemn contract, invoking blessings on those, who observed these faithfully, and curses on those who broke this eternal hereditary and national contract between the two. (Thutub & Dolma: 1908)

There was nothing unusual about this act of the Bhutia patriarch. Amalendu Guha informs that once the Ahoms, the Thai migrants to Assam, were settled down in Upper Assam and realized the significance of ploughing the paddy fields and scrapping the land surface to a dead level, they too incorporated Maran and Barahis in their political structure. Not only they, but a few of the tribal chiefs and headmen were also admitted into even the respectable Ahom clans and the rest were transformed into peasants doing militia duty like the Ahoms (Guha 1987: 170). Similarly, anthropological literature informs of the practice of blood-brotherhood among the various communities from many communities as the forms of social and political alliance.

It appears that Phuntsog, the Bhutia prince, had managed to buy a level of peace in the land from the Lepchas, the autochthones of the land. But there was another community which possibly still had reservation on the new dispensation and they were the Limbus, though some of them were won over by the Lamas and were persuaded to join the new faith and earn a new nomenclature: Tshongs. The Namgyal establishment invariably talked about an ethnic commonwealth of communities as the original inhabitants of Sikkim. It appears that there was sufficient dissension among the various communities of Sikkim in the middle of Phuntsog's rule and he was forced to call for an ethnic conclave in 1663 in which an agreement known as the Lho-mon-tshong Gsum was signed:

...Henceforth confirming to the command of his majesty (?), the humble (12) ministers and leaders of Lho, Mon and Gtsong have met here with the desire for unification and solidarity and hereby make the statement that there shall not be separate governments of Lho, Mon and Gtsong. During the previous Mon Pa war (13) people from all the different ethnic groups intentionally rebelled and this has been remembered. Henceforth with from this year (1663) take hold (of this order) and in accordance with orders of the Lord the Chos-rgyal laid down the affirmation and grasps the solution and so the humble and dedicated minister Dag shar (affixed his) seal.... (Mullard 2011: 142-3)

The point to be noted here is that though some of the members of the nobility and the aristocracy would marry with Limbus, in course of time, no Limbu was elevated to the status of the aristocracy, kazihood. So much so, that even the maternal uncle of one of Namgyal kings was murdered by the mechanizations of the Bhotia courtiers. It appears that unlike the Lepchas, the Limbus, in spite of their various contributions such as the very nomenclature of Sikkim (Sukhim, 'new home'), were not completely assimilated within the Namgyal state structure even after Sikkim's claim on the Limbuan as part of their domain.

Though there is not much mention of the two other Lamas after coronation of Phuntsog, Lhotsum Lama remained in Sikkim to guide the king in the theocratic state craft. He established the famous Pemiyagtse (Pemiyangchi) monastery and laid the tradition that the chief abbot of the said monastery would be entitled to crown the Namgyal kings. Then a series of monasteries were established and the king was commanded to rule as per tenets of the religion, thus justifying the nomenclature, Chos-rgyal, the religious king or the Dharamraja. The Kalons and Jongpens were left to mind their estates and contribute to the upkeep of the kings. Moreover, they were commanded to maintain two establishments each: one in their respective estates and another one at the king's court. However, at the kings' court, the capital was bereft of attributes of a township: there was no town, no market, no commerce and industries. So much so that there was no state police or standing state army; rather, whenever the contingency arose; ethnic groups raised their forces to fight against the adversaries. The kings were invariably week and were manipulated by their strong armed courtiers. Out of a total of a dozen Namgyal rulers from 1642 to 1975, there were half a dozen of them who ascended the throne at the ages ranging from zero to fourteen years of age, making them vulnerable to manipulation by others. The Namgyal rulers remained obliged all along to the monastic order for their smooth reign in such a situation. The Bhutia highlanders avoided residing in the hot, humid and wild Morung foothills below the Dorji-liang hills in the south leaving it vulnerable to rulers from the Gangetic plains in the south, Bhutan in the east and Nepal in west in course of time.

The entire divine and mythical narrative of the founding of the Namgyal dynastic rule in Sikkim suggests a series of legitimatizing criterion. First, Phuntsog Namgyal was a descendant of an Indian Khatriya king and a Tibetan king of antiquity. Thus, his ancestors were claimed to have ruled over Himanchal Pradesh in India and Kham in Tibet. In this way, he was not an ordinary mortal, rather he was something larger than life among the men. Second, the Namgyal dynasty was established in Denzong, which could be verified by visiting the coronation site, the stone slab at Yoksom, other historical landmarks and the original monastery at Pemiyangtse established by venerable Lhatsun Gampo. Third, stories of contracted blood brotherhood between the Lepchas and the Bhutias chiefs and the ethnic alliance of Lho-Mon-Gtsong are repeated time and again to hammer out Lepcha-Bhotias or Bhutias' ethnic antiquity vis-à-vis the immigrant ethnic Nepalis of Sikkim. The appearance of these themes in seventeenth-century sources has to be understood as legitimatizing mechanisms of the newly-formed state and monarchy and not as a reflection of the political reality of state formation in seventeenth-century Sikkim. However, it was far more complex and it was brought about, not by religious invitations to the first Chos-rgyal, but by conquest, alliance formation, and subjugation of the population under the figure of the Chos-rgyal. The reason they appear in the later historical narratives is to characterize the formation of the Sikkimese state as the fruition of divine policy (Mullard 2012: 27).

Sikkim as a British Indian Principality

Chronologically, Sikkim was the first among the three principalities in the Eastern Himalayas – Sikkim, Nepal and Bhutan – where a political party was formed, a popular democratic movement against the feudal dispensation was launched and a popular government was formed. Thus, it is in the fitness of things that we first undertake the analysis of those pioneering endeavours. Sikkim, the smallest and centrally located among them, was a dynastic theocracy ruled by the Namgyal family since 1642. It was ideally located on the shortest trade route between Tibetan capital, Lhasa and Calcutta, the commercial capital of the British Indian Empire. Soon after the Anglo-Nepalese War of 1814-15, the British decided to control the affairs of Sikkim decisively with a view to facilitating the trade across the Himalayan passes and for that they took a number of steps from 1817 after signing the Treaty of Titaliya with 'Sikkimpati Maharaja'. By the end of the nineteenth century, Sikkim was reduced to a small ordinary feudatory strictly under the control of the British Political Officer, J.C. White from 1888 onwards. And its 9th Namgyal ruler, Thutub Namgyal, was imprisoned at various locations in the newly created district of Darjeeling. After his demise, his eldest son succeeded him, but he died in mysterious circumstances within a few months. Consequently, his step-brother, Tashi Namgyal, was crowned as the eleventh ruler of the principality, who was destined to rule his kingdom for almost five decades till he died in 1963. Though educated at Mayo Princes' College, Ajmer and trained by Sir Charles A. Bell ICS, Tashi Namgyal was happy to leave the state to be ruled by his Kazi courtiers under the overall control of the British Political Officers in Gangtok.

On the other hand, the princely state of Sikkim had an archaic aristocratic system in which Bhutia-Lepcha Kazis (aristocrats) and Nepali *thikedars* (contractual developers of the allotted land with immigrant Nepalese labour) were not only the landlords, but were also permitted to run their own police force, jails, courts, and revenue administration. They used to collect land rents from the tenants and apart from that they used to administer the forests in their localities in a wanton manner. There were four types of unpaid compulsory labour which every tenant was subjected to and defiance of which led to heavy corporal punishment, confiscation of their property and other forms of indignities. Among them, especially *kalobhari* (the black load, it was a popular nomenclature among the coolies, because of the fact that the heavy head load was wrapped in black colour tarpaulin so that it did not get damaged while carrying across the snow bound Himalayan passes) was much abused by the Kazi aristocracy. Normally, most of the Kazi households and even the Lamas used to trade with Tibet and goods were transported by the coolies manually. The Political Officer had fixed the rates for hiring the labourers. But the Kazis abused the provision during the period of the Second World War when consumer goods were required to be sent in considerable quantity and within the shortest possible time. Kazis used that provision to transport their commercial goods in considerable quantity with indentured labour free of cost. Naturally, it was resented and when the coolies opposed, they were mercilessly flogged. And any voice raised in opposition to the system resulted in repression and public flogging and no political rights were recognized in the system.

The oppressors had their own private police force, jails of their own, and had the judicial power to try alleged criminals. 'The state police were an ill-trained mob disunited and openly partisan with one side or the other. As upholders of law and order in the countryside, they were no less than the local bullies. Many of them freely collected exaction because the people were habituated to submitting to the lessees and their henchmen', writes J.S. Lall, the first Dewan of Sikkim in 1949. In such a situation, anti-feudal activists such as Tashi Tshering, Sonam Tshering, Kezang Tenzing and others, who had suffered at the hands of Kazis' goons, got together and organized a welfare society: Praja Sudharak Samaj at Gangtok in the early 1940s. Kazi Lhendup Dorji, a scion of Chyakhung Kazi Khangsharpa family, had founded a similar forum known as Sikkim Praja Mandal in 1945. And from south Sikkim, some of the All India Gorkha League (AIGL) activists such as Gobardahn Pradhan, Dhan Bahadur Tiwari and others had founded the Sikkim Praja Sammelan at Temi Tarku. Though they wished to, but politically these fora were inactive and tried to do some or other social service to keep themselves active and alive.

The Ruler Reacts to Impending British Withdrawal from India

But before that, the ruler, Tashi Namgyal, was a worried man as he felt that the British were leaving India without advising him about the future status of Sikkim. He confided to the Political Officer, Basil J. Gould that he would like the status of Sikkim as a British protectorate to continue in the event of the British withdrawing from India. Gould informed him that it was not possible as Britain was far away from Sikkim and it would not be possible for them to safeguard Sikkim from that distance. In fact, he advised him to send a delegation to Delhi to meet the Cabinet Mission sent from Britain for working out a framework of the future political set-up in India. Gould also added that if a similar delegation from Bhutan would visit Delhi with the same purpose that would help the matter well. Thus, Maharaj Kumar of Sikkim, Palden Thondup Namgyal and the Bhutan Agent, Sonam Tobgyel Dorji, visited Delhi and waited on the Cabinet Mission. They were advised to return and wait for instructions on the future course of action. On 10 August 1946, the Political and Foreign Department, Government of India, New Delhi, sent a 'Note' to the Political Officer of Gangtok on the policy to be followed in near future as far the political status of the eastern Himalayan kingdoms was concerned. The 'Note', informed the Political Officer, A.J. Hopekinson, states (Sinha 2008: 63):

> In practice, it may well prove difficult to secure a tidy solution of [the] future of Nepal, Sikkim and Bhutan, and even the eastern marches of Kashmir. This will largely depend on the future policy and fate of China and hence of Tibet. The Government of the (Indian) Union must be prepared for complications on Northeast Frontier and evolve a policy to meet them. This may well have to be that of maintaining all the principalities in virtual independence of India, but as buffer, as far as possible, (as) client states. There may be greater advantages in according Sikkim a more independent status than seeking to absorb Bhutan as well as Sikkim in the Indian Union, adding a communal problem of Buddhism.... The Government will be well advised to avoid entering into fresh commitments with any one of these frontier states or seeking to redefining their status. Their importance is strategic in direct relation to Tibet and China and, indirect to Russia. Such adjustment of relations with the (Indian) Union can fully be affected by those political and strategic considerations ... account of which, it is hoped, the treaty will take rather than the political niceties, which do not help defence policy.

Indian Protectorate of Sikkim and Her Last Ruler, Palden Thondup Namgyal

Soon after Independence, the Government of India signed a standstill treaty with the Maharaja of Sikkim, followed by a formal treaty with that principality in 1950. This treaty was signed on three subjects, foreign relation, defence and communication, which Sikkim surrendered to the Indian Union. On rest of the subjects, it was the internal administration of the Maharaja, which was run on an archaic feudal autocracy. Incidentally, these were the three subjects, on which other Indian principalities had merged with the Indian Union. The Government of India signed treaties with Nepal and Bhutan on the same old pattern set forth by the British. Coming back to Sikkim, the above Note left behind by the British Imperial power was possibly unknown to the popular political leaders engaged in organizing democratic movements in these principalities and anticipating support from the Indian Union. The treaties signed by the three rulers had a provision that the Government of India would not interfere in their internal administrative matters.

Palden Thondup Namgyal, born on 4 May 1923 and the second son of Sir Tashi Namgyal, was an incarnation of his uncle, Sidkeong Tulku, the Gyeshe Rimpoche (the prince abbot). The Prince, popularly known as Maharaj Kumar, who was supposed to be a Precious Jewel theologically, was held in high esteem. He was schooled for monkhood prior to his brother's death in an aircrash and was recognized as the spiritual head of the two important monasteries of Rumtek and Phodang. He was given secular instructions at St. Joseph's Convent in Kalimpong, St. Joseph's College in Darjeeling and Bishop Cotton College in Simla to prepare him as the successor to the Namgyal throne. He was then seconded to the Indian Civil Service (ICS) probationers' course in the Administrative College at Dehradun like princes of other similar States (Rustomji 1987). His friend from Dehradun days, Nari Khurshid (N.K.) Rustomji, found him to be a complex personality: 'a shy, timorous, lonely and lost individual' (Rustomji 1971: 21). In his considered opinion, Sikkim belonged to the Bhutias: the Kazis were, after all, his courtiers. Lepchas were, in any way, the loyal subjects and the rest (read the ethnic Nepalis) were intruders, and thus the responsibility of the protecting power of Sikkim, i.e. the (British or Indian) government. He was stubbornly opposed to any accommodation of Nepalis, (who constituted two-thirds of the population of Sikkim by 1951) in the Sikkimese establishment as he took it as the surrender of his legacy.

The Maharaj Kumar saw himself as a Bhutia ruler of his kingdom, and grudgingly accepted Lepchas as his associate subjects simply because of the fact that if he would not, the mythical legitimacy of his regime would be vulnerable and stand alone among the subjects. Thus, he was determined to make a stand in defence of the Lepcha-Bhutia communities against the democratic aspirations of the Nepalis.

He wrote to his friend, Rustomji, way back on 12 April 1949, that when he was only 25 years of age:

I am all for fulfilling the wishes of our Bhutia and Lepchas, real wishes. But I will be sooner damned than let these mean conspirators and job hunters (read Nepalis) have their way, if I can. We are on the verge of getting our independence of sorts like Bhutan and I think we have achieved a miracle in not having to accede [to the Indian Union]. Out greatest drawback is that the P[olitical}] O[fficer] and the Government of India seem to favour the other side, and we have to proceed so that we give you people [the Indians] no chance to butt in. The second trouble, which I have a feeling is common, is the unruly Nepalese element against whom I cannot take action as I would like to have.... (Rustomji 1987: 27)

So in his scheme of things, Sikkimese Nepalis did not figure in his domain and this stubborn attitude ultimately turned out to be his undoing, as the events in the early 1970s showcased that. He saw Sikkim in his own image, and stubbornly believed that others must do the same and this insistent belief eventually resulted in the obliteration of the Namgyal dynastic rule in Sikkim. He appeared to be something like a Shakespearean tragic hero who lost everything at the end: his wife, the crown prince, throne, kingdom, patrimony, friends and supporters.

Birth of Political Parties

British Political Officer and the Namgyal courtiers had created such a reign of terror that nobody could openly dare to assemble for any public cause. Thus, inspired by the movement for independence in the Indian plains, some educated and enlightened Sikkimese such as Tashi Tshering, Kezang Tenzing and Sonam Tshering met to discuss the state of affairs in Sikkim on the pretext of a picnic party at Bhotia School, Gangtok in 1947 and they decided to form a reformist forum, the Praja Sudharak Samaj. Earlier they had petioned to the authorities against forced labour and oppression of the landlords. And they pleaded for paying rent directly to the state bankers instead of lessees, as was the practice till the 1940s. Their petitions were not only ignored, but they were also charged with spreading Nepalese communialism.

In course of time, the Samaj leaders such as Sonam Tshering was physically assaulted by the Kazis' goons for openly raising the cause of the forced labour. Similarly, two Nepali *thikedars*, Gobardhan Pradhan and Dhan Bahadur Tiwari of Temi-Tarku in South District, who were exposed to populist movements in Darjeeling, stealthily met at Thakurbari at Rangpo on the plea of worship and picnic. However, the police offcer smelt a rat, paid a surprise visit to the picnickers and went back to report that there was nothing objectionable being done. On that day, 14 August 1946, they established another such forum, Sikkim Praja Sammelan, for redressal of the plights of the commoners (Subba 2012: 63-4). Inspired by the movement for independence in the Indian plains, some educated and enlightened Sikkimese such as Tashi Tshering, Kezang Tenzi, a descendant of the illustrious Cheebu Lama, the Lepcha Kazi of Chyakhung, Lhendup Dorji Khangsarpa (or L.D. Kazi) and an ascetic turned politician, Krishna Das Ray Chaudhury, established a third organization called Sikkim Praja Mandal in western Sikkim in 1945.

The Praja Sudharak Samaj of Gangtok had the benefit of the seasoned counsel of Tashi Tshering, an English educated former employee of the Political Office, who alone of all the champions of change, had understood politics and administration, and had the gift of articulating his views. The Gangtok Party (Sikkim Praja Sudharak Samaj) decided to hold a public meeting at the Gangtok football ground – then known as Polo Ground – on the 7 December 1947. The two parties from Temi Tarku and Chyakhung were invited to participate. Tashi Tshering (had) composed his pamphlet, *A Few Facts about Sikkim*, which was translated into Nepali by Chandra Das Rai, who also took upon himself to cyclostyle enough copies for distribution among the masses. (Basnet 1974: 76)

Among the other speakers, there were Tashi Tshering, Kezang Dorji Tezang, K.D. Ray Chaudhury, Helen Lepcha, nee Sabitri Devi, and Captain D.S. Lepcha.

That was an unprecedented political meeting, in which Sikkimese heard their first political speeches for the first time. Again, Basnet informs us what happened in the meeting:

Appearing with the stalwarts was a young man, Chandra Das Rai, 24, from Namchi. He was asked to read the Nepali version of the paper, 'A Few Facts about Sikkim', which he did with gusto, lacing his reading with witty remarks. The crescendo of applause that followed his speech marked him as a budding hero in the inchoate politics of Sikkim. All the speeches were in Nepali language, the language of an overwhelming majority of the population and the *lingua franca* of Sikkim. Later that evening, the three associations formally merged together and formed a new party called the Sikkim State Congress (SSC). Tashi Tshering was elected President of the party, Dimik Singh Lepchpa as the Vice-President and Kashiraj Pradhan as the General Secretary, consciously disabusing the charge of possible Nepali Party by the Durbar. It was decided that a five-member delegation should call on the Maharaja and present the 'three-fold' demand of the Sikkim State Congress. The three-fold demands were: (a) abolition of landlordism; (b) formation of an interim government as a precursor of a democratic and responsible government; and (c) accession of Sikkim to the Indian Union. (Basnet 1974: 77)

It appears that the Sikkim State Congress was organized as the Sikkimese counterpart of the Indian National Congress (INC) and affiliation to the parent body was sought (Tshering 1960). The party petitioned to the ruler for a drastic change in the political structure (Memorandum....1960: 7) with their three-point demands. Apart from formulating and presenting political issues of radical significance, the Sikkim State Congress started to impart political education to the masses through campaigns and movements. In no time, it became the party of the masses, reflecting their aspirations. Though its popularity was more among the Nepalese, the State Congress took special care to appear as the forum of consensus and avoided any overt identification with a particular community. This was the political forum, which was careful to represent all the important ethnic groups and region of the state. They launched agitation in favour of their demands.

Columnist Sunanda K. Datta-Ray, writes that it was the 20 year old Maharaj Kumar, Palden Thondup Namgyal who envisioned a 'federation of the Buddhist units such as Sikkim, Bhutan and Tibet' in 1947 (Datta-Ray 2013: 64-6). And with a view to counteracting Namgyal's alleged strategy to galvanize Lamaist conclave against India, a nervous Political Officer, Harisher Dayal, drafted Tashi Tshering out of a mob to organize Sikkim State Congress. The author had heard this formulation once before from a scion of the Libing Kazi, Tashi Tobden, in 2008, a few months prior to his fatal accident. In fact, it was Sir Basil J. Gould, Hopekinson's predecessor, who advised the Bhutanese and Sikkimese scions on the steps to be taken in the uncertain situation after the Second World War and impending British withdrawal from India. It was Gould's ideas to think of a Buddhist Federation of Tibet, Bhutan and Sikkim and send a representation to the Cabinet Mission in Delhi, which Sikkim and Bhutan did. Incidentally, Gould was a scholar in Buddism, who is known for book, *Lotus in the Crown*. This was the precise argument with a view to justifying the Crown Prince's known role to get the Sikkim National Party (SNP) organized to counteract the efforts of the Sikkim State Congress.

Durbar Reacts by Organizing its Own Political Forum, Sikkim National Party

Andrew Duff, an author, writes that the above demands of the SSC 'posed irritating challenge (to the Crown Prince, Thondup)'. He could accept the first demand:

> he knew that the land laws needed to change, but he also knew that the problem was deeply ingrained and could not be addressed overnight. As for the second, he was willing to consider change, but he also had grave concerns. For decades the ethnic make-up of Sikkim had been altered with the wide scale immigration from Nepal. Any move towards more representative government would give Nepalis more power. Thondup was deeply concerned by the obvious implication that the Buddhist community might lose its strong connection with the land in the face of the growing Nepali population.... It was the third demand, however, that Sikkim should join India that Thondup found most frustrating. He was certain that such a move was incompatible with Sikkim maintaining its identity separate from India. (Duff 2015: 34-5)

And thus,

> 1. Resolved that with regards to the question of abolition of landlordism in Sikkim, the party would approach His Highness the Maharaja for an early consideration ... a time-honoured institution, like the one in question, cannot be suddenly wiped out of existence root and branch, without giving rise to graver consequences, such as, administrative difficulties and disruption.
>
> 2. Resolved that the proposal of introducing a responsible government

in Sikkim shall not under any circumstances accede to the Dominon of India. (Documents: 1960)

And who had drafted these lines on palace stationery? It was the same character who happened to be the Maharaj Kumar (the crown prince) of Sikkim and he was present in the little crowd on the occasion.

This party had few clear political objectives. It was an organization of the Kazi aristocrats and the neo-rich Bhutia courtiers who sought to safeguard Lepcha-Bhutia interests against the alleged Nepali-dominated Sikkim State Congress. The Sikkim National Party stood for an independent Sikkim with special treaty with India. This party could not assume the character of a mass party, did not spell out any ideological commitment, and was mainly a defender of the status quo in Sikkim. It was a political forum floated by the Crown Prince against the expressed advice of the Political Officer. It was not only funded by the Durbar, but even the paper work such as the resolutions, etc., were also drafted by the Crown Prince and not those half-wit functionaries such as Gyaltensen or Sonam Tshering, who had never accomplished such an exercise in their life. However, the brain behind this facade of the political forum worked out the resolutions on 30 April 1948 by which all efforts were made to thwart the populist demands of the Sikkim State Congress and resolutely maintain the status quo in the principality. From its very inception, the SNP remained a party under the leadership of the affluent Bhutias with the backing of the lamas from various monasteries. The National Party leadership was convinced that the State Congress was committed to wresting power from the ruler and establishing the 'tyranny of the majority'. The indomitable Tashi Tshering rightly termed it as the 'anti-thesis of the State Congress'.

Anti-feudal Agitations, Formation of a Popular Government and its Dismissal

As an answer to the mechanization of the Crown Prince, Sikkim State Congress organized on 22 October 1948 its next session at Namchi and reiterated its threefold demand and decided to agitate for that.

And for that, the SSC decided to open its branches in every village, canvassed in favour of three demands against abolition of Kazis and *zamindars*, establishment of people's government and joining India as a democratic move. They pleaded with the people that they were not against the king, but they were certainly against the oppressive administration run in the name of the king. The Durbar ignored their plea and went ahead with sabotaging SSC by placating Sikkim National Party. Out of desperation, the SSC sent its President Tashi Tshering and one of the General Secretaries, Chandra Das Rai, to Delhi in December 1948 to impress upon Pandit Jawaharlal Nehru to act in favour of their demands. Nehru gave a patient hearing to his visitors and explained the intricacies of their demands and advised them to go back and strengthen their movement among all sections of the Sikkimese.

The Sikkim State Congress organized a series of no-tax campaigns, non-cooperation movement and non-violent agitation against the autocratic administration. Its leaders courted arrest in favour of their three-point demands. They also lobbied to convince New Delhi of the urgency of drastic political change in Sikkim. To some extent they were able to impress upon New Delhi about the partisan attitude of the ruler towards the Sikkim National Party. Armed with organizational experience and fraternal assurances from the politicians in New Delhi, the State Congress embarked on the second Satyagraha movement in May 1949. The demonstrators barricaded the royal palace and the ruler ran away to take shelter in the Political Office. The hyperactive Crown Prince tried to drive away from the palace to the Political Office for confabulation, but the agitating volunteers of the SSC blocked his way by laying themselves in front of his vehicle. The indomitable Namgyal Tshering, the Vice-President and C.D. Rai, the General Secretary of SSC mounted on the hood of the jeep being driven by the prince and managed to secure the keys of the vehicle forcing the beleaguered prince to stage a retreat to his den, the palace.

As the popular agitation continued unabated, the Maharaja was forced to hand over the administration to the Political Officer, who advised him and the SSC to negotiate among them to break the stalemate. After prolonged negotiation, the Maharaja agreed to install a five-member interim government inclusive of two of his nominees. In this way, the first popular government of Sikkim was installed on 9 May 1949 under the leadership of the President, Sikkim State Congress, Tashi Tshering and it included Dimik Singh Lepcha and C.D. Rai of the State Congress, and Dorji Dadul and Reshmi Prasad Alley were the two nominees of the Durbar. This ministry was installed without defining the scope of its power and functions of the ministers and even the role of the chief minister. On most important issues, the Durbar and its nominees disagreed with the chief minister. Moreover, the Durbar's nominees proved to be unenthusiastic about the popular government, which was also not in a position to liberate the masses from the feudal autocracy. The ruler refused to introduce agrarian and administrative reforms insisted by the chief minister. Out of desperation, the State Congress leadership embarked on questionable political gimmicks with vulgarity. Meanwhile, the Maharaja had been trying to convince New Delhi that popular government in Sikkim meant anarchy and political instability. This led the Government of India to act 'in the interest of law and order'. All of a sudden, the Political Officer sent for all the five ministers on 6 June 1949 and curtly announced the summary dismissal of the ministry in the name of the Government of India. This action on the part of the Government of India came as a boost to the Durbar and a rude shock to the democratic forces, which had not traded for such a strong reaction from New Delhi (Sinha 2008).

Ethnic Balancing of the Parity System

Under the pressure from the Government of India, Sikkim State had to involve the political parties in the affairs of running the administration. All this resulted in an ethnic policy of parity between the Nepalese on one side and the Lepcha-Bhutia combined on the other. This was a skewed contrivance to deny about 75 per cent Nepalese population of Sikkim their due representation as they were equated with about 25 per cent Lepcha-Bhutias in political representation in the elective bodies of the State. The Sikkim State Congress was some way persuaded to participate in this charade of democratization in the state. But its rank and file was not reconciled to it. Thus, many of the leaders and most of the followers walked out of the party. They formed a separate political party in course of time – the Sikkim National Congress, under the leadership of one of the former founders and the presidents of Sikkim State Congress, Lhendup Dorji Kazi.

The elections to the State Council were held periodically from 1953 to 1973 and Executive Councillors were appointed from the elected councillors in spite of a variety of charges levelled agasit them. Lal Bahadur Basnet, the Joint Secretary to the Sikkim National Congress, issued a statement on 10 September 1966 on the functioning of the Executive Councils in Sikkim:

> No sane person, certainly no sane Sikkimese, could for a moment, accept the fact that the present Executive Councillors are people's representatives in any sense of the term. It is generally accepted that in Sikkim and elsewhere, they are in effect, are the agents of the Sikkim Durbar and no more. Their continuation in the office (elected in 1958 for a period of three years term) without a fresh mandate from the people constitutes the greatest affronts to democracy and is possible in Sikkim, where autocracy blandly poses as democracy. What the Chogyal practices runs counter to not only what he preaches.... But then, apparently, such contradictions abound in the 'Welfare State of Sikkim'. (Sinha 2008: 143)

And these 'Executive Councillors' gave a public statement to revise the Indo-Sikkimese Treaty of 1950, for which they were not entitled.

At last, the State Council Elections for the last time were held in January 1973 and the results were challenged by all the political parties other than king's own outfit, the Sikkim National Party in May 1973. King Palden Thondup Namgyal ignored the political outcry of the foul play and got busy in concentrating on the golden jubilee celebration of his coronation. But this time, his subjects were in a different mood. It appears they had enough of the royal foul play and perhaps they had decided to have a showdown with the ruler and resolve the issue of their representation for all times to come. On the other hand, the ruler presumed that the agitation was a passing phase as in the past and did not pay serious attention to it. And ultimately that cost him dearly, whatever he had: kingdom, queen, crown prince and his life at the end.

The American Queen and Her Initiative to Introduce a Novel Court Culture

In 1963, twenty-years old American Hope Cooke came in the life of Maharaj Kumar Palden Thondup, who was double her age with two sons and an infant daughter. In spite of the opposition of the tradition-bound Sikkimese clergy and aristocracy, they got married in March 1963 under visible publicity blaze. However, 'this was the first occasion in the history that foreigners from different continents were being invited to grace a Sikkimese royal wedding and it was important that they should go back with them with the impression not of a medieval, feudal backwater but a progressive, enlightened country of standing of its own to do so. The plethora of foreign diplomats and relatives, however, with their old-world morning coats and western regalia, almost outnumbered the Sikkimese gentility, who seemed relegated to the position of back stage observers. And the expenses incurred on the festivities was out of all proportion to the country's resources', noted his loyal friend of four decades (Rustomji 1987: 64-5).

The coronation of the Namgyal couple in 1965 was conducted in even in a more ampler style than the wedding. Foreign dignitaries of the highest diplomatic level attended. In the words of Namgyal's friend, Rustomji, who felt a sense of unease:

> ...that more importance was attached to attending to the requirements and seating of the guests from abroad than to high ranking dignitaries of Sikkim itself.... It became obvious that Hope relished playing queen. She was gifted with a sense of theatrical and the part offered infinite possibilities.... Hope realised, however, that unless public opinion within Sikkim itself could be effectively mobilized, there was little prospect of the raising of Sikkim's status under the Treaty (with Indian Union) being seriously taken note of. It was this view she gave encouragement to the activities of the Youth Study Forum, an organization established the objective of highlighting the need for safeguarding Sikkim's identity and countering any move to bring the country under tighter control of the Protecting Power. Members of the Youth Study Forum enjoyed the patronage of the Palace and were also assisted in obtaining scholarships for study in various disciplines abroad. (Rustomji 1987: 76-7)

Hope had taken over as the Chief of Public Relations to the ruler by the end 1960s. Former Maharaj Kumar, by then the Maharaja (not the Chogyal: one who rules as per the tenets of Chho, religion: an ancient nomenclature of the Sikkim rulers, which the Government of India agreed upon in 1965 as a friendly gesture without changing the term legally) was slowly getting obsessed with the idea of his international persona. The ruler did not hide his desire to project his small kingdom as a member of the UNO in the near future. And for that the couple felt that it was the protecting power, which was the biggest obstacle on the way. As an example of Indian illegality and exploitation, Hope wrote an article in the *Bulletin of Tibetology*, Gangtok, 1965, pleading a case for the restoration of Darjeeling to Sikkim. The Indian public got enraged on that and the issue was raised in the Indian parliament. When pressed for his views, the Chogyal pleaded that that was not his official position; rather Hope's article was an academic exercise. However, slowly, the ruler was getting obsessed with his 'claimed mission to fulfil commitments to Bhutia-Lepchas cause'. He was so taken to his own claimed commitment that he forgot his commitment to the ethnic parity between the communities. In the year 1967, the Sikkim National Congress, led by Kazi Lhendup Dorji, won 8 out of 14 elective seats in the Sikkim State Council elections. Instead of honouring L.D. Kazi by offering the post of Senior Executive, the Maharaja caused defection to the SNC Legislature Party and offered executive posts to the defectors. By then, it was loud and clear that the ruler was determined to deny any legitimate role to his alleged political enemy, Lhendup Dorji Kazi, who stood for the common Sikkimese.

The Ruler Overplayed His Game and Lost the Principality

The above developments led to some serious considerations at the highest echelon of the Government of India (Ramesh 2018)[1]. It appears that the government had finally decided to clear the pitch for the Maharaja of Sikkim, as he had played enough nationalistic politics at the cost of India by taking its support for granted. And it was not to be anymore. When he tried to engineer victory to his Sikkim National Party in 1973 elections to the State Council by letting its candidates win 8 seats, three opposition parties (Sikkim National

Congress, Sikkim State Congress and Sikkim United Front) got together and challenged the rigged verdict by taking the issue to the public. While the ruler was busy celebrating his golden jubilee, the people at large had marched in a huge body to the capital defying the police and facing their bullets. Naturally, the administration collapsed and a Joint Action Committee of the three political parties demanded cancellation of the last election, introduction of electoral reforms and a fresh election on one man, one vote principle. The agitation for the electoral reforms had reached the villages; police posts were deserted and volunteers of the Joint Action Committee were running the administration in the interiors. The political parties reached the Political Officer and requested the Government of India to intervene in the matter.

There is another side of the Sikkim saga. It is claimed that the Indian armed forces disarmed the Sikkim Guard personnel, in which there were some casualities. So much so that even the Maharaja's palace was put under military guards. Sunanda Dutta Ray claimed (Dutta Ray 2013) that among the mob, which resorted to violence against the state establishment and supporters of the Maharaja in Gangtok and elsewhere were a good number of outsiders, mainly from Darjeeling and even from Nepal. It is also alleged that there were a good number of construction workers engaged in road repairs and improvement and many of the plain clothes sepoys of the CRPF (Central Reserved Protection Force) posted to guard the state establishments were among the agitators. The charge was that the so-called mass uprising was stage managed by the Indian establishment. Who will verify such claims? The Maharaja who could not save himself against his own people, how long would he survive by blaming the protecting power? The tragedy was that all through the Maharaja believed that the protecting power, the Indian Union, would ensure continuation of the Royal family and interests of the minority Bhutia community at the end. He seemed to be so sure of it that he went on defying the advice advanced to him time and again by the Indian functionaries. At last, it appears that the obstinate Maharaja was determined to take the plunge in darkness blindly.

The Foreign Secretary of India paid a visit to Gangtok and a tripartite agreement among the ruler, political parties and the

Government of India was signed in May 1973. Consequently, election to a 32-member State Legislative Assembly on the basis of 'one man, one vote' under the supervision of the Election Commission of India was held in 1974. Results of the election to the new assembly was a foregone conclusion: all but one seat were captured by the Sikkim Congress party, a formation of the above Joint Action Committee. Lhendup Dorji was elected the chief minister and the newly-formed government asked for closer ties with the Indian Union. Meanwhile, having realized that all her dreams of Sikkim had gone awry, Hope Cooke, the queen, decided to leave her husband and Sikkim for good.

It appears that the ruler was not reconciled to the changing situation. As if he was waiting for an opportunity to play his last card by trying to internationalize the recent changes in the principality. And he used the occasion of Prince Birendra's coronation in Kathmandu to air his side of the story. He was invited to the celebration of King Birendra's coronation to Kathmandu in 1975, which was an unprecedented development in the history. He was advised by the power to be not to visit Nepal, but he did go to Kathmandu by road and addressed the assembled press as and when the occasion arose. All these developments did not endear him to the Sikkimese people and there was a demand for his removal as the ruler of the state and merger of Sikkim in the Indian Union on floor of the State Legislative Assembly. So much so that a plebiscite was ordered in Sikkim to choose between Namgyal's rule or popular democracy. The result was a foregone conclusion: the Sikkimese people overwhelmingly chose democracy. Ultimately, Sikkim merged with the Indian Union and the 333-year Namgyal dynastic rule came to an end in May 1975. Unfortunately, he was so unceremoniously removed that nobody thought of compensating him for the loss of his kingdom, as it had happened in case of other princely states, and providing for his and his dependents' upkeep.

NOTE

1. On November 1970, P.N. Haksar had sent a note to the Foreign Secretary (FS), T.N. Kaul, while keeping the prime minister informed:

   I had suggested to FS that we should carefully consider and review the underlying assumption of our policy in Sikkim. We have had several meetings. Broadly two points of view have crystallized themselves:

That our economic, social and political policies must be designated to improve the people of Sikkim, so that they feel that their destiny lies with India.

That have regard to our policies in the past and what we have done in Bhutan, there is really no escape from leading Sikkim to a stage where it becomes a sovereign independent state tied up with India.

My own preference is for the first alternative. Be that as it may, we have to deal, for the time being with the Chogyal. He is going to impress upon us the need to let Sikkim exercise greater autonomy and responsibility. He will stress as his reasons: the restiveness of his educated classes, particularly the young, under the influence of the spirit of our times and India's own anti-colonial ideals; the infectiousness of developments in Nepal and Bhutan; and the dangers of resentments growing if the natural aspirations of the Sikkimese to do more on their own is denied....

The pressure for change really centres around him and are sufficiently (354) manageable without any basic concessions on our part. PM might take the following line with him....

The existing relationship has been as helpful to Sikkim as to India. Where we have been found insufficiently considerate or overtly restrictive, we are prepared to have a fresh look and meet all genuine grievances not only sympathetically but also generously. But grievances should not be manufactured or harboured till they become disproportionate; least of all by those elements in Sikkim, the ruling hierarchy, who owe their whole position to the Indian presence. We have an impeccable record of not interfering in Sikkim's domestic politics, and we have relied scrupulously on him alone. We always wish to do this and he should look upon us as his active supporter. The pressures he feels from his educated elite are very understandable and we should like to help him meet them. They cannot be met by giving in to illusions about Sikkim becoming free, prosperous and neutral like an Asian Switzerland if only India would relax its hold....

...We should exhort the Chogyal to create a feeling of mutual trust and confidence instead of subjecting us to one manoeuvre or another and to pressures of various kinds....

Without doubt, this note was to trigger a change in Indira Gandhi's approach to the Chogyal. He had been a protégé of her father and she herself had a fond personal relationship with him. But she could be unemotional when larger national interests were involved.

Two years later, Haksar was to take this forward and fired a second salvo that was to lead to Indira Gandhi's actions in April 1975. This is what he had told the prime minister on 14 March, 1972:

I try to keep track of the goings on in the Ministry of External Affairs. The Foreign Secretary had spoken to me about his visit to Sikkim. But I have long felt that we really have no policy in regard to Sikkim except to wait upon Chogyal's varying moods. The Foreign Secretary says that he found him 'chastened mood'. With great respect, this makes no sense to me....

There was a time in 1947 when the people of Sikkim were with India. Thereafter, we developed a great fondness for the Sikkim Durbar and now we wait on his frowns and on his smiles....(355)

I tried at one stage to organize some thinking about our policy towards Sikkim. Nothing came out of it. The basic question is what are the sanctions behind 'Permanent Association' or 'protectorate' or anything else. In this later half of the twentieth century, a sanction political framework has to be people if that framework is to prove durable. And we have totally alienated the people of Sikkim....

We had a similar sort of policy towards Nepal of alternating between Pro-Consulars's stances and abject subjection to His Majesty. Until a year and a half ago, we succeeded in restoring to our policy in Nepal a semblance of rationality....

We must not deluge ourselves. The Chogyal wants independence, a membership of the United Nations and he is gradually eroding our will....

My own view is that until time the PM has made up her mind, she should not see the Chogyal in order to put a seal to the so-called 'Permanent Association'. In my view, we are not utterly helpless. We can make a new beginning. We can establish contacts with the people of Sikkim, develop relationships and earn their goodwill and use that as a real lever against the vagaries of the Chogyal. If we decide on such a policy, I have no doubt that in the space of two years we shall get the Chogyal running to us for protection against his own people. Otherwise, he will be taking us for a ride all the time.

In this cold blooded note, Haksar was wrong on the time it would take for the Chogyal to change his approach. It was not two years as Haksar had predicted, but it took three years. But, by the time it was too late and he had burnt all the bridges with Smt. Indira Gandhi. For the moment, the prime minister had agreed with the broad approach that Haksar had delineated. Three months later he was at it again and, on 1 May 1972, he made his views known once again to the prime minister before a meeting of the Political Affairs Committee of the Cabinet:

... It is true that we do not like having the only Protectorate in Asia, and it might well suit our interests to meet the aspirations of the Sikkimese people. It is, however, doubtful whether they want independence rather than democracy. The latter would endanger the Chogyal's position, while giving him independence would endanger the people's aspirations for democracy. He has always shown absolutist tendencies.... (356)

... The Chogyal has been very careful not to support us on our problem with China in a way that might antagonize Peking. Even on Pakistan, his support to us has been very lukewarm.... Such caution in relation to China and Pakistan indicates a desire to play off these powers against us which Nepal has been doing.

... PM has repeatedly advised the Chogyal to mend his anti-Indian ways, but I am not aware of any improvement. Partly this is our fault, since the Dewan we have given him plays the courtier rather than giving him correct advice, but essentially it is the Chogyal's own approach to any exract concessions by creating difficulties for us. Before we agree to any treaty revision, therefore, we should first try to prevail upon him to create a more harmonious working relationship.

At this stage we should tell him we are not averse to the type of changes he has suggested, and would be glad to help him achieve Sikkimese aspirations, but these must be based on two realities:

(i) Sikkim is militarily vulnerable without India's military presence, and
(ii) Sikkim also has domestic stresses which only an Indian presence can contain.

These weaknesses expose Sikkim to interference from China and possibly Nepal. Since such interference would harm his interests more than India's, we both need to maintain a relationship which allows us to protect Sikkim from external military pressure and domestic political instability. We need assure that a partial revision of the treaty would not lead to a further demand a few years hence for a total revision which would exclude us totally from Sikkim.... If he does not agree, we should tell him that we are working over his draft to try and make it safeguard our rights and interests against unilateral erosion....(Ramsesh 2018: 354-7)

REFERENCES

Basnet, L.B., 1974, *Sikkim: A Political History*, S. Chand, New Delhi.
Documents, 1960, 'Inside Sikkim', *Mankind*, February, New Delhi.

Duff, A., 2015, *Sikkim: Requiem for a Himalayan Kingdom*, Penguin Random House, Gurugaon.

Dutta Ray, Sunanda K., 2013, *Smash and Grab: Annexation of Sikkim*, Tanquebar, New Delhi.

Guha, A., 1987, 'The Ahom Political System: An Enquiry into State Formation in Medieval Assam: 1228-1800' in *Tribal Politics and State Systems in Pre-Colonial Eastern and North-Eastern India*, ed. S.C. Sinha, K.P. Bagchi, Calcutta.

Lall, J.S., 1953, Fortnightly Report, Private papers of Baleshwar Prasad, Sub File No. 18, NMML, Teen Murti House, New Delhi.

Mullard, S., 2011, *Opening the Hidden Land: State Formation and Construction of Sikkimese History*, Brill, Leiden and London.

Namgyal, T. and Y. Dolma, 1908, *History of Sikkim*, MSS.

Patterson, G.N., 1963, *Peking Versus Delhi*, Fabre & Fabre, London.

Ramesh, Jairam, 2018, *Intertwined Lives: P.N. Haksar and Indira Gandhi*, Simon & Schuster, New Delhi.

Rustomji, N.K., 1971, *Enchanted Frontiers: Sikkim, Bhutan and Northeast Frontier of India*, Oxford University Press, Bombay.

_____, 1987, *Sikkim: A Himalayan Tragedy*, Allied Publishers, Bombay.

Sinha, A.C., 2008, *Sikkim: Feudal and Democratic*, Indus Publishing Company, New Delhi.

Subba, P., 2012, *Sikkimma Dostro Kranti in 1993*, (in Nepali: *The Second Revolution in Sikkim, 1993*), privately published by the author, Gangtok.

Unknown, 1963, *Sikkim: A Concise Chronicle*, Published by Royal Wedding Committee and Printed by Sikkim Durbar Press, Gangtok.

PART C

The Personae

7

Zaphu Angami Phizo and the Naga National Council

For whatever else Phizo may be remembered, no one can deny his genius in welding the Nagas, a people divided by tribal and clan rivalries, into a people united by the fire of nationalism. He was referred as a 'Moses of his people' and it was he who spelt out loud and clear what was in the heart of many Nagas, namely, an independent nation. It was he who gave expression to the unexpected desire of the Nagas and continued to be their spokesman even in exile. He completely dominated the rapid development during the decolonization of Naga territory. (Horam 1988)

A passionate nationalist, he was … exceedingly devious and frustratingly inflexible.… It is difficult to present him in easy terms, but it cannot be gainsaid that to his countrymen, in spite of his failings, his steadfastness has assured him entry into a legend as the progenitor of their nationalism. He will be for time immemorial be their greatest hero.… It must, however, be remembered that Phizo never set out to be liked; to please was not his way of doing things. His guiding philosophy was: I am annointed to set my people free – the Lord called me early in the morning of my life, all, is born of the spirit. (Steyn 2016: xiii)

The man who ran the most powerful insurgency in India … was a little man, hardly more than five foot four inches tall, impeccably dressed in a dark, three-piece suit … the legend of Nagaland.… Phizo was very conscious of the paralysis on the left side of his face and took great pain in most of his appearances and photographs, to be seen with the non-paralyzed side. (Hazarika 2011: 87)

The write-up below is mainly based on Pieter Steyn's brief biography, *Zapuphizo: Voice of the Nagas*, which in the words of the author is 'not the complete story'. And there is another slim book by an Angami Naga scholar, who warns the readers that 'this book is not

FIGURE 1: ZAPHU ANGAMI PHIZO
(*Source:* Photograph by the author)

at all meant to be a biography of Phizo. The aim of this book is to provide inside materials to those who are interested in the Naga affairs' (Zinyu 1978: ix). Zapu Phizo, an Angami Naga from Khonoma village, traces his ancestry from the legendary hero Merhu, who founded Merhumia clan of the village. Like Naga tribal villages, there were other two founding clans of Khonoma: Semomia and Thevomia.

Social Profile and Struggles for Carving a Space for Himself

Phizo was born on 16 May 1904 at Khonoma and was named Zapu Phizo, meaning, 'may his name be well-known' (Steyn 2016: 38). However, the other biographer gives his year of birth as 1903: 'Phizo was born in 1903 at Khonoma' (Zinyu 1979: 3). He is supposed to have grown up in solitude. He was less sturdy than most of the Angami boys and was less interested in the company with persons of his own age. He lost his father, Krusietso, in 1914, while he was very young. After clearing his village school, he came to Kohima, the headquarters of the Naga Hills district, in the province of Assam and joined the American Baptist Mission School. With a view to augmenting his limited resources, he worked as a part-time janitor in the school and herdsman to the mission's cows. At the age of 18, he got baptized on 12 December 1922 and since then he had displayed a strong faith in the Gospel of Christ and tried to work under the Christian ambit. He was admitted to the Assam Government School, Shillong in 1923. He proved but an average student. 'He was more noted for his bucking the system and display of independence than excellence in his studies'. He left school in 1927, when he appeared for his Entrance examination, which he could not clear as he failed in mathematics. Though he is known for being in the company of books, but failure in Matriculation examination led to the end of his formal education.

Hunting for Vocation and Learning the Ways of the World

Phizo applied for and obtained the agency of the B.B. Kirkbride Bible Company of Indiana, USA to promote their edition of the Thompson Chain Reference Bible. It was a superbly produced book priced at Rs.

100 apiece, for which there was a very limited market in Nagaland. Earlier, he had tried to start, after borrowing money from friends at 3 per cent interest, a rubber tyre retreading company at Dimapur with the intention to open ultimately a rubber tyre factory for supplying tyres to motor vehicles plying on the roads. He did have enough confidence to run the enterprise, but he could not attain any expertise in this industry. Thus, the enterprise was a failure leading him into a huge debt. However,

> Phizo never lacked self-confidence and never doubted he could make good as a businessman. He started various ventures which included importing canvas shoes to undersell competitors, locally made lemonade, (import of) rice from Manipur, and a motor tyre retreading company with five of his cousins. At all worked systematically, showing considerable organizing ability, but his options were limited and he was not really cut out for commerce. His choice of collaborators was not wise. The result of his ventures were in the main disappointing, and at least one ended in financial recrimination. (Steyn 2016: 47)

All these failures turned him into a laughing stock to his fellowmen. He was not able to repay the debt to his lenders. Zinyu informed in 1979 that there were still some people at Khonoma, who said that sooner or later when Phizo returned home, they would try to recover their money with interests from him.

> Khonoma villagers often termed Phizo as the builder of castles in the air, and the collapse of his tyre factory became a living example of his failures.... He refused to surrender to defeat and still persisted in dreaming of and aiming at lofty things. For Phizo was a man of strong determination.... Whatever he determined, he would pursue it in spite of any kind of hurdles in his path. 'Phizo does not bother whether his objective is right or wrong so long as he attains it', thus said one of his associates. And he would refuse to budge until he is satisfied. (Zinyu 1979: 4-5)

At the age of 26, he married Jwanne Kent of the Rengma community on 9 August 1930. It appears simply ludicrous that a private wedding celebration be attended by the most powerful man in the district, J.P. Mills, ICS uninvited. And that also, when the groom did not want the guest to spoil his day by attending it. But Phizo's rebuff was royally ignored by the presiding deity of Naga Hills district and the big man made his presence on the scene. It becomes clear that Phizo had taken an incident involving him with the Deputy Commissioner to his heart. It so happened that Phizo had decided to investigate natural oil seepage at Mokokchung and for that he was hauled up before the Deputy Commissioner, Mills. Phizo was found guilty of meddling in matters which did not concern him and was proscribed on that occasion for leaving Kohima area for the next three months. And that made him to try his luck in Burma as a business man.

He travelled to Rangoon in 1934 by a ship owned by the British India Steamer Company, hoping to secure an agency of Sun Life Insurance Company of Canada. He already had an agency of selling the Bible. Now he added to that a sub-agency of the Canadian Insurance company. With the best of his efforts, these two agencies were not functioning in Burma to his satisfaction so far as earning was concerned. He left Rangoon and moved up on the Irrawaddy River at Yenangyaung, the headquarters of the Burmah Shell Oil Company. With a view to providing inexpensive loan to the needy factory hands, he borrowed money from a Canadian source and opened his concern, the Commercial & Banking Cooperation. His venture took off, but he landed in serious trouble with the fellow moneylenders, who were exploiting the needy labourers by charging exorbitant interests. They instigated his bankers to file suits against Phizo for money embezzlement. With lot of difficulty, he extricated himself from this messy endeavour and came back to Rangoon. Soon he hit upon the idea of producing face cream in partnership of a chemist, which was again doomed for failure. At last, he sought and got the job of stevedore supervisor in the Rangoon docks.

Phizo, the Japanese Collaborator

By then the Second World War was on in full swing and the Japanese on 11 December 1941 had mounted an attack on Tenasserim, the southernmost tip of Burma. There was an exodus of Indians from Burma back to India. Phizo did not see any reason why he should retreat to India. It was a fact that the Japanese intelligence service was in touch with Phizo, a fact on which he had been reluctant to talk.

Phizo and his brother Keviyally provided intelligence inputs to the Japanese field forces about logistics and movement of the armed forces in the province of Assam. Phizo claimed that he had been meeting Netaji Subhas Chandra Bose, who would always salute him first, which the latter would reciprocate. But he claimed that he never tried to be close to him, as he knew that Bose was a diehard Indian patriot and possibly in Bose's India he did not see any future for him. Till then, there had been no evidence on the part of Phizo to dabble in Naga politics. Incidentally, he could not fool Charles Pawsey, the new Deputy Commissioner of Naga Hills District, who was collecting reports on his activities.

Phizo's biographer reports:

> Phizo deliberately sat on the sidelines. He gauged it would be politics to show support for Bose on his arrival in Rangoon, yet he was reluctant to commit himself irrevocably to Bose's aims for India as a whole. He agreed with Ba Maw's public outburst: 'In my view Asia cannot be free unless India is also free. If we wish to destroy anti-Asiatic stronghold which is India', but he preferred not to allow Bose to know about his own bilateral talks with the Japanese. In any case, he conjectured that an ardent nationalist such as Bose would be unlikely, when the crunch came, to permit Nagaland to float away even before he had a chance to take control of his own motherland. (Steyn 2016: 59)

Thus, his relationship with Bose was polite but distant, if at all there was any. Apparently, this was Phizo's cock and bull story, spun much later in London to prove the point that he was always a visionary for the cause of Naga independence.

The Japanese mounted attack on India in March 1944 and proceeded to Manipur plateau and Kohima in Naga Hills district, where they met with stiff opposition from Manipuris and Nagas under the command of the British officers. Bose's Azad Hind Fauj could not pose any serious challenge to the defending British forces on the eastern frontiers of Assam. A classic case of Japanese intense invasion is cited in Deputy Commissioner's Tennis Court at Kohima, in which the invaders were soundly beaten back in a hand-to-hand fight. The defenders chased, harassed, and ambushed the starving Japanese retreating forces, who were advancing in the hope that they would be welcome by the Indians. Moreover, they did not receive contingent logistic support from their own armed forces. Theirs was a most humiliating retreat from the Indo-Burmese frontiers, as the starving Japanese were harassed and ambushed all the way.

A former Japanese diplomat is quoted by Pieter Steyn, describing the plight of the retreating Japanese soldiers:

> On September 27, 1944, our expeditionary forces of 270,000 men marched to the gate of Imphal in Manipur, India, and met defeat. Most of the forces perished in the battle or later died of starvation. The disaster at Imphal was perhaps the worst of its kind yet chronicled in the annals of war. One of the Regimental Commanders who survived the retreat, called on me in his tattered uniforms. I hardly recognized him. He told me how ranks had thinned daily as thirst and hunger overtook the retreating columns, and how sick and wounded had to be abandoned by hundreds. In order to avoid capture these men were usually forced to seek death at their own hands. Only 70,000 of the original force survived at the end. (Steyn 2016: 61)

Major-General Ichida, Assistant Chief of Staff of the Japanese Burma Area Army, formally surrendered all the Japanese forces in Burma on 13 September 1945 in Rangoon to Brigadier Armstrong of Britain's XII Army. Phizo and his brother were arrested as the Japanese collaborators against the British during the war. They were imprisoned in Rangoon Central Jail, which was some 13 miles away from the town. They were interrogated closely and there was enough corroborative evidence against them for their trial. For that, they were to be repatriated to India for trial along with other Indian prisoners. However, for some reasons, Phizo was released from gaol after 8 months with a gift of facial paralysis. At this stage, Phizo's family was helped by an Indian army officer, Col. Rashid Yusuf Ali. After a gap of 10 years, Phizo and his family returned from Burma to India in 1946. He found to his surprise that the post-War Naga Hills district was not the same as the old one; it was in a political turmoil. Two points need to be kept in mind: first, Phizo was a complete failure in all his commercial ventures since 1930; and second, he came back home with a stigma of a Japanese collaborator, at least in the eyes of the British administration. And that was the time the British were negotiating with the Indian leaders the terms on which they would withdraw from their Indian Empire. Naturally, there were wild rumours and apprehensions among the frontier communities as they had been politically sheltered under the provision of Excluded Areas in the Province of Assam which were taken care of by the British bureaucracy.

The Deputy Commissioner of the district, Charles R. Pawsey, was busy in assessing the damages and arranging for the relief in the war-torn district. As many as 12,000 dwelling units were completely destroyed by Allied bombing even in the dispersed Naga settlements. Apart from the material losses, the British were confronted more with moral, psychological and political consequences of the Japanese invasion. Though Nagas helped in all possible ways in the British war efforts, they noted that the British rulers of the district were not invincible as presumed earlier. There was also a large sum of money afloat in the hills in the form of remittances from the Nagas working abroad in the Coolie Corps. Somehow, an idea emerged from the administration that in the event British withdrew from India, hill districts should join the successor state provisionally for a period of 10 years. And that is one of the points negotiated by the Governor of Assam with the NNC known as Sir Akbar Hydary's Agreement. By then with a view to preparing the Nagas for the future, Pawsey encouraged the Naga Club to be turned into the Naga Hills District Tribal Council (NHDTC) in April 1945. But it did not appear to be a success. He got an experienced Naga government officer in Kevichusa and other government employees to turn the NHDTC into the Naga National Council (NNC) in 1946. Initially, it was supposed to be a forum devoid of politics but for social reconstruction in the aftermath of the Second World War in the Naga Hills district.

Naturally, an unemployed Phizo was desperate to find space in the fast-changing political scenario in the late 1940s of the Naga Hills district. He began with a re-reading of the Sir Akbar Hydari Agreement. He did know the controversies regarding clause 9 of the agreement between the two parties. With a view to shift the entire blame on the Government of India, he travelled to Shillong and got it endorsed by Governor Hydari and Premier Gopinath Bordolai. It was Nari Khurshid (N.K.) Rustomji, the Advisor to the Governor, who was instrumental in taking Phizo to the two dignitaries of the Province of Assam. He had a foresight to record his impression of Phizo:

What struck me about Phizo at the first meeting was his extraordinary thoroughness and pertinacity. He was armed with neatly typed, systematically serialized copies of all his documents relevant to the Naga problem and he gave the impression of carrying single-handedly in his small briefcase the destiny of the entire Naga people. (Rustomji 1971)

Indian Union, Naga National Council and Insurgency in the Naga Hills District

A recent study has recorded the complexity of the Naga Movement:

For over six decades, the Naga Movement rejects and rebels enclosure into post-colonial India and aspires to realize Naga independence through the barrel of gun, in doing so presents itself as a people's movement. A ceasefire is in place since 1997. However, this manifests itself… as a period of relative political stasis … While the antecedents of the Naga uprising trace back to the era of late colonialism. In more concrete form the Naga nationalist project took off in the 1950s.… A.Z. Phizo (1951), the erstwhile president of the Naga National Council (NNC) and the prophet of Naga nationalism, pronounced, as he orchestrated a near millennial movement galvanized by a messianic, salvific promise of Naga political and spiritual redemption. 'I always have a feeling that God, our Heavenly Father, our Creator, is with us and guiding us. What is there for us to fear? Phizo added'. (Wouters 2018: xii)

The Founder-Secretary of NNC, Theyiechuthia Sakhrie, had sent a memorandum to Jawaharlal Nehru, the President of Indian National Congress: (a) The Council stands for solidarity of Naga tribes, including those in the un-administered areas. (b) The Council strongly protests against the grouping of Assam with Bengal. (c) The Naga Hills should be constitutionally included in autonomous Assam, in free India, with local autonomy and due safeguards of interests of the Nagas. And (d) the Naga tribes should have a separate electorate (Steyn 2016: 70). In response to that, Nehru had replied that:

…the Naga territory in Eastern Assam is much too small to stand by itself politically and economically.… The Naga territory must form part of India and of Assam with which it has developed such close association. (Hazarika 2018: 53)

Sir Andrew Claw, the last British Governor of Assam, handed over charge of the administration to his successor, Sir Akbar Hydari, in May 1947. Sir Hydari realized the gravity of the turmoil among the Nagas and signed a comprehensive nine-point agreement with the Naga leaders on 9 June 1947 at Shillong. However, the last clause turned out to be most controversial, which stated: 'after ten years of the agreement's implementation, the Naga National Council will be asked whether they require the above agreement to be extended for a further period, or a new agreement regarding the future of the Naga people arrived at'. This last provision of the agreement turned to be vague: while a section of the Nagas interpreted that after 10 years they would have a right to self-determination. The Government of India meant that the agreement may be extended or negotiated, but the issue of self-determination was ruled out.

A group of Nagas paid a visit to Delhi to apprise the Indian National leaders of their points of view, but could not manage to meet either Nehru or Patel in those eventful days. However, they managed to meet Mahatma Gandhi at Bhangi Colony in Delhi and acquainted him of their points of view of Naga Hills vis-à-vis the Indian Union. They tried to convince Gandhi that the Indian Union intended to forcefully take over Naga Hills. Gandhi disapproved the idea of forceful integration of Naga Hills in India and allegedly agreed to oppose it himself (Zinyu 1979: 21; Steyn 2016: 73-4). Sajal Nag records that Mahatma's concept of Ram Rajya fitted perfectly with Phizo's Naga way of life and he claimed:

> Nagaland is a wonderful country where there is no political party, no class distinction, no class feeling or caste system, no complaint of maladjustment, no paupers, no (family without) property, no liquor ban, no opium den, no dancing hall, no brothel, no law for death penalty, no law to imprison a person, no land tax of any kind. It is purely a country of people, owned by people, managed by the people for the common interest of the people. Every village is a small republic and has its own council and assemblies established from time immorial and it is dynamically alive. Nagaland is a country of Mahatma Gandhi's dreams. (Nag 2002: 145-6)

After meeting Mahatma Gandhi in July 1947, some of the Nagas like Zapu Phizo announced that they would declare their independence on 14 August 1947 before India became formally independent. Thus, a section of the NNC went ahead and declared independence of Naga Hills district on 14 August 1947. They claimed to have sent telegrams informing New Delhi and the UNO, which were aborted by the alert district administration. Hazarika records referring to W.G. Archer's note,

> the Naga Flag was raised at the Kevichusa residence, but (it) was taken down by (Deputy Commissioner, C.R.) Pawsey and that Mrs. Kevichusa was 'in hysterics'; one note says that there were twelve efforts by the 'Kevichusa group' to send telegrams announcing Nagaland's freedom but Pawsey intercepted all of them and ensured that no telegrams were sent. (Hazarika 2018: 52)

There is another version of the same incidence. It was to streamline the materials and cash afloat that Pawsey

> facilitated the formation of NHDTC in April, 1945, and whose mandate it became to unite Naga tribes to effectuate reconstruction after the damage caused during the War. Less than a year later, the Council had rechristened itself as the NNC, and became the platform for debates on Naga's political future. Initially the debate was between those who envisaged a genuine Naga autonomy within Assam and India and those who insisted that only an independent 'government of the Nagas, for the Nagas, by the Nagas' (Kevichusa) would ensure Nagas' welfare. (Wouters 2018: 19)

This led to a division within NNC, and a split group calling themselves the People's Independent League', of which Z.A. Phizo was a member. By then, a new Naga leader was emerging on the political horizon of Naga Hills, who elbowed out the moderates from the NNC and placed his followers among the office bearers of NNC. In him, the Nagas had found their spokesman and he championed their cause ceaselessly, fearlessly and even fanatically. Moreover, though religion, Christianity, was mentioned earlier also, but it was Phizo who introduced Christianity as a factor between Indians as Hindus and Nagas as Christians. He coined the slogan, 'Nagaland for the Christ'. On the other hand, T. Sakherie, the Secretary of NNC, was a cool, level-headed, competent and articulate operator. However, the destiny of the Nagas began to shift fast under the emotive and theological spell of Phizo. Slowly and steadily, he was consolidating his hold, influence and his network of supporters.

There is another side of Z.A. Phizo, as being very vindictive. For illustration, Phizo did not like Charles Pawsey ICS, the last British Deputy Commissioner, who had his own reasons to believe that Phizo was a Japanese collaborator during the Second World War. Phizo chose the moment when Pawsey 'was about to leave Kohima for home in 1948. Having packed all his belongings, Pawsey was about to go away. At that moment Phizo entered the bungalow (uninvited) and ordered Pawsey in a rather rude manner to leave Nagaland immediately. It was a moment of utter defeat for Charles Pawsey who had rather ruled over Nagaland (now Naga Hills district) throughout the Second World War.... He, however, told Phizo that he would be watching from England his relations with the Indians.... In fact, since then the relation between the Nagas and the Indians had never been good till Nagaland became a separate full-fledged state of India (Zynyu 1979:12).

As ill luck would have it, Phizo would be forced by circumstances to seek asylum in the United Kingdom in 1960 and would live in that country for the next 30 years till his death on a British subject passport. The irony of fate is such that even that document was arranged courtesy of the same Charles R. Pawsey (Steyn 2016: 111). We meet Sir Charles Pawsey very soon again in the context of Phizo's advocacy of the Naga cause in UK in 1966 in a meeting called by Rev. Michael Scott. It so happened that J.H. Hutton ICS and former Deputy Commissioner of Naga Hills district and author of two monographs on Nagas had blasted Phizo's presentation of Nagas' independence from India. In fact, he had pleaded that Indians had been generous to the primitive Nagas by granting them a state in the Indian Union. It became so hot for Phizo that he decided to walk out of the meeting.

> The one man to emerge with (on the occasion) was Charles Pawsey. When Phizo was about to leave the hall, he stood up, called him by name, and shook hands with him as if they were old and close friends. (Steyn 2016: 142)

Coming back to Naga Hills of 1950, Phizo went to Calcutta to see off one of his nephews, Charlie Iralu, to the United States of

America, who proceeded for higher studies. The intelligence agents got a smell of him, and he was arrested and put behind bars in the infamous Presidency Jail of Calcutta. He remained in jail for six months without trial under some old sedition law. That was the time his wife was travelling in a jeep with her baby son from Kohima to Khonoma and the jeep met with an accident. The lady was badly injured and her two-year old little son instantly died. She was brought to the Welsh Mission Hospital, Shillong for treatment. By then, the Governor of Assam, Sir Akbar Hydari was dead and his successor, Jairamdas Daulatram had taken over the office of the Governor. After J.P. Mills' departure as the Advisor Tribal Affairs (ATA) to the Governor of Assam in 1948, it was the old hand N.K. Rustomji ICS, who was the ATA to the Governor.

Zapu Phizo Moves to Centre Stage of Naga Insurgent Politics

The Nagas boycotted Independence Day celebration on 15 August 1947, Republic Day celebrations on 26 January 1950, and they did not form a District Council stipulated under the new Constitution unlike other hill districts of Assam. Moreover, they boycotted the first General Elections held in 1952 for the State Assembly of Assam and Parliament of India. All these resulted in violence. The NNC agitators coerced the government employees to dissociate themselves from the government offices. When the agitators began snatching guns from the police force, armed police were called in. That led to further violence and retaliation. As president of NNC, Phizo planned to force through a referendum on the total Naga independence by the earliest. Thus, in December 1950, NNC called for a plebiscite on Naga independence in April, which was ultimately held on 16 May 1951. The NNC claimed that 99.9 per cent Nagas voted for independence, but nobody knows how they came to that figure without any polling ever held, votes ever counted and any authorized person ever making an announcement as such. They claimed that they had informed the Government of India and the foreign embassies. This was something like a repeat performance that of declaring independence on 14 August 1947, which never reached anywhere beyond Khonoma, or Kohima.

Records his biographer,

> Phizo, driven by his determination, made the same mistake as many other politicians before him (had done). He used subtlety to get the answer he wanted. On May 16, a vast crowd gathered at Kohima from all over Nagaland. He spoke to them with emotion and conviction in language they could understand, and was calculated to touch the most sensitive Naga mind.... His oratory became a series of repeated questions: 'Do you want to be free?' Yes. Do you want to love Nagaland? Yes. Do you want to live under a black (Indian) government? No ... He ended rhetorically: 'Do you want independence?' If you are independent, you will enjoy life as we had it before the British came.... Phizo was naturally jubilant (on the alleged result of the plebiscite). But the euphoria faded when there was no response either from Nehru, or from any other quarter. Murkot Rammuny summed up the situation as follows: 'This Naga independence plebiscite was an article of faith with Phizo. He wanted to convince the government of India about the genuineness of his demand but the indifferent reaction it created, frustrated him (possibly all the more)'. (Steyn 2016: 85)

Phizo possibly believed in relentless publicity camouflage. He painted India to be a Hindu state without any evidence. He believed and kept on repeating that unlike his father, Jawaharlal Nehru had allowed Hindu conservatives to dominate the government. In his formulations, 'black Indians' were not to be welcome in his Nagaland. During his so-called plebiscite one of the frequently raised question was: Do you want to live under a black (Indian) government? He claimed that he was apprehensive of 'Indians' infiltrating in Naga Hills. Phizo reasoned:

> Steps should be taken to prevent attracting an unwanted flow, not only of Indians, but (also) of people from East Pakistan (Bangladesh), Bengal and Nepal. Unless Nagaland was the undisputed master of its destiny, he foresaw migrant people being given preference, then dominance over Nagas. That would presage an insidious spread of corrupt practice so prevalent in India. (Steyn 2016: 84)

Prime Minister Nehru had invited Thakin U Nu, the prime minister of Burma, to Kohima on 30 March 1953 to sign an agreed boundary between the two countries, which covered Naga Hills district. His idea was to display to the Nagas that the Government of

India attached so much importance to them and their land that such important events could be held among them. But it was not to be. It so happened that local Deputy Commissioner (DC), Barakakti, was approached by the powerful Village Headmen Association with the proposal to welcome the honoured guests, as per Naga tradition. Without taking the prime minister into confidence, the inarticulate DC refused their request on the plea that a high dignitary such as the prime minister should not meet the humble village headmen. The Nagas, naturally, took it as a great insult to them and their tradition of welcoming dignitaries. The next day when the main function was over, Nehru stood up to address the assembled audience largely manned by the village headmen, who stood up, turned back, uncovered their buttocks, bent their head down and walked off the venue. Everybody was stunned and the entire show ended in a fiasco. Naturally, it was an unprecedented event. Nehru remained the prime minister for the next 11 years. He did everything possible for the Nagas and Nagaland, but he never visited them again.

Now Phizo's version of the event was recorded by his biographer (Seyn 2016: 88-92), which suggests that it was he who had organized the fiasco. Barakakti, Deputy Commissioner at Kohima and possibly his next man in the administration used to drink liquor and quarrel between themselves.

Barakakti vetoed the presentation of NNC address (to the visiting dignitaris). He went further, he issued an order forbidding any address whatsoever, either in writing or speech, to be given at any of the scheduled public meetings. He did not have the least idea of the psychology of the Nagas. The Nagas will hear anyone, but also want to be heard. His democracy, equality and classless society make him feel equal to anyone. Based on that equality it is right to be heard, and he is patient to hear anything spoken to him. An opportunity was lost.... Many of the Naga elders and notables had walked for days from distant villages to hear Nehru. Naga fashion, they had also come prepared to talk to him. When that right was denied to them, they decided that if the Prime Minister would not talk to them, they would not hear him either. Consequently, when Jawaharlal Nehru rose to speak, he witnessed a walkout by the entire public meeting for the first and only time in his long political career. Mortification showed plainly on his face....

Till then, the Government of Assam had been handling the issues of security in the Naga Hills district as it was a district in the state. After the events of 1953, the central government decided to impose emergency in the district with a view to maintaining law and order. Central forces were ordered to instil confidence among the citizens who would like to work within the parameter of the rule of law. It was rumoured that Nehru had said that 'he would be glad to meet Phizo'. Later, it was officially clarified that, in fact, Nehru had said: 'I would meet him only if he does not repeat his demand for independence'. His biographer records Phizo's reaction to that.

> The possibility of a face to face meeting between the two men was missed again (was there a possibility of their meeting face to face missed in the past?) by both sides. Phizo adamently refused to oblige Nehru and the latter's retort bore his personal autocratic imprint. The result was a directive issued in early 1956 to the General Commanding Officer, the Eastern Command, for stringent measures to be taken to quell all Naga intransigence. (Steyn 2016: 95).

Major-General R.K. Kochar was appointed to command the Indian formations in Nagaland in April 1956. He immediately issued an order of the day cautioning his troops on anything which might be termed violence against the innocent people. However, he resolved to express his stern intention to maintain law and order. There were attacks and counterattacks between the armed forces and the rebel armed forces. In between the villagers suffered because the insurgents invariably take shelter in the villages for food as well as logistics. In the retaliation, villagers suffered heavily. In answer to that, the Naga army sacked a police station and half a dozen policemen were killed. On another occasion, an army convey was attacked on way to Imphal and a senior army officer was killed on his way to Zunheboto in the Naga Hills. By 1957 the Government of India decided to bring eastern Naga inhabited areas of Tuensang from North East Frontier Agency (NEFA) along with the Naga Hills district. It is informed that the little hill district had to the extent of about 30,000 troopers posed on duty in 1957.

The peace-loving citizens in the district were sandwiched between the armed forces trying to establish normalcy and the NNC insurgents retaliating their intrusion in their areas of operation. NNC created such a reign of terror that anybody disagreeing with their point of view was afraid of one's life. T. Sakhrie's murder on 18 January 1956 reminded the peaceniks of the risk involved in the move. However, there were Nagas, who were willing to probe how much accommodation New Delhi was willing to make for creating a conducive environment. Meanwhile, armed forces were engaged in their ceaseless efforts to flush Phizo out from his hideout. Finding no corner safe enough to take shelter, Phizo managed to smuggle himself out of Nagaland in a coffin in early 1957 to East Pakistan (Hazarika 2018: 101). In this exercise, he was helped by some Rengma and Zeliangrong Nagas. Sanjoy Hazarika recalls that Phizo's corpse would be transported back to Nagaland after more than three decades in May 1990 in a similar way.

Z.A. Phizo and T. Sakhrie belonged to two different clans from village Khonoma. When Phizo was cooling his heels in Burmese jail as a Japanese collaborator, Sakhrie was the leading light among the educated Nagas. He was the founder secretary of the NNC and he was the main spokesman of the Nagas when 'The Nine point Agreement of June 1947' was signed with the Governor, Sir Akbar Hydari. He did hold clear views on the distinct identity of the Nagas away from the Indians from the plains. He was intelligent, suave, sociable and pragmatic in his approach. He was at the same time, pragmatic against a dogmatic Phizo. He had watched the political developments in the Naga Hills district vis-à-vis Government of India from mid-1940s to mid-1950s. He had come to the conclusion that a confrontation with the Government of India would not be in the larger interests of the Nagas. He stood for a negotiated settlement with the Government of India against Phizo's emphasis on open confrontation and armed rebellion.

As normally happens, in a volatile situation, reason fails to impress the crowd and emotive arousal creates a psychosis of crisis, in which clash is left to be the only option. Rest is recorded by the historian of insurgency in north-east India, Sanjoy Hazarika:

> As days passed, the division between Sakhrie and Phizo began to flare openly and Sakhrie quit the NNC. At a critical meeting in Khonoma, Phizo

confronted Sakhrie and attacked him bitterly. 'You do not deserve to live', he roared.... The first prominent moderate among Naga nationalist leaders was seized when he went to meet his lover at a village near Kohima. Sakhrie was tortured brutally and then killed. But, till the end, Phizo denied any role in his death. (Hazarika 2018: 99)

Phizo Slips off from the Naga Hills to Pakistan and then to the United Kingdom

Phizo clarified his position to his biographer that he was not running away from Nagaland. He had to weigh carefully what he hoped to achieve and what it was possible to achieve. He had the confidence of the movement behind me, but he had to ask himself: Did he have enough confidence in himself to handle the task? He wanted to tell the whole world that India was escalating war on the Nagas and to stop India from acts of aggression against Nagaland. I was our only hope. He had to leave Nagaland because Nagaland was virtually sealed off from the rest of the world by India. He claimed that:

> My leaving Nagaland was clear to Nagas. It was by their will that I went to establish link with the Western world, China and Burma ... with anyone who would listen to me. The Naga Federal Government was in place – as the president of the NNC I had responsibility for foreign affairs. Before I left I told our people to stand fast, never to yield, to fight to death. They have not yielded an inch. Our intelligence network has improved. We now receive timely warning of nearly all their offensive moves. We can never be defeated, and I shall stay here as long as my people wish.

The biographer made a query: 'But, having regard to November 1957, was it not true that some members of NNC were gradually gaining recognition as advocates of accommodation with India. The whole political ball game in Kohima seemed to be changing in favour of such a move?'

> A splendid silence followed, ... but the interviewer was left feeling like a school boy rebuked for contradicting his headmaster. His (Phizo's) glare said it all. The discussion for the time being was over. It would be resumed in a calmer atmosphere when an opportunity arose. Phizo, although not a vindictive person, did allow the intolerant side of his character to break

through when he supposed his political judgement on Nagaland affairs to be under attack. (Steyn 2016: 100-3)

Phizo had reached East Pakistan through the Naga Hills-Cachar-Silchar-Tripura bordering a forested region and was ultimately led to Dhaka. Against his expectation, he met with a cold reception in Pakistan. Let us have Phizo's own word on his reception in Dhaka: '

> It came as a great shock that contrary to expectation we were confronted by unfriendly government officials when I reached Dhaka. At that time (Gen.) Ayub Khan was the defence minister of Pakistan and I expected him to be sympathetic [to our cause] ... he [had] commanded a battalion of the Assam Regiment at one time and knew the Nagas. And also, because India and Pakistan were enemies and we had often collected a small quantity of arms in the past from Sylhet. Instead of facilitating my passage (to the West), I was confined to quarters in the Dhaka police compound. I was not allowed outside, but I could receive visitors. During my detention only Pakistanis I met were intelligent officers who were very guarded about their identity. They suggested that Assam rightfully belong to Pakistan and tried to get me to say I agree. (Steyn 2016: 101)

Phizo at last managed to reach Karachi, the capital city of Pakistan at the time, in early 1960 after hanging on in Dhaka for more than two years. His nephew from America, Charlie Iralu, had reached Rev. Michael Scott with the fate of Phizo. Rev. Scott was an Anglican priest, who championed human rights and had specialized on exposing the colonial abuse of minorities. Phizo did not find Karachi any different from that of Dhaka so far as his cause was concerned. One day, suddenly he was handed over an El Salvadorian passport in the name of Prudencio Llach. At long last, he reached Switzerland on 5 March 1960. Charlie had been working on Rev. Scott to extricate his uncle Phizo from Switzerland to Britain. At last on 12 June 1960, Rev. Michael Scott and his charge, Z.A. Phizo, reached Heathrow Airport. After a lot of legal rigmarole with the immigration authorities, Phizo was permitted to enter Britain under an assumed name as Commonwealth citizen. It is another matter that he would remain in the United Kingdom for the next three decades till his death on 30 April 1990.

Naga Peoples Convention (NPC) and the Creation of the State of Nagaland

Meanwhile, things were not going as expected among Phizo's protégés in NNC in Nagaland. A group of Nagas came to believe that other than the programme of NNC, they should explore other possibilities also. Normal life for the common people had become intolerable between the two sets of armed contestants. So a Naga Peoples Convention (NPC) was called at Mokokchung and they appealed to the Government of India to cease the armed operation and let them lead a normal life. The government responded that as long as armed insurrection by the NNC was on, there would be pacification drive against their excesses. Two more Naga Peoples Conventions were held and a strong plea was made that a state of Nagaland be created with an elected State Legislative Assembly and a Cabinet of Ministers within the Indian Union. There were large many politically active persons such as Dr Imkongliba, Shilo Ao, Chiten Jamir, Hokishe Sema, Jassokie, Akum Imlong and others, who came forward. On the other hand, things were not the same as before in the NNC camp. Dissension was emerging at the top level in Naga Federal Government (NFG) and its armed wing leading to dissociation of two key figures of the movement: Kaito Sukhai and his brother, Kughato Sukhai.

At last, the Naga Conventionalists reached approached the Government of India with their resolutions and discussions were held in a number of rounds. At the end, the Parliament of the Indian Union passed a bill for the creation of the first ethnic state of Nagaland consisting of Naga Hills district and Tuesang Frontier Tract, in 1960. We have mentioned above that formation of Nagaland as a state was inaugurated by the President of India in 1963; elections to the State Legislative Assembly were held in February 1964 and a popular government led by Shilo Ao was formed soon thereafter. Phizo termed these developments as of no consequence. For him elected functionaries in the State of Nagaland were quislings and formation of the state of Nagaland was meaningless, to say it mildly, because nobody bothered to reach him for his approval. In his views, the NPC leaders were 'reactionaries', traitors and stooges of the Government of India'.

They are puppets of the Indian government and in no way (they are the) representatives of Nagaland. They want India to downgrade my country to a state within India, but I predict that is a sure way to civil war. The Naga people will never accept it. (Steyn 2016: 110)

Within six months of that an amnesty was offered to the NFG and re-grouping of the villages for the reason of security was abandoned. The third chief minister of the state and a future governor of an Indian State, Hokishe Sema, termed the Conventionalists (who by then had termed their forum as the Naga People's Organization (NPO) as the 'peace-makers' (Sema 1986: 94). However, in Phizo's view, it was he, the president of the NNC, who held the final key of Naga destiny in his hands. Thus, in spite of the State of Nagaland functioning with all the formal structure, curfew continued to be clamped in the state all 24 hours and insurgents continued to operate as before perhaps more ferociously. Naturally, security agencies had to be more stringent to prove the point that the dawn of statehood had made a difference.

Finally, an accord was reached between the Government of India and Conventionalists, Nagaland became a state within the Indian Union. Asked for his reaction, Phizo expressed his amazement:

I am sometimes dismayed at the numerous times people in Nagaland have worked against me. With such friends who needs an enemy! But I remind myself that the kingdom of God is within us and nothing can defeat us. If we believe that we shall receive power from Him. The struggle will end only when our goal is achieved. The Naga National Council has never accepted the so-called Shillong Accord, which came later. At heart every true Naga yearns for freedom. I hope to witness our triumph. (Steyn 2016: 150)

The Government of India began to liberally allocate funds to Nagaland for welfare schemes and infrastructure with a view to catching up with the sister states in the Union in terms of socio-economic development. Such amount of money was invested frequently in rehabilitating many of the NNC cadre and functionaries so that they could lead a secured life.

While such surrender-cum-rehabilitation schemes are often negotiated individually, they were occasionally concluded *en masse.* When the Revolutionary Government of Nagaland (RGN) surrendered in 1973, roughly 1500 of its cadres were inducted in the Border Security Forces (BSF) in

Nagaland and subsequently they lived their lives on government salaries. Its commander, Scato Swu, in turn, was rewarded with a Presidential nomination into the Rajya Sabha (the Upper House of the Indian Parliament). Over the years, a significant number of NSCN cadres have been similarly rehabilitated. (Wouters 2018: 152)

Phizo was possibly a doubtful biblical creature, who saw fault everywhere and in everyone. Look at his assessment of the persons, who were allegedly associated with the cause of the Nagas:

The blunder had begun with Sir Andrew Clow (the Governor of Assam) and his rigid pedantic attitude (in rejecting Robert Reid's Crown Colony proposal); (Prime Minister Jawaharlal) Nehru, who was snared by his philosophy and vision of future Indian greatness; Sardar (Vallabhbhai) Patel held true to his reputation as the Iron man of India; (V.K.) Krishna Menon (the Defence Minister) considered any mention of ethnic independence a treasonable propaganda; Bishuram Medhi (the Chief Minister of Assam) was a comic and (the Governor) Daulatram in Assam upset everyone by his arrogance; (the Foreign Secretary) Y.D. Gundevia at the foreign ministry toed Krishna Menon line; (the Prime Minister) Indira Gandhi, when she came on the scene and under great pressure, she was persuaded to meet the Naga aspirations half way, but it is doubtful she ever really understood the root cause of Naga unhappiness. A successor prime minister, Morarji Desai, at his stringent best, could not unbend or showed, 'What is there to settle?', he asked, 'If you want to persist in independence, I have nothing more to say. I will certainly exterminate the rebel Nagas. I have no compunction in that. (Steyn 2016: 110)

On the other hand, Phizo's host in London, Mrs Morton, said of him:

He was a bundle of contradictions. The paradox, as I saw it, lay in the fact that alongside his role as a devout Christian was his role as a warrior leader who felt no compunction in planning the death of a political adversary.

When Phizo was asked if he felt discouraged in getting attention to the Nagas' cause in the West, he replied with candour, philosophically: 'God gave me a strong body and a dream I can never give up. I did not come here (United Kingdom) because it was easy, but I was troubled on every side, perplexed often, I did not despair.' His biographer writes after that: It was to be a clear case of the longer he remained in the West, the more his difficulties would multiply. The 1960s were the years of decolonization, crimes and the Beatles. Great change in political and social structure throughout the world took place. He was always hard-put to find a suitable moment to press for international recognition. But, as he waited, the right time never seemed to come his way.

Nagaland Peace Mission

At last, Phizo could persuade his mentor Rev. Michael Scott to make some moves with that of the Gandhian peaceniks like Jai Prakash Narayan and his one time good friend, now the chief minister of Assam, Bimala Prasad Chaliha. With consent of the Government of India, a three-member Naga Peace Mission was formed and they soon moved to Nagaland and got in touch with the NNC camp. The three-member Mission met with six representatives of the Naga Federal Government (NFG) at Sakrabama in the Chakesang area. They persuaded them to agree for 'ceasefire' as the minimum requirement for proceeding to establishing normalcy. The NFG put certain conditions, which the Mission promised to examine along with proposals from the other side, but they did reiterate what they meant by ceasefire as the minimum requirement for the next step. At last, the terms for suspension of the operations were thrashed out and it was sent to the Government of India. Both sides showed eagerness to come to a meeting ground and let peace have a chance. Thus, an agreed term of ceasefire between the NFG and the GOI was signed on 10 August 1964.

The Mission continued to work from Kohima. It had created lots of expectations from the beginning because of the stature of the three-member Mission. Delegations from both sides were led by Y.D. Gundevia, the Foreign Secretary, Government of India and Zashei Huire from the NFG respectively. There were long, tiring discussions, arguments and counter arguments among the members with a view to thrash the various points out. Two delegations met on 4-5 May 1965 and Nagas came with the fresh demand that Phizo should be associated with the next higher level of talks. The Government of India agreed to the proposal but Phizo refused to come to India for talks

(Nag 2002: 271). Delegates were getting restive to clinch the issues. Phizo claimed that he had lost interests in the Peace Mission, as he was not willing for anything less than Naga independence, while the Indian delegation was negotiating every issue within the parameter of the Indian constitution. Keviyallay, Phizo's youngest brother, had just returned from England, met with B.P. Chaliha in Shillong and informed him that his brother did not accept proposals of the Peace Mission. Meanwhile the Mission itself had a problem on its hand. Rev. Scott was found to have tried to internationalize the Naga issue on behalf of the Peace Mission without taking other members into confidence. Thus, activities of the Mission came to a standstill. Scott was ordered by the Government of India to leave India immediately as his activities were found to be prejudicial to the interests of the country. All his papers and documents were confiscated. The other two members, J.P. Narayan and B.P. Chaliha, too dissociated themselves from the Mission. Scott came back to England exhausted but he was unrepentent. He was saddened because his high reputation in India was thus dissolved in to thin air. As he is known to 'suffer from an excess of zeal', within a few weeks he was ready with a pamphlet: *Naga Problem: India's or World's.*

A meeting was called at Caxton Hall in London on 21 July 1966 with a view to launching of the above pamphlet by Michael Scott. Along with the interested individuals, the media were invited *en masse.* Charles Pawsey, the former DC of Nagaland, was reluctant to come, but he had to because he had to accompany J.H. Hutton, ICS, who had articulated British approach to North-East Frontier areas right from 1918. Moreover, he was old and deaf. Pawsey's apprehensions largely came true:

> Hutton, in spite of long years of absence from Nagaland (since 1938), still considered himself the leading expert on Naga affairs. He had been incensed upon reading his pre-publication copy of Scott's booklet, and scathingly ridiculed the whole concept of Naga independence. Before anyone could speak after Michael Scott's introductory words of welcome, the old man launched his diatribe. He described his former 'subjects' as head-hunters, who if left to themselves would return to 'the state of savagery in which the British had found them'. His advice to the Indian Government was to 'offer a thumping reward to anyone bringing in the head of a rebel. In this way

this independence nonsense will soon be brought to an end'. Such an outburst coming from a man of Hutton's stature shocked the meeting and even quite-spoken Pawsey failed to pacify the irate professor. Visibly upset, Phizo rose to leave the conference room.... To say the least the occasion was not a success. The participants hung around for a while, then drifted away. Nothing concerning the conference ever appeared in any of the national newspapers. (Steyn 2016: 142)

Phizo had come to Britain with the high hope that his frequent reference to Christ, Christianity and slogan of 'Nagaland for the Christ' would move the West in his favour. He had forgotten that it was the British, one of largest imperial powers of the world, which had allotted all the eastern frontier districts including the Naga Hills district to the province of Assam, which became an integral part of the Indian Union. Queen's British government could not go back to alter their stand for a doubtful claimant, who was a Japanese collaborator during the Great War. And the United States of America and the rest of the West would naturally follow the British precedence in this context. He had already written to the President of the UNO in 1960 with no response. In April 1967, Phizo travelled to the United States of America and his efforts were rebuffed by and large. When he came back to England, two of his former colleagues, Vizol, an ex-soldier from the Angami village of Visema and an elderly Manipuri Tankhul Naga, Suisa, who had travelled from India, were waiting for him. They were sent to him by their colleagues in the Naga movement to convince him for negotiating a peace accord with the Indian Union. Phizo exploded at the very idea and the emissaries were told to go back and tell their sponsors that 'there will be no compromise'. M. Horam informs that two of them were sent to Phizo with the permission of the Government of India to consult before signing an accord (Horam 1990: 134).

Shillong Accord between the GoI and the Underground Nagas 1975

There were peaceniks like Rev. Longri Ao and other Baptist church leaders, who reached the Governor, L.P. Singh, to explore the possibilities of a peace initiative. The State of Nagaland was already under President rule, as Chief Minister Vizol had lost the majority in the State Assembly. Naga Federal Government (NFG) was willing to explore the possibilities of ending the conflict.

Thus, from May to November 1975, protracted negotiations in jungle hideouts and Shillong were conducted. The talks were conducted by Assam State and local level officials.

> On the Naga side, Keviyallay, Phizo's younger brother, emerged as a key player. He was recognized as the contact man by all sides. His also was an invidious role. He has the onerous task of trying to reconcile his brother's adamant stand on Naga sovereignty with New Delhi's equally adamant intention to maintain the sanctity of its inherited frontiers.... Keviyallay played what cards he had dexterously, and throughout kept Phizo advised of developments. By return, and at each critical stage, he received messages from Bromley to stand firm.... On 23 October (1975) members of the Peace Council met with the governor to inform him that the NFG had agreed to talks to finalize the manner in which they would accept India's terms. Two weeks later, a delegation of six, selected by Zashei Huire, the NFG president arrived in Shillong with authority to sign an accord with the Indian government.... It was a cold and foggy evening in Shillong on 11 November 1975. Rain battered down. In the Dubar Hall of the Raj Bhawan, the governor's residence, L.P. Singh and his advisors faced Keviyallay and his colleagues. Each participant read in silence his copy of what was destined to become known as the 'Shillong Accord'. Then came the subdued signing of the master copy and a last minute dramatic gesture on the part of one of the federal delegates, Veenyiyi Rhakhu refused to append his signature. (Steyn 2016: 155)

What did the Accord contain? The Accord had three points only:

1. It informed that 'the following (six) representatives of the Underground organizations met the Governor of Nagaland, Sri L.P. Singh, representing the Government of India, at Shillong on 10 November 1975: 1. I. Temjenba, 2. S. Dahru, 3. Veenyiyi Rhakhu, 4. Z. Ramyo, 5. M. Assa; and 6. Keviyallay.
2. There were a series of four discussions. Some discussions were held with the Governor alone; at others, the Governor was assisted by two (of his) advisors for Nagaland.... All the members of the Liaison Committee, namely Revd. Longri Ao, Dr. M. Aram, Shri

L. Lungalang, Shri Kenneth Kerhuo, and Shri Lungshim Shaiza, participated in the discussion.

3. The following were the outcome of the discussions:
   (i) The representatives of the Underground organizations conveyed their decisions, of their own volition, to accept, without condition, the Constitution of India.
   (ii) It was agreed that the arms, now underground, would be brought out and deposited at appointed places. Details of giving effect to this agreement would be worked out between them and representatives of the Government, the Security Forces and the members of the Liaison Committee.
   (iii) It was agreed that the representatives of the Underground organizations should have reasonable time to formulate other issues for discussion for a final settlement.

Subsequently, a Supplementary Agreement to the Shillong Accord (clause ii) on 5 January 1976 was signed at Shillong by four representatives of the organizations and the Governor, L.P. Singh (Zinyu 1979: 81-8).

Was Phizo a party to the Shillong Accord through his brother Keviyallay? Reading between the lines one colud see that Phizo was indirectly a party to the Shillong Accord. And that episode practically ended his invisibility in Naga affairs. But Phizo always believed in the principle of 'heads I win, tails you lose'.

> From all accounts, Phizo did take the news calmly. He did not blame the messenger of bad news. He understood the motives in the lead up to the accord at Chedema. There had always been a possibility that India might, at the last minute, be magnanimous in victory and invite him to return unconditionally. No such invitation ever came, not even a sounding-out by the Indian High Commissioner's office in London. Just an arrogant silence. (Steyn 2016: 157)

From the sanctuary of Upper Burma, the Chief of the NNC armed wing, Thuengling Muivah issued a stern reprimand to the signatories of the Accord, but used his spleen to accuse Phizo of complicity in the affair. However, there is no denying the fact that the Shillong Accord marked a watershed in the modern history of Nagaland. Great adjustments of thought had to be made. It also had one redeeming feature, that of leading to the release of Naga army prisoners, who had been languishing in stinking jails of Hazaribagh and Agra. When the biographer probed him further: How did he assess the situation? Phizo reasoned:

> Broadly speaking, the so-called Shillong Accord had strengthened Naga nationalism. The people have a clear choice: either they become Indians or live as free Naga.... Muivah and Isak Swu accused me of being supportive of what had taken place in Shillong. They have created the National Socialist Council of Nagaland (NSCN). They had become too much influenced by the ideology of China and rejected me and NNC. They forgot that God is their rock and redeemer. I abided by the decision of the NFG that I should remain in Britain until the time was ripe for me to return.... (The rise of NSCN) was morally divisive. Many communications have passed on between us, but to no avail.... (Thuengaling) Muivah drew up a manifesto in which he presented the NSCN as the true voice of Nagaland and reviled Christianity as an insidious danger ... he asserted that I had failed to condemn the so-called Shillong Accord, and he lauded socialistic altruism over his description of me as a treacherous, capitalist and egoist who had betrayed Nagaland. Muivah and Isak Swu tried to confuse the people, but failed. Both the Tankhul and Sema regions from which they come refused to recognize them. I could not, of course, ignore the threat the NSCN posed, but I am confident the the NNC and NFG together will remain the symbol of free Nagaland. (Steyn 2016: 159-60)

The Shillong Accord created optimism for the future among the new generation of the Nagas. The prolonged deliberations at the working level among the representatives of the government and the underground organizations along with the liaison group of the noted unattached Nagas gave a level of authenticity. The liaison group began its work in earnest. They were aware of the fact that there was huge gulf between the two sets of operators; there was a problem of trust; also there was difference in the working styles at both the ends and there were people in both the sides who openly expressed their reservations of the outcome of the Accord. The biggest stumbling block was the newly emerged splinter group of the NNC in the form of NSCN, which openly charged Phizo for conniving in the Shillong Accord. And it was a serious challenge to Phizo's standing in the Naga imagination and political leadership of NNC. It was apparent that the long absence of Phizo from Nagaland had reduced him to a mythical figure who was divorced from the real scene of action and actors. No doubt, Muivah and Swu's NSCN had stolen the thunder from Phizo's NNC.

Zinyu wrote in 1979 that

> Phizo had refused to accept the Shillong Accord. Phizo claimed that those who signed the Shillong Accord did not get a mandate or authority from the Federal Government of Nagaland. Furthermore, he said, those signatories might have been shot dead from the back, if they had refused to sign the agreement.... He did not bother whether his stand was unrealistic, as asserted by several Nagas such as Vizol, the then chief minister of Nagaland, so long as he thinks that he is morally and legally right. But Phizo says that Vizol's government was a puppet government and Vizol had been acting as a puppet chief minister of a puppet state. He did not care whether his relations are with him or not, so long as he believed that his activities were justified in his own eyes. (1979: 55-6)

The writer of these lines remembers vividly the visit of the Chancellor of North Eastern Hill University, Shillong, in early 1977, where he was on the faculty. The honourable Chancellor of the University happened to the newly elected prime minister of the country, Shri Morarji Desai. His was a formal visit to the university. A delegation of the Naga Students Federation called on the honourable Chancellor with their charter of demands and they had secured a prior appointment for the meeting with him. The moment the delegates were ushered in presence of the big man, he fired upon them, 'Who are you?' They answered, 'We are Nagas'. 'I shall talk to Indians only' and the visiting students angrily walked back. Reminded of that Shillong incident, I cannot understand why Morarji Desai and Phizo met in England. These two perennially angaries, opinionated, inflexible, arrogant and politically unusual characters could not even agree to be civil to each other. Their meeting ended in more rancour and it was a big fiasco to the discredit to both (see the text: Zinyu 1979: 48-53).

From 1975 to 1990, no extraordinary things happened in Nagaland. The state government functioned as per the laws and more than once, the terrorists mounted armed attacks on the chief minister. Violence in Nagaland was taken to be as a routine matter. Underground

Nagas and the state government co-existed side by side. In fact, almost all the states in the neighbourhood of Nagaland suffered from some or other type of insurgency in those days. And it was often said that the NNC was the mother of all the insurgencies in the region. Phizo was invariably charged by some of his former friends to live in luxury in Britain away from the ground reality of Nagaland. In fact, slowly his glamourous image of an angry rebel needed to be dusted. In reality, a more sparkling star was shining on the Naga insurgent horizon in 1980s and that was of NSCN led by T. Muivah and I. Swu.

A recent study informs that after the 1975 Shillong Accord, the authority of the NNC and influence of Phizo had corroded from Nagaland.

It had since split into several factions while most of the cadres that stayed with the original NNC and FGN were now disarmed and aging. He (the respondent) also accepted that with the dwindling of the NNC came the rise of the NSCN, which now superseded the NNC in power and influence. Athe (the respondent) nevertheless insisted thst it was in the NNC, and not in the NSCN-IM or any other NSCN faction, that the historical legitimacy of the Naga struggle was vested. In support of this view, Athe invoked the 1951 plebiscite as having given the NNC the legitimacy to represent the Naga argument for independence. Athe's reasoning is disagreed with the NSCN-IM which at the time of its establishment insisted that by signing the Shillong Accord, even if under duress, the NNC had relinquished once for all, its legitimacy to represent Nagas politically. In a statement issued in the 1980s, the NSCN (had) stated: 'Countrymen, your sovereignty is no more in danger of the Shillong Accord.... it is securely in the hand of the National Socialist Council of Nagaland. (Wouters 2018: 96)

Phizo Passes Away in England

Phizo's biographer posed possibly a last question to Phizo:

The creation of Nagaland as a state is now an established fact. True also is the moral damage the flow of easy Indian money had had on a section of the Naga people. Could it be said that with hind sight it was a mistake for Phizo to leave (Nagaland) for the West in December 1956? Could not his on-the-spot personality have prevented political errors and also worked for greater unity throughout Nagaland? 'Many things might have happened. The effect of the NNC sending me to internationalize our situation is now history. There was so much to do; I hoped to achieve much for my people. I tried, and still (I) do so. I do not think they will judge me a failure', responded Phizo. (Steyn 2016: 160-1)

Zapu Angami Phizo, the president of the Naga National Council (since 1950), died on 30 April 1990 in Bromley in the southern English county of Kent, Great Britain. His death brought an end to an era and a spontaneous resurgence of (the Naga) communal unity at the same time. A seven-man delegation arrived immediately (from Nagaland) in Britain to take his body back to Nagaland. The body was brought from London in a commercial flight. Writes the historian of the regional insurgencies, Sanjoy Hazarika:

> After T. Sakhrie's death, Nehru had ordered the army to the Naga hills to crush the revolt. Phizo fled, first to East Pakistan, having been smuggled out of his beloved Angami hills in a coffin, and then turned up in Britain under a Peruvian (?) passport. He was never to return to his native hills, except, ironically in the very way that he had left Nagaland: in a coffin. (Hazarika 2018: 99)

From Dimapur his body was taken on a slow but dignified procession to the local stadium, covered by the NNC flag. Tens of thousands of mourners filed by the coffin of India's first great rebel. The entire State cabinet, top officials of the state, *gaon buras*, relatives and friends stood and watched the spontaneous outpouring of grief. It was in death, finally, Phizo attained the position that he had always had in the hearts and minds of his people.

Phizo: The Man and his Legacy

By nature, a frontier community is a part society across the national borders, and frontier men, similarly, are defiant of natural obstacles. They are fighters and hunters and for them, loss of life is taken as a part of the normal play of everyday game. Phizo was a typical frontier man, defiant, persistent and resolute in his mission. Moreover, he was a passionate nationalist, exceedingly devious and frustratingly inflexible, but was sincere to Naga culture and its claimed stand on independence. His biographer notes his inconsistencies and warns his readers to remember that Phizo never set out to be liked: to please was not his way of doing things. He belived and claimed that: 'I am anointed to set my people free; the Lord called me in the morning of my life, all, is born of spirit'. In his case, it was a rare non-conformism, which was the combination of his charismatic personality, complex background and unfathomable mystery generally surrounding him.

Despite his laudable sentiment to be honest, he did fall short of his claims. His first notable lapse could be the failure after 1956 to use his influence on the Federal Government of Nagaland in the matter of executive appointments, with the result that the dissenting elements were left with no option, but to work with the Government of India. His second failure may be identified with his inability to recognize honest intentions of those who disagreed with him. For illustration, Sakhrie's life would have been saved for posterity leading to avoiding bitterness between the two clans for many decades and a better cause for the Nagas. And third, he claimed to be a good Christian and invariably referred everything in biblical terms. However, while he could appreciate and applaud an Anglican priest in Revd Michael Scott, he failed to see any merit in Naga Baptist missionaries, who staked their neck for the cause of peace and harmony. He was supposed to have an excellent memory and was slow in forgiving.

Phizo claimed:

> I am not a politician as the word is understood in the West'. He said, 'I am neither a capitalist nor a socialist. I am a Naga from inside out. First, because there is no alternative; second, because I am a son of the soil; third, because there is no better social, political or economic system than the way a Naga lives. I made a mistake in over-estimating the will of those I had left behind in Nagaland to resist the pressure put on them by India; I made another mistake in believing that in the West (that) the truth would conquer. That was not so. Having come here I could see the world too distracted, too divided. I thought of myself as a student of history, but I have discovered I have a lot to learn. (Steyn 2016: 133)

Phizo never courted greatness. For him, religion and politics were not separate. However, he could claim to strive for 'Nagaland for Christ' and play his ethnic politics to buttress his claim even among the animist communities. But he could charge Nehru for non-existent

Brahminical bias. Possibly he had high hopes from the Shillong Accord. But as years passed, in spite of his constant claim to be the president of NNC, he had little control over it and its armed wings over the years. In fact, emergence of NSCN in Nagaland had galvanized the discordant Naga youth at the cost of NNC. His biographer noted a certain sadness creeping in him about that. Then he advances an absurd argument, which is rather confusing and at the same time mischievous:

> A key to the Naga tragedy was the confrontation, which characterized the relationship between Phizo and Jawaharlal Nehru. Both were men of a mission, Phizo's being just as duty-bound as that of Nehru. If either had been a lesser man, they might have sunk their differences and found a common basis on which to work. Both had suffered for their beliefs. Nehru was generally known as a large-hearted liberal, but he was shackled to orthodox Brahminism (?) and his vision of Indian hegemony in South Asia(?). Phizo was throughout unswervingly messianic; he never deviated, never compromised; his perspective was of (either) good or evil, everything which was not truly in line with Naga sovereignty, and therefore good, was tainted. The disaster which overtook the Indian Army in the Himalayas (in 1962) changed Nehru. He then could not move fast enough to secure his strategic eastern flank: the state of Nagaland was born (in 1963), unloved, politically divided, and a pattern for further break-up of the north eastern region. Phizo was perhaps correct in holding the view that Delhi had blundered, but sadly his remedy was not an acceptable alternative ever. (Steyn 2016: 166)

Posterity will demand Phizo to account for the sacrifices, sufferings and untold hardship of three generations of Nagas, who invested everything they had in his improbable dream. In the long run, Phizo was a total failure in his personal life as an entrepreneur, as a politician in public life, and as a person who caused much misery to his family, clan, tribe and and Nagas at large. He was inflexible, arrogant, cliquish, vindictive and politically prophetic and acted as if the biblical truth of Naga politics started and ended with him. For a second generation convert like Phizo, Christianity might be all and end all, but the rest of the world had moved much ahead on secularization in international politics. Moreover, Naga nationalism might be the most critical issue of existence for Phizo, but for the rest of the world, it was a non-issue so far as international set-up was concerned. Thus, try as much as he could from his base in London with sympathetic individuals, but so-called Naga nationalism could not convince the international forums anywhere at any time. At the fag end of his life, disenchantment began to dawn on him. Perhaps again, he was unfair to himself and his associates to pitch his goals too high, which remain far away still in spite of all the struggles, sacrifices and sufferings of the last seven decades. However, he will be remembered by the generations to come in this part of the world as the most glorious rebel of South Asia who would inspire them to rise to every cause of alleged injustice and human suffering.

REFERENCES

Hazarika, Sanjoy, 2011, *Strangers of the Mist: War and Peace*, Penguin Random House India.

_____, 2018, *Strangers No More: New Narratives From India's Northeast*, Aleph Book Company, New Delhi.

Horam, M., 1990, *Naga Insurgency: The Last Thirty Years*, Cosmos Publications, Delhi.

Nag, Sajal, 2002, *Contesting Marginality: Ethnicity, Insurgency and Subnationalism in North-East India*, Manohar, Delhi.

Sema, Hokishe, 1986, *Emergence of Nagaland*, Vikas Publishing House, New Delhi.

Steyn, Pieter, 2016, *Zpuphizo: Voice of the Nagas*, Routledge, Taylor and Francis Group.

Zinyu, Mhiesizokho, 1979, *Phizo and Naga Problem*, Nagaland Times Press, Dimapur, Nagaland.

Wouters, Jelly J.P., 2018, *In the Shadow of Naga Insurgency: Tribes, State, and Violence in Northeast India*, Oxford University Press, New Delhi.

8

Sheikh Muhammad Abdullah and the (Jammu and) Kashmir Quagmire

I chanced to read a book in Hindi, *Naye Bharat Ke Naye Neta*[1]!, by the eminent Marxist Indologist and multilingual author, Rahul Sanskritayan, while I was still in high school. As the title of the book indicates, it was devoted to the life histories of various regional leaders who had taken up the cause of the downtrodden common people at the cost of their careers since the 1930s. And all the life histories detailed in the book, were of those who were known as Marxist leaders. Two names, I still remember whose acts were described in the book besides others, were Sheikh Muhammad Abdullah and Kunwar Muhammad Ashraf. The very first chapter of the book was devoted to the life history of Sheikh Muhammad Abdullah, who hailed from the Kashmir Valley and his family was engaged in making and selling of the famous Kashmiri shawls. The Sheikh claimed (Abdullah 2016: 24-5) that his great-grandfather was a Dattatreya Kaul Brahmin, Raghu Ram, who got converted to Islam. He was the posthumous sixth son of his father, Sheikh Muhammad Ibrahim, who had married thrice and had five other sons and three daughters. It was a joint family of shawl traders, who could manage their household with thrift. After attending the local *makhtab* (Primary school teaching through the medium of Urdu), he passed his matriculation in 1922 at the age of 17 from the Punjab University.

Sheikh Abdullah passed his FSc and was expecting to be nominated for a medical course by the Maharaja, but he could not get it. He made a second effort for the nomination for the medical course, but once more he was rejected. Then he joined Islamia College, Lahore for a BSc course, on a promise from Thakur Janak Singh, a senior

FIGURE 2: SHEIKH MUHAMMAD ABDULLAH
(*Source:* Photograph by the author)

member of the Maharaja's Council and a relative that he would send him abroad for higher studies, but nothing came out of it. Then he joined Aligarh Muslim University for an MSc degree and Law course, and passed MSc in second division in 1930. As he was the first Muslim from Kashmir to get an MSc degree, he applied for the nomination by the state for further studies in Europe, but it was summarily rejected on the grounds that he had crossed the age limit for nomination. Naturally, he writes in his biography:

> My continuous deprivations had convinced me that expecting justice from the (maharaja's) system was like expecting milk from stone. In course of time I could see my individual failures reflective of the failures of a whole community. I was becoming aware of the mesh that lay under my feet indistinguishable from the ground I stood upon. My community was captured in that mesh.... A community, crushed over centuries, was wriggling out of its deplorable situation. I did not know that I was sitting on the crater of a volcano and that nature was burning within me a sacred torch with which to blow up the crater. The valley of roses and tulips (of Kashmir) was going to erupt into a conflagration. (Abdullah 2016: 16)

He had no choice but to accept the job of a school teacher in the state service.

Social Background and the Iniquitous Feudal Regime of the Maharaja

Kashmir was a classical case of feudal exploitation by a Hindu Dogra Maharaja from Jammu, who was oblivious of the bulk of his toiling Muslim subjects who were not only extremely poor but were also denied the minimum of basic rights for human existence. In the summer of 1924, the labourers at the silk factory rose in revolt against the excessive persecution and assembled at Huzuri Baugh in Srinagar demanding their rights. The government sent armed soldiers with spears, who harshly inflicted corporal punishment on the agitating labourers. They later took out a huge demonstration parading through the city of Srinagar with their wives and children for the first time in the history of the state, but the state government refused to do anything about their demands. That was the year the British Viceroy of India, Lord Reading and his wife were on a state visit to Srinagar. The Muslim notables of the town and many of them were courtiers and holding some or the other offices in the government, had drafted a memorandum listing the grievances of the people. It was presented to the Viceroy while he was riding in an open procession. The Viceroy passed on the memorandum to the Maharaja for further action. Instead of redressal of the grievances, that led to further suppression in the Valley and most of the signatories of the memorandum were severely punished for their audacity.

In the late 1920s, the Maharaja had appointed Sir Albion Banerjee as the prime minister and foreign minister of Kashmir. Banerjee tried to address himself with the basic issues of state administration with the hope that the situation might improve. He also made a plea for mitigating the injustices meted out to the masses. His proposals were put in the wastepaper bin. Banerjee was made of a different metal; he resigned from his post and went to the press to expose the misdeeds of the Maharaja's regime. In March 1929 he issued a statement in Lahore:

> The state of Jammu and Kashmir is a victim of all sorts of injustice. The majority of its population comprises Muslims, who are utterly illiterate and who lead a life of destitution. They are treated as dumb-driven cattle. There is no liaison between the masses and administration. Nor are people afforded a chance to find a redressal of their grievances.... The administration has never permitted emergence of public opinion. The number of newspapers is almost nil. The main reason for the backwardness of the state is the abject poverty of the people for all their goodness and intelligence. They are simply denied [the basic] amenities of Life. (Abdullah 1982: 50)

The Maharaja owned the entire land in the state, cultivable as well as the rest in Kashmir Valley, which were given in allotment as *jagirs* to his kinsmen, courtiers, functionaries and hangers-on. The tillers of those lands were extremely poor Kashmiri Muslims, who could have only one-fourth share of the produce. Though they had to work for all the year round on their fields, but their share of produce would barely suffice the consumption needs of their family for three-four months in a year. If they dared to pluck a little of ripe products from their own cultivations for their starving children, punishments would be harsh corporeal injuries. In such as a situation, they would migrate to the plains of Punjab for any work available to them, to the extent of working even as coolies in the urban centres at any price, they would even resort to begging for food.

Political Initiation

The Maharaja had instituted a civil service recruitment board for selection of candidates for various services. The people who supervised the selection tests, set the papers and examined and consolidated the results, were all non-Muslims. While Hindi and Sanskrit were made elective languages, Urdu, Persian and Arabic had no place in the selection process. The government would fill up 60 per cent posts independent of the board. For the rest of the 40 per cent posts, the government could reject any candidate without providing any reason for it. Moreover, there was an upper limit of 22 years of age for a candidate to be selected. Apparently the regime appears to be tilting deliberately against the Muslims, who constituted the majority of the subjects. With a view to creating awareness among the educated Kashmiri Muslims, Abdullah and his friends organized a Reading Room with him as the Secretary. With a view to attracting the attention of the authorities, the Reading Room people decided to send a memorandum to the authorities indicating its unfairness and other drawbacks. Two representatives of the people who had filed the memorandum were asked to meet the government representatives, who intimidated the representatives for their audacity instead of listening to their grievances. Their memorandum was seen as an outburst of impotence and frustration of the disgruntled Kashmiri youth.

As a punishment for his political activities, the Director of Public Instruction (DPI), McDermott had transferred Sheikh Abdullah to Muzaffarabad, but he refused to join. He was asked for the reasons for refusing to go on transfer. Abdullah responded that he was committed to the service of his people and was determined to restore the dignity they had lost. Moreover, he had been doing his duties from 10 o'clock to 4 o'clock. The examination results indicated dedication for his work at the school. The DPI responded that he was on government duty for all 24 hours and defying the government rules amounted to disobedience. Abdullah responded that in that case he would resign from his job. When he came out of the director's office his friends were waiting outside for him. He informed them that for the Kashmiri nation, he had resigned his teacher's job with tears in his eyes, which made the people emotional. A large number of the assembled friends followed him up to his house. This incident was published in *Inqilab* from Lahore, which prefixed Sher-e-Kashmir (Tiger of Kashmir) Sheikhs' name for the first time, which got stuck with him for all times to come.

Once free from the government job of a teacher, he dedicated himself completely in the cause of the toiling and impoverished Kashmiris. He and his friends began organizing public rallies in different parts of the city, which were attended by a large number of men and women against the state apathy for their lot. Abdullah's voice had a thunderous resonance, which was tempered with Muhammad Iqbal's couplets and poems. By then Maharaja Hari Singh had returned from Europe and he was advised to open some dialogue with the people with a view to knowing their problems. The Maharaja at last invited a representative delegation of the Muslims to meet him with their demands. At last, a seven-member delegation was chosen on 21 June 1931 to represent the Muslims of Kashmir to wait on the Maharaja. However, an unexpected turn of events changed the entire context of the Kashmiri political scenario. It so happened that a non-descript person from North West Frontier Agency, Abdul Qadeer, who had come as a butler of Major Abbot, an Englishman on a holiday to Srinagar, offered *namaz* at the Hazaratbal shrine. At times he would make speeches on the pitiable conditions of Kashmiri commoners. One day, pointing his finger to the distant palace of the Maharaja, he exhorted his listeners to pull the royal edifice down by force. The following morning he was arrested, charged with sedition and rebellion under various clauses and put behind bars. Naturally there was an upsurge of sympathy for Abdul Qadeer as he had spoken in favour of the Kashmiri Muslims. On 12 July 1931, Abdullah and his associates held a rally at Gao Kadal in Srinagar and condemned the government for holding his trial in-camera.

Next day, on 13 July 1931, was decided to hold an in-camera trial of Qadeer and for that a large number of people assembled. The

Governor, Raizada Trilok Chand, who had reached the scene with a huge police force, rebuked the jailor for not arresting the members of the audience. The police began indiscriminate arrests on the scene of the onlookers, which provoked them and they began throwing brickbats on the police force. The Governor, possibly out of nervousness, ordered the police to open fire and guns were cocked on people, who were offering their prayers by then. In this indiscriminate firing as many as 22 persons were killed on the spot and hundreds of people were injured badly. There was hardly any arrangement to shift the injured to the hospitals for their treatment or even first aid. In the melee, the injured persons ran helter skelter to save their lives. After that a reign of repression ensued and a regime of panic was created in Srinagar to cow down their morale. The aggrieved Kashmiris decided to commemorate the day (13 July 1931) as Martyr's Day every year thereafter.

Next day, on 14 July the Dogra army raided the mosque and a large number of persons were arrested including Sheikh Muhammad Abdullah. Moreover, the repressive regime resorted to clamp public curfew for 19 days besides the route march by armed forces to intimate the people. But residents of Srinagar went on demanding the release of their leaders from the prison. The regime asked for a written guarantee from them for not making inflammatory speeches in the future, which the prisoners refused on the plea that they were not revolting, but would not agree to surrender their right of free speech. At last, Abdullah and his associates were released from the jail after 21 days. Subsequently, some influential Kashmiri religious leaders close to the regime, mediated between the regime and the public leaders. Their efforts led to signing of a pact with the people and the regime by the prime minister of the state and the Muslim representatives on 26 August 1931.

This development had a lot of significance for the struggling people. First, it was the first document agreed upon by the prime minister and the representatives of the Muslims of the Valley. Second, the movement itself was a disorganized outburst of the suffering people. Thus its organizers too needed breathing space to take stock of the situation. Third, a lot of wild rumours about the movement, regime and the public leaders were afloat in the Valley; for that the regime desired the leaders to help explain the situation to the masses. To facilitate that the government provided transport to travel to different locales in the interiors. The movement leaders took advantage of that to reach the masses at the grassroot level for their purpose. On 21 December 1931, while collecting funds for the movement, Sheikh Abdullah was arrested and a reign of terror was let loose by the local Governor once more. But after intimidation and offers of allurements by the authorities, he was released from jail. On 3 October 1931, the Maharaja celebrated his 36th anniversary and for that he held an open court, which was attended largely by the loyal courtiers. The ruler also made some vague announcements to invite a memorandum from the various communities. The community leaders were invited to present their memoranda to the Maharaja in person on the appointed day. The ruler appeared on the scene after making the public leaders wait for a considerable period of time, took the memoranda in his hands and promised to look into them and quickly vanished back to his palace. On 23 January 1932, Abdullah was again arrested, taken to Central Jail and put in solitary confinement in an apathetic condition.

Birth of All Jammu and Kashmir Muslim Conference

A General Council of the elected Muslim representatives of Kashmir was held on 14-16 October 1932 at Patthar Masjid Srinagar. The Council decided to organize a new forum, the 'All Jammu and Kashmir Muslim Conference', with its flag and clear objectives. Sheikh Muhammad Abdullah was elected the President of the Conference. The Founding President of the Conference made it clear that the forum had been formed not only for the welfare of the Muslims, but for the restoration of rights of the people of the state. He pleaded for the provision of women's education and stepping up of social reforms. He went on:

> we have made it clear again and again that the Kashmir movement is not a communal movement, but one aimed at redressal of the grievances of all communities. And I assure the brethren of the state, Hindus and Sikhs, that we are determined to remove their hardships as in the case of Muslims. Our State cannot progress if we do not learn to live in harmony with each other.

And that is possible only when we respect the legitimate rights of each other and sort out our difficulties among ourselves. Hence, the Kashmir movement is by no means a communal movement. (Abdullah 1982: 123)

Meanwhile, there was continuous demand for inquiring on the reasons for frequent firing on the unarmed crowd of Srinagar. At last, the Glancy Commission was appointed by the Ruler to examine the past firings and make recommendations with a view to minimizing such eventualities in future. The Commission submitted its report on 22 March 1932 and after three weeks the prime minister issued an ordinance on 10 April 1932 approving the recommendations following the Maharaja's assent. The following recommendations of the Commission, when they were made public, there was a wide sense of relief among the masses:

- Places of worship taken over by the government be thrown open to the devotees.
- Education, especially at the primary level, should be broad-based and quantitatively improved.
- Muslims should be offered government jobs, especially in the educational sector. A special officer should be appointed to monitor the progress in providing education to Muslims.
- Academic qualifications for government jobs should not be fixed too high.
- A recruitment policy should be devised, whereby each community is entitled to government service.
- Property rights to government land should be passed on to those who till it.
- Forced labour should be abolished.
- The state authorities should pay immediate attention to the promotion of the arts and crafts to ensure a quick end to unemployment (Abdullah 1982: 130-1).

But the administration was determined to keep Abdullah under their control by force. Thus, he was arrested along with his friends and detained in Udhampur Jail. However, they were released on 7 August 1933. Once they reached Srinagar, there was a huge rally held in Abdullah's reception to the city. That very year in October 1933, Sheikh Abdullah got married to Akbar Jahan, who was the daughter of Michael Harry Nedou. The Nedous were the leading hotelier of Kashmir with branches of their hotel spread in other leading cities of India.

Sheikh Abdullah in Political Ferment

Under the pressure from public demand, the Maharaja instituted a State Assembly known as the Praja Sabha. It was a bizarre institution. The Maharaja kept for himself the power to legislation and he could veto any bill passed by the Assembly. There could be no debate on royal expenditure and expenses incurred for the armed forces. Moreover, he could nominate anybody, anytime for any purpose and any stretch of time to the Assembly. Disgusted with the worthlessness of proceedings in the Assembly, all the members with the exception of one, decided to stay away from the proceedings of this farce of the Assembly. However, this was the time all the elected members of the Assembly got closer to each other. Sheikh Abdullah met Jawaharlal Nehru at Lahore for the first time. They discussed the politics going on in Kashmir at the time and Nehru suggested that salvation of Kashmiris lay in leaving the narrow grooves and joining the national mainstream. He met another notable Congress leader from Kashmir, Saifu-Ud-Din Kichlew at Amritsar. Again he called on an ailing Muhammad Iqbal, who had made a common cause with Muhammad Ali Jinnah, whom he considered as a politician, but termed Jawaharlal Nehru as a patriot with the pride of Kashmiris. That was also the time the short-sighted Maharaja gave away Gilgit Agency to Britain on a long lease of 60 years in 1935, which would prove disastrous for him, as the British Commander of the Gilgit Agency surrendered it to Pakistan as soon as the so-called tribal raiders mounted their attack on Kashmir in 1947. Its purpose for the British was to mount espionage against the USSR, an ideological adversary of the Western Bloc of countries. In this context, one may remember how grateful was Gulab Singh, the founder of the dynasty to the British, that he had sent a contingent of 7,000 troops to crush the 1857 Sepoy revolt against the British rule.

The Sheikh, along with Bakshi Ghulam Muhammad, met with Jawaharlal Nehru at Lahore and travelled with him to North West Frontier Agency. They both were guests of Badshah Khan aka Khan Abdul Gaffar Khan, the leader of famous Red Shirt volunteer force. They travelled for days together and discussed national and international politics and a possible policy for their political parties. Abdullah put the idea to make the Muslim Conference broad-based and alter its nomenclature to the National Conference on 24 June 1938 before the working committee of the party. The party debated the issue threadbare and recommended it to the Executive Committee for acceptance. Meanwhile, the political atmosphere of the state was vitiated by the regime with the imposition of Section 144 and banning all types of political activities. A number of leaders of the Conference addressed the people defying the draconian order and for that they were harshly punished. Sheikh Abdullah was jailed for six months for defying the curfew and addressing the rally without permission. On 10-11 June 1938, the Muslim Conference held its special session at Shahi Masjid, which was presided over by G.M. Sadiq. An important leader of the movement, Chaudhuri Abbas advocated the change over of the Conference in the following words:

> Eight years ago we founded our organization under the name of the Muslim Conference. The name will not do now. It is time that we give a new name.... A misunderstanding is being created that Sheikh Muhammad Abdullah and his companions have sold our movement or that they have been bought over by the Congress. It is being rumoured that we have become lackeys of Gandhi. But I want to tell you we are neither dependent on the Congress nor on the Muslim League. We respect both Gandhi and Jinnah. Yet we will never allow them to decide our destiny for us. Gandhiji says the people of the state should bow before their rulers. We do not agree. Jinnah Sahib says that the majority community of the state ought to win the trust of the minority community. We accept this idea. We welcome the help of the Congress and the Muslim League in our endeavour to seek our demands. But cannot pawn our conscience with any external party.... We are making a bold move. You must remember the services of Qaide-e-Azam Sher-e-Kashmir and ignore what our critics have to say. (Abdullah 1982: 174-5)

Out of 176 delegates attending the Muslim Conference, only four of them cast their votes against the changeover. Thus, now the

Conference had turned to be All Jammu and Kashmir National Conference and a large number of non-Muslims from the State joined the forum and became its functionaries in course of time.

Since then, the All India Congress Committee began inviting the president and the functionaries of the National Conference to attend its annual sessions at various places. Apart from fraternizing the National Congress and various left-oriented leaders and intellectuals, the National Conference welcomed the Muslim League leader, Muhammad Ali Jinnah and his associates as well. Jinnah came to Srinagar first in 1935 and Sheikh Abdullah and Mirza Afzal Beg called on him and pleaded to take up an intricate case of a Muslim lady being fought in the Court. Jinnah demanded Rs. 1,000 per appearance in the court for pleading the case. When pleaded for being lenient, he responded that that his principle was not to lower his fee and he might donate some of the fee for a cause if asked for. He invited Sheikh Abdullah to visit him in Delhi, which the Sheikh did in the company of Mirza Afzal Beg, visiting him at his residence at Aurangzeb Road at Delhi, for two hours. When they were parting, Jinnah as if admonished the Sheikh:

> I am like your father and I have greyed my hair in politics. My experience is that Hindus cannot be trusted. They will never be your friends. All my life I have tried to befriend them. But I did not succeed. (Abdullah 1982: 223)

In May 1944, Jinnah came to Kashmir again and the National Conference gave him a warm reception at Pratap Park in Srinagar in a meeting attended by nearly a hundred thousand people. Abdullah briefly welcomed him and after that Jiya Lal Kilam made a welcome speech in English. Jinnah in his reply said that he believed that the grand reception accorded to him meant an endorsement of the policy of the Muslim League of which he was the president. This led to the exit of Kilam and many others from the meeting. Jinnah and Liakat Ali Khan, the General Secretary of the Muslim League, were advised not to meddle in the local issues of the Kashmiris. But Jinnah was not the one to take anybody's advice. On top of it, Jinnah began addressing in a park at Baramullah where a young and enthusiastic worker of the National Conference, Muhammad Makbool Sherwani, raised the slogans: 'Sher-E-Kashmir Zindabad; National Conference Zindabad'.

Jinnah was unnerved and decided hurriedly to withdraw from the scene. He walked up to his car and drove straight to Rawalpindi in Punjab. He had issued instructions to his lackeys in the breakaway faction of the so-called Muslim Conference of Kashmir that in no case they do anything that would annoy the Maharaja and they should shout, 'Maharaja Zindabad'.

During his stay in Kashmir, people of different views would come to see him. When one of the National Congress volunteers, Ali Muhammad Tariq, who was smart and an extrovert, asked Jinnah, 'Will the future of Kashmir be decided by the Kashmiri people themselves?' Jinnah angrily exclaimed, 'Let the people go to the Dal Lake'. Abdullah informs that the irrepressible Tariq gave the remark wide publicity. However, the Sheikh held Jinnah in great regards. This was reflected in his speech he made after the tribal raids on 30 October 1947, when he took over as prime minister:

> Pakistan is not our enemy. And we still have regards for Jinnah Sahib that we had earlier on. It is our hope that the Kashmir dispute is resolved through dialogue. For that even if I have to go to Pakistan to meet Jinnah Sahib, I will certainly go. But at that time, Jinnah was drunk with power. He thought it beneath his dignity to talk to a nation that had no military equipment. But when the balance of power tilted against him, he was suddenly awakened, but by then it was too late.... A major part of the dispute of Kashmir has something to do with Jinnah Sahib's recalcitrant and undemocratic disposition. (Abdullah 1982: 231)

Jinnah was an obstinate person and had a split personality. He began his career as a popular Congress leader, who rose to the top rank of the leadership. But once Gandhi's populism turned out to be the catch word of the Congress, Jinnah's elitist and exclusive lifestyle had few takers and thus he travelled to England and got busy with his legal career. Temperamentally, in terms of his upbringing and background, he had not even a remote connection with the common people. Neither was he interested in observing even the basic tenets of Islam, as he could not do without his peg of scotch and bacon. A country such as Pakistan was born out of a tornado of hatred. Historian Bipin Chandra rightly said that a religious Mohandas Karamchand Gandhi founded a secular Indian Union and a secular Mohammad

Ali Jinnah was instrumental in giving birth to a theocratic Muslim state of Pakistan.

Jinnah felt that he was smart enough not to commit anything on paper about his ideas of Pakistan and leave every detail pertaining to fate of the people deliberately for his bargaining at the end as a pleader. When pressed for the future blueprint of Pakistan under the Muslim League, the famous Qaid-e-Azam had blurted out: 'What is the hurry?' Jinnah's

> phraseology was a master stroke in ambiguity. At no point did Jinnah elaborate on anyone of the technicalities that will surely follow the cleavage of the country (the British India) into twins. He said nothing about boundaries, or demographic shifts, administration or minority rights. He had no blueprint for national governance. The image of the new nation, Pakistan, dangerously fluid, a ghost-like garment that would fit anyone who cared to dream of it. (Basu 2020: 126)

Jawaharlal Nehru, in the view of Sheikh Abdullah, was an enigma, as various strands of his personality in the form of virtues and vices make it difficult to form an unambiguous assessment of his personality (Abdullah 1982: 250). A Kashmiri by origin, he possessed an extraordinary charm. Raised in an elitist high society, he was liberal-minded and non-conformist in his approach. Possibly he was an inseparable part of the British liberal tradition. It is said that he even thought and dreamt in English. Much earlier in life, he turned a Marxist – not an orthodox one, but a pragmatist one. It is said that he had a streak of Machiavellianism, as he was a great devotee of Chanakya and his famous work, *Arthashastra*. He was a sentimentalist and his personal charisma was such that anybody could fall a victim of his charm. He had a fascinating personality, in which strands of English taste, Hindu delicacy and Muslim nobility were inseparable sublimal strands. In matters of friendship, he would go to a great extent.

Sheikh Abdullah went to Delhi to acquaint the Cabinet Mission of their demands on Kashmir. He met Mahatma Gandhi and suggested to him that the right to accession should go to the people of the state and with a view to securing that right the National Conference would launch an agitation. But the Mahatma did not agree to the suggestion.

The Cabinet Mission went to Srinagar on 19 April 1946 and returned to Delhi on 24 April. The Sheikh had sent from Lahore a telegram stating the position of the National Conference to the Cabinet Mission. He reached Kashmir in May 1946 and began addressing public meetings at different places. In a particular meeting at Zaindar Mohalla he said that contributing one rupee each, Kashmiris would scrape together seventy-five hundred thousand rupees and return the amount to the Maharaja with which his great grandfather, Gulab Singh, had purchased Kashmir a hundred years before, a fact on which Urdu Poet Muhamad Iqbal had written:

They sold the farmer, the field, the stream, the orchard
They sold a whole nation and for what a throw away price.

When Jawaharlal came to know of the situation in Kashmir, he invited the Sheikh for talks in Delhi. But the Sheikh was arrested on 20 May on the border of Kashmir when he was on his way to Delhi in response to a call from Nehru and he was detained in the quarter guard at Badami Baugh. The great Muslim League leader, Jinnah, termed the Muslim Conference as a movement of the hooligans, masterminded by a foreign agency, the Soviet Union. Only Jawaharlal Nehru stood with the National Conference movement. He decided to go to Kashmir to stand by the Sheikh, but the President of Congress, Maulana Azad and Mahatma Gandhi prevented him from going to Rawalpindi, as he was urgently needed for the ongoing discussions with the Cabinet Mission. But having said that: 'I am a man of the people, so I must go', Nehru proceeded to Kashmir. Once he reached the border, he was stopped and offered one of two parked cars for returning to Delhi. He refused and he was arrested and kept in a nearby guesthouse. Meanwhile, there was a stalemate in the ongoing discussion between the parties and thus there was pressure on Nehru to return to Delhi. At last, Lord Wavell sent his personal aircraft to bring him back to Delhi. Once he was back in Delhi, he issued the following statement exposing the feudal tyranny of the Maharaja:

Everybody with some awareness of Kashmir knows of the great respect that Sheikh Muhammad Abdullah enjoys there. The darling of even those living in remote parts of valley, he is their 'Lion of Kashmir'. His personality is surrounded by countless tales and folk songs. In respect of the popular movements in the states, he is my greatest and most valuable friend. I seek his opinion on every important matter. Nobody should think that we would desert him or his friends simply because the Kashmir government possesses a few guns. We are determined to stand by the Kashmiris and their leaders in their hours of trial. Right now in the beautiful valley, people are being killed. It is clear that the State government is crushing the people's movement. (Abdullah 1982: 261)

The Government of Maharaja Hari Singh had clamped Section 144A of the Indian Penal Code, which the Sheikh and his associates had violated and that they were tried in the court for that, Nehru had arranged a leading advocate, Asaf Ali from Patna, to plead Abdullah's case against the battery of the government pleaders such as Bhullabhai Desai. But that was the day of Asaf Ali, who pleaded in the court:

Slaves have a birth right to revolt and the Kashmiris have the same right to revolt against the Amritsar Treaty. We are in 1946, when the British cabinet has announced that India has a right to freedom. We are in the age when the whole world is abuzz with a demand for the freedom of the masses. It is sin even now to say that the government of this state too should be based on people's consent and not on the abominable, century-old sales deed likely to be rejected by the highest court of the world.

Even Jawaharlal Nehru donned the barrister's black gown and attended the court to defend the Sheikh. The verdict was out on 10 September 1946 and the Sheikh was awarded three years' imprisonment each for three cases running concurrently and a fine of Rs. 500. Jawaharlal Nehru commented on the case:

People's movements informed with an impulse or cause generally throw up personalities who become the symbols of these movements. By the same token Sheikh Muhammad Abdullah has become the most outstanding, illustrious and living emblem of the Kashmiri aspirations. Looked at from this point of view, Sheikh Muhammad Abdullah's legal case has assumed a magnitude for above that of an ordinary individual. In fact, a whole nation has been put in the dock. To be more precise, it has been a hearing in the people's court about the government officials who tried in vain to deflect the course of a great mass movement. It is amazing to see that the rulers have forgotten the lessons of history with their brains too softened to understand the logic of contemporary events. The people of the state have started a revolt against the state's armed forces, which is not going to end with this case , but will continue until it reaches its logical conclusion. (Abdullah 1982: 265)

Pakistan Attacks Kashmir, Accession to India and Sheikh's Release

Sheikh Abdullah was sent to various old forts converted into jails, which were not livable because of poor maintenance. Mahatma Gandhi visited Kashmir from 30 July to 3 August 1947. On his return to Delhi, he gave a statement that Sheikh Abdullah was tremendously popular and the Maharaja had lost the trust of his subjects. The Kashmiris would be pleased only when the Sheikh would be released from prison. He termed the Treaty of Amritsar as a 'Sales deed', and when it expired, Kashmir's sovereignty should be made over to the people. Meanwhile, British India was divided into two dominions: India and Pakistan on 15 August 1947. That unnatural division of territory and mixed population resulted in extensive tragic violence between the two countries. There were extensive communal riots occurring between the Hindus and Muslims and large number of refugees were migrating from India to Pakistan and vice-versa. Houses were burnt, properties were looted, destroyed and burnt and women were raped and abducted. Homeless, dispossessed and injured, men and women were travelling in hordes in opposite directions in search of security and home. All said, the partition of British India resulted into a horrendous tragedy. Kashmir was not untouched from this grim scenario. The Hindus from Punjabi-speaking western parts such as Muzaffarabad of Kashmir were attacked by violent Muslim mobs and ran towards Jammu to take shelter. In this grim scenario, if Kashmir was to be rescued, it was only Sheikh Abdullah who could possibly help to ease the situation. Maharaja's brother-in-law, Kunwar Nischant Chand, visited the Sheikh in Badami Baugh Cantonment Jail and after a series of meetings, it was decided that the Maharaja and the Sheikh should meet. The meeting ended with a positive note and there was plain and frank speaking on the part of the visitor. After that, he returned to Badami Baugh Cantonment Jail.

Sheikh Abdullah was released from the jail on 29 September 1947 after one year, four months and eleven days instead of a term of three years. It was a fact that circumstances forced the Maharaja to release him against his wishes. The Sheikh was accorded a rousing reception when he was released from the prison and taken away in a spectacular boat procession to Srinagar. The Sheikh expressed his views in the rally:

> The issue before the state of Jammu and Kashmir is: Should we accede to India or Pakistan or opt for independence? It is a fact that I am the President of the All India States Peoples Conference, whose policy is unequivocal. Pandit Jawaharlal Nehru is a close friend of mine and I respect Gandhiji. It is also a fact that the Indian National Congress has rendered us great help in our struggle. Despite all this, the most important criterion that will determine our accession is the interest of our people. I am not going to interfere in the matter. Our foremost obligation now is to shake off the Dogra rule. After that, if the people decide to join Pakistan, I will be the first man to endorse their decision.

Meanwhile, Jinnah's Pakistan had adopted various ways to get Kashmir for itself at any cost. They reached the Maharaja for accession, who dithered as per his habit. They depended heavily on the Muslim Conference and fifth columnist among the National Conference, which did not work, as their followers had no support among the masses. They invited a number of National Conference leaders and tried to entrap them through various deceptions. So much so that they had designed to invite Sheikh Abdullah as a guest of their President, put him in some godforsaken obscure place virtually in captivity, and form a 'government' allegedly under his leadership and send their army in his claimed support. But unfortunately, the Sheikh had no time to spare for travelling to Pakistan as he was terribly tied up with the burning issues in his home state. G.M. Sadiq, a senior functionary of the National Conference, was in Pakistan at the time. He had a taste of their hospitality and how could he manage to get away with difficulty to Srinagar is another story. At last, they mounted allegedly a tribal raid on north-western Kashmir abated by their armed forces and regional leadership of the Muslim League. The climax was reached when the raiders had reached Baramulla and burnt the electric power station and stopped electric supply to Srinagar when the

Maharaja was busy celebrating the annual Dussehra festival. These vicious attacks were the worst form of atrocities: murder, arson, loot, destruction of properties, rape and abduction of women. The raiders were so barbaric that they raped and killed fourteen nuns at Saint Joseph Mission Hospital and murdered the Mother Superior of Hospital and an English couple point blank. The attackers inflicted all sorts of atrocities to all the Kashmiris, but they especially targeted Hindus and Sikhs. As the raiders were allegedly two days march away from the Maharaja's capital, Srinagar, he decided to move instantly to Jammu, the main support base of the Dogras, in the midnight. In such a situation, an old Congressman, Saif-U-Din Kichlew, who was visiting Srinagar from his home town, Amritsar, rushed to Delhi and requested the Congress leaders to rush with the help before it became too late.

The Maharaja requested for instant armed support from the Government of India, but it could not be accomplished, as he had not accessed to the Indian dominion. Once he signed the Instrument of Accession, air-borne military aid reached instantly to beleaguered Kashmir. The raiders were chased away from the cities of Uri and Baramulla and a huge chunk of territory and helpless citizens were rescued from the clutches of the attackers. The Indian armed forces worked in most adverse condition as it was difficult to maintain required logistic support because of poor infrastructure. However, the Indian Army displayed instances of bravery, ingenuity, and initiative to salvage the bad situation and turn them into a favourable one. The Indian Commander, General Thimmaiyya, mounted a fleet of tanks at a height of 13,000 ft Zojila Pass and rescued Dras, Kargil and Ladakhi Kashmiri subjects from the north. Brigadier Sen's troops recovered Uri from the Pakistani hold and that shattered Pakistan's dream of conquering Kashmir. The defeat was particularly painful to hypocrite President Jinnah, who pretended that he did not know anything about the attacks on Kashmir and it was a local affair mounted by some tribal raiders unknown to him.

Apparently, Maharaja's administration had not planned anything for the security of Kashmir Valley before they hurriedly left Srinagar for Jammu to save their skin. In the absence of effective administrative machinery, chaos prevailed everywhere and all sorts of rumour were afloat. In such a situation, volunteers of the National Conference came forward to mount guards on strategic locations and important installations. Moreover, the Government of India came to know that certain highups in the administration at Jammu were instrumental in the massacre of some Muslims in Jammu. The Government of India realized the gravity of the situation and Prime Minister Jawaharlal Nehru wrote a letter to the Maharaja on 13 November 1947:

> If there is anybody who can deliver in Kashmir, then that person is Sheikh Muhammad Abdullah. I have a high opinion of his moral integrity and mental calibre. Without him no satisfactory solution to any issue is possible in Kashmir.

Abdullah records: a bizarre situation was created by Maharaja Hari Singh. He had appointed M.C. Mahajan for a period of five years as the prime minister. Then he appointed the Sheikh as the Chief Executive of Administration, who took charge of his office on 30 October 1947. He was the first Muslim from Kashmir to be ever appointed as the head of the administration in the Dogra regime. In fact, four Dogra kings from 1846 to 1947, had appointed 28 prime ministers, but not a single Muslim was ever given a chance. Even in the adverse circumstance such as Pakistani attack on Kashmir, J.C. Bali, Deputy Inspector General of Intelligence, reported to Nehru in a personal letter:

> In Jammu, the Dogra and Rajput soldiers are responsible for the disasters and bloodshed there, as the tribal raiders from Pakistan are elsewhere. Like brigands, they set fire to the Muslim villages, abducted women and rape them. The silence of the Maharaja and the ruling clique encourages them in carrying out such barbarous acts.

On a visit to Jammu, Jawaharlal Nehru consoled sufferers publically and snubbed the Maharaja in private. Sheikh Abdullah also told the Maharaja of the atrocities committed on Muslims in Jammu and warned him of the consequences.

Gandhiji, as a one-man-army, was crusading against the communal violence in India at the time. He had high hopes from the non-partisan and non-communal atmosphere of Kashmir and he had publically acknowledged Kashmir the beacon of hope during the communal holocaust. When he learnt of what had happened in Jammu, he asked Sheikh Abdullah about it. When Sheikh Abdullah affirmed it, a sad Mahatma angrily asked, 'Why are you silent about the curtailment of the Maharaja's powers? If you do not speak up, you will be betraying the trust of your people?' However, Sheikh Abdullah's adversaries in the corridors of power in Delhi were quiet for the moment, but the preparations were afoot for the ambush that was to be laid in 1953 had started. Sheikh Abdullah alleges that 'it was supervised by India's "illustrious" Home Minister and the Iron Man, Sardar Vallabhbhai Patel' (310). He had no doubt in his mind that had 'the sage of Sabarmati' survived, the 1953 events would not have happened.

Sheik Abdullah Takes Over the Office of the Prime Minister of Kashmir

Gandhiji had got a wind of the communal riots engineered at the highest level at Jammu in the state. Thus, he spoke in his famous prayer meeting on 27 December, 1947:

> The maharaja had got the reports about countless killings of Muslim men and abduction of women in Jammu. He should own it up. He has direct command of the Dogra army, so he should be held responsible for whatever has happened. Sheikh Abdullah came to Jammu and tried to calm the tempers. In view of whatever has happened in Jammu, the Maharaja ought to step down and give Sheikh Sahib and his people the opportunity to repair the situation.

Prime Minister Jawaharlal Nehru is said to have written a letter to Patel alleging that the ministry of states was ignoring his instructions openly. Citing the principle of collective responsibility of the cabinet and the leadership of the prime minister as the key principles of functioning in a democratic system, he wondered how could the ministry under him function as independent of such principles. The effect of the letter was such that Sardar Patel offered to resign at the end of December 1947 and had even framed the letter as such, but did not press for it. Once Gandhiji came to know of it, he tried to restrain Patel. Not only that, Gandhiji asked Sheikh Abdullah to meet Patel and request him not to press for his resignation. Sheikh Abdullah did so and also informed the sharp eyed and experienced home minister that the prevalent practice of diarchy (of a prime minister and a Chief Executive of Administration) was not functioning in Kashmir to anybody's advantage. It is to the credit of Sardar Patel that he agreed to dismiss M.C. Mahajan as the prime minister. Consequently, the Maharaja appointed Sheikh Abdullah as the prime minister. The new cabinet of eight ministers representing the various communities residing in the state led by the Sheikh Abdullah was sworn in on 5 March 1948.

There was a basic difference between Maharaja Hari Singh and Sheikh Abdullah because the two represented two different political cultures. The Maharaja belonged to the feudal order and was unable to accept the new dispensation and swallow the populist policies of Sheikh Abdullah, the latter, on the other hand, while a charismatic leader and a superb orator in Kashmiri, was imbued with a bitterly anti-Dogra and anti-monarchical attitude. Sheikh Abdullah really represented Kashmiri opinion, the numerically majority in the state. The Maharaja, in turn, commanded traditional loyalty of the Dogras, who constituted a majority in Jammu region. In this conflict, Sheikh Abdullah had an advantage of wholehearted support of Jawaharlal Nehru, the prime minister. As against this, the Maharaja was closely in touch with Sardar Vallabbhai Patel, the Minister of Home Affairs, who often stood up for him, writes Karan Singh (1983: 86-7).

The Maharaja was advised politely, but very clearly by Sardar Patel on 29 April 1948 to absent himself for some time from the state by appointing the Crown Prince Karan Singh as the Regent to carry out his duties and responsibilities in his absence. And that had to be done in the national interest. Hari Singh was shocked to hear the advice from the home minister; he was extremely upset with the development and he took some time to reconcile to the fast changing realities. It was an extremely delicate situation for the young prince (Karan Singh) still in his teens to fathom a sensitive, difficult, intricate and intriguing development in which history had placed him. Luckily, the prime minister and the home minister, both were sensitive about the delicate responsibility thrust upon the young prince and they did their best to groom him in the new role with all the required care. Karan Singh met Jawaharlal Nehru and Sardar Patel subsequently, who acquainted him about the delicate and complex issues at hand. In fact, the Crown Prince spent three weeks with Sardar Patel in Dehradun before he travelled to Kashmir. At last, the Maharaja and Maharani left Delhi on 20 May 1948 and the Crown Prince left for Srinagar by DC3 aircraft. Incidentally, on the same day, a proclamation was issued by the Maharaja:

> Now, therefore, I hereby direct and declare that all powers and functions, whether legislative, executive or judicial which are exercisable by me in relation to the State and the government, including in particular my right and prerogatives of making laws, of issuing Proclamations, Orders and pardoning offenders, shall during the period of my absence from the State be exercised by the Yuvaraj Shri Karan Singhji Bahadur.

That very day, the Regent was welcomed by Sheikh Abdullah and his cabinet of ministers at Srinagar and a new chapter began in the history of Kashmir (Singh 1982: 100-2).

India took the issue of the invasion of Kashmir by Pakistan to the United Nations Organization (UNO) on the advice of the British prime minister. Within no time, it was realized that the Kashmir issue had turned out to be an issue of power play among the powerful members of the Security Council of the UNO. Sheikh Abdullah took part in the deliberations of the Council as a member of the Indian delegation. Moreover, he also tried to reach to delegates of Pakistan to find some common ground to work out a possible formula between the two countries to remove the bitterness. He desired further that if Pakistan would agree, India and Pakistan could jointly ensure Kashmir's independent autonomy. But he was rebuffed by the Pakistanis, so much so that they did not desire to even look at him in those days. Under these circumstances,

> the Security Council kept on despatching its arbitrators and delegations to Kashmir, who enjoyed their visits and then, submit their reports. Sometimes, it would be a Dixon, and sometimes a Graham. Sometimes, there was talk of sending Admiral Nimtenz and sometimes Sweden's Gunnar Yoring to supervise a referendum. Thus, the matter kept on hanging on fire. (Abdullah 1982: 337)

Background to Sheikh Abdullah's Arrest and Incarceration

Sheikh Abdullah was a self-made man, who was proud of his sacrifices made for the cause of Kashmir against the iniquitous Dogra regime. He was headstrong, dedicated to the cause of the poor, and always ready to uphold the dignity of ordinary men and women. He was non-partisan in his behaviour, who did not believe and operate in factional politics. He was egalitarian in his approach, but was not a member of or aligned to any socialist or a communist party at the all India level. He was proud of his friendship with Jawaharlal Nehru and had the highest regards for Mahatma Gandhi. These two luminous political stars of Indian politics naturally attracted Sheikh Abdullah to the Indian National Congress party. Moreover, as he had well identified himself with anti-feudal and anti-monarchical approach of the Congress party, he was confident of their support. Furthermore, he felt that detailed programmes of the Congress hammered out in the open public sessions ensured their commitments for the future. Against this background, he found Muhammad Ali Jinnah, a formal, distant and an arrogant individual, who had decided to carry the Muslim India in his pocket.

Sheikh Abdullah had not bargained to be in politics for a career, but he had emerged as a crusader for the cause of the suffering masses. Moreover, he had first hand experience of suffering at the personal level because of the iniquitous feudal regime of the Dogras. Even in the Congress, he respected Maulana Abdul Kalam Azad and Khan Abdul Gaffar Khan, but found them away from the common Muslim masses. He had no answer to the question, why did the common poor Muslim masses follow theological, feudal, obscurantist, and orthodox leaders and did not possess mass leaders from among them. In such a situation, the Sheikh Abdullah had large many admirers in every walk of Indian life, but he remained largely a regional leader of Kashmir, whose splendid sacrifices made for the cause of Kashmiri people perhaps did not reach beyond Kashmir by and large.

In October 1950, the General Assembly of the UNO adopted a resolution advising Kashmir to form a Constituent Assembly to frame its constitution on the basis of adult franchise. It was to be an assembly that should include the representatives of every section and class of people from every unit of the state. The Head of the State of Jammu & Kashmir issued a proclamation on 4 April 1951 instituting and convening the Assembly. The Constituent Assembly would have a hundred seats: 25 of them were set aside for the areas occupied by Pakistan where elections could not be held as they were not within the Indian control. For the rest, elections were held in September 1951 and the National Conference got most of seats in the newly created Assembly. G.M. Sadiq, a senior member of the Conference, was elected Speaker of the House and thus Constituent Assembly got going with its programme. The business advisory committee of eight senior members of the Assembly had drawn four important issues to be considered by the Assembly:

1. To frame a constitution for the state in keeping with the aspirations of the common people.
2. To ratify the action taken to abolish *jagirdari* and *chakdari* systems.
3. To abolish the hereditary rule of the Dogra dynasty.
4. To take a decision regarding the Accession of the State (Abdullah 1982: 365-6).

The above issues were debated in the House and as the above points were identified after threadbare discussion among the members of the Assembly. By and large, the first and the last issues listed above took no time to decide on, as the leadership was clear on them and they were accepted easily. Even other two, 2 and 3 numbers listed above were also something like action taken before and they had to be ratified by the Constituent Assembly. But these issues had regional ramifications, as they were intimately linked with the past power and privilege of Jammu region and the vested interests thereof, which had their powerful patrons in the corridor of power in New Delhi. It is a fact that the Dogras were the most ruthless rulers of the Kashmiri masses, who were dispossessed of everything. Other Hindu courtiers, such as the Rajputs, the king's caste and kinsmen, were the one who held the most of the *jagirs*, they were powerful elements who still commanded influence. Moreover, the Brahmin priests and courtiers, who wove the theological legitimacy in favour of the royalty, were another component of the Jammu circus, which was naturally ranged against Abdullah's radical land reforms. All these conservative elements from Jammu had formed a formidable front against the pro-poor moves of the National Conference. At times, they had a great patron in the personae of Sardar Vallabhbhai Patel, the Union Home Minister. When he was no more, his place was taken over by the newly founded conservative political forum, the Bharatiya Jana Sangh. All these elements were naturally ganged up against Sheikh Abdullah and Jawaharlal Nehru.

There was another reason why the Sheikh was attracted to the Congress for the fact that the Congress stood for a plebiscite in Kashmir with a view to deciding the future of the Kashmir, while the Muslim League under Jinnah was determined to take Kashmir for themselves without any reference to the people. And that is why when the Maharaja was dithering in his decision in favour of India or Pakistan, Pakistan mounted an attack on Kashmir camouflaged as tribal raids. The British had given a choice to the rulers of the Princely States in India to decide to join any one of the two dominions. There was a popular perception that a Princely State in British India was known as Hindu or Muslim State as per the religious affiliation of the rulers. For illustration, Jammu & Kashmir was known as a Hindu state because its ruler was a Hindu though its bulk of population was Muslims. On the other hand, the Nizam of Hyderabad and Nabob of Junagarh were Muslims, but the majority of their subjects were Hindus. The rulers of Hyderabad and Junagarh tried to join Pakistan, which India objected and demanded to hold a plebiscite in the states for deciding the choice of the people. On the same ground, India had committed in the United Nations Organization that there would be a plebiscite in Jammu & Kashmir to decide on which of the two countries, India or Pakistan, the people would like to join. Thus, when the Constituent Assembly was in session in Srinagar, it decided for an elected head of the state, a prime minister and a separate flag for the state.

On 15 November 1952, the Constituent Assembly of Jammu & Kashmir had met and elected the Regent, Karan Singh as the Sadar-e-Riyasat, the Head of the State, for a period of 5 years. After two days, on 17 November 1952, the Regent drove to the old Rajgarh

Palace on the Jhelum, where the Constituent Assembly of the State was in session. The Speaker of the Assembly, G.M. Sadiq and ministers of the cabinet led by the prime minister, S.M. Abdullah, and the members of the Assembly welcomed him. Soon after that, the Chief Justice Wazir Janaki Nath of the High Court administered the oath of office of Sadar-e-Riyasat to him. Ironically, Karan Singh, very aptly summed up the development: 'I was at once the last representative of the old (feudal) order becoming, by the consent of the people, and the first servant of the new (democratic order)' (Singh 1982: 147).

Enters Dr Shyama Prasad Mukherjee in the Kashmir Imbroglio

The Praja Parishad, a forum of Jammu region, which was aligned with the newly-formed Bharatiya Jana Sangh, was agitating for Kashmir's complete merger with India. Shyama Prasad Mukherjee, the founder President of the Sangh, desired to enter Kashmir against the prevalent practice of getting an entry permit issued from the Ministry of Defence, the Government of India. When he applied for the permit, it was denied to him, but he persisted and entered Kashmir with a lot of publicity, as his was a political move. Naturally, he got arrested on 8 May 1953 and put behind the bars in Srinagar. Mukherjee was insistent on Kashmir's complete merger with India. Sheikh Abdullah and his colleagues met him and tried to convince him, why it could not be accomplished at the time, but he remained unconvinced. Shyama Prasad Mukherjee died of heart attack on 23 June 1953 while in jail. Naturally, his sudden death led to a lot of rumours. One of the rumours was that his death was not a natural one. Shyama Prasad Mukherjee was not an ordinary individual. He was the son of famous Sir Ashutosh Mukherjee, former Vice-Chancellor of Calcutta University. S.P. Mukherjee himself had occupied that august chair. He was also a member for some times of the Indian federal cabinet led by Pandit Nehru. And it is alleged that Shyama Prasad Mukherjee was one of the first batch of five luminaries, loaned (or deputed) by the Rashtriya Swayam Sevakdal (RSS), to launch the Bharatiya Jana Sangh. So there was a big stir on his death at different levels. Though it was a bungling on the part of the Ministry of Defence, Government of India, it was projected as if it was the Sheikh Abdullah who had master-minded the whole affairs of Shyama Prasad Mukherjee's demise.

By then merger of Junagarh and Hyderabad was settled as per the satisfaction of the Indian leadership. So far as Kashmir was concerned, even the world opinion was turning uninterested in the acrimonious debates and unending charges and counter-charges by both the parties on the floor of the UNO. The Indian opinion veered to the point to accept the reality. There was a public fatigue: let Pakistan hold what they captured by force once, but what remains with India, let India be happy with it. Then the bombshell was dropped that Kashmir will have a separate head of the state, its own prime minister and a separate flag of its own. It was considered something going back on the process of integration of the Indian Union. On the other hand, the apologists of Kashmir development argued that Kashmir had merged with India only on three subjects: defence, foreign relations and communications and for the rest it was independent to have her own way. On top of that Shyama Prasad Mukherjee's demise occurred in captivity in Kashmir. He was not only the President of the Bharatiya Jana Sangh, but also a freedom fighter and a top raking national leader from the sensitive State of West Bengal. It was difficult to ignore the issue as a local event of no consequence. On the other hand, there had been bickering within the fold of the National Conference leadership. The atmosphere was surcharged with some apprehension. Even there were demands of Sheikh Abdullah's dismissal and arrest published in the Indian press.

Sheikh Abdullah too had a premonition. He writes in his biography:

> Karan Singh had already a secret missive for my removal. The zero hour had been fixed. The entire strategy was being put in place with an eye on details. In my innocence, I carried the cross of duty on my shoulders. Of course, when I looked around me, I saw my companions, from whom I had alienated myself from all and sundry, after my life. (Abdullah 1982: 397)

The Sadar-e-Riyasat Karan Singh writes that there were two factions in the National Conference: one led by M.A. Beg and other, led by G.M. Bakshi, G.L. Dogra and D.P. Dhar. While the issue of the abolition of monarchy and choosing a Sadar-e-Riyasat was accomplished fast by getting resolutions passed in the Constituent Assembly, but other vital issues such as relations with the Government of India regarding judiciary, finance and administrative services were left hanging on fire. The factional fights between the two groups became more pronounced and slowly Sheikh Abdullah began to veer around the hardliners in this controversy. Karan Singh met the prime minister in Delhi twice, once on 21 April and again on 23 May 1953 and acquainted him with the fast changing scenario in Kashmir. The PM informed him that he had no answer from the parliament on the issues pertaining to the Delhi Agreement, as he could not get answers to his letters from Sheikh Abdullah. Furthermore, writes Singh in his biography,

> It was clear that he (Jawaharlal Nehru) was deeply disturbed, but he had not quite made up his mind how to deal with the problem. He was particularly hurt, even bewildered, at the hostile manner in which his old protégé and friend, Sheikh Abdullah, was acting, and agreed with me when I remarked that unlimited power seemed to have brought out the Sheikh's worst fascist and totalitarian tendencies. (Singh 1983: 153-4)

The Arrest of Sheikh Abdullah

The prime minister asked Sheikh Abdullah to visit Delhi on 3 July 1953 and meet him for some important discussion; Sheikh Abdullah turned it down. Then the PM sent the venerable Maulana Abdul Kalam Azad to Srinagar so that Sheikh Abdullah could take advantage of that visit and convey his views categorically, but it was not to be. Singh received a signed copy of the memorandum on 7 August by which, Sheikh Abdullah had asked one of his ministers, Shyam Lal Shraf, to resign from his cabinet of ministers. On the next day, he received a copy of the memorandum sent to Sheikh Abdullah by the deputy prime minister of Jammu & Kashmir, Bakshi Ghulam Mohammad, the Finance Minister G.L. Shraf and the Health minister, Shyam Lal Shraf. The five page document squarely blamed Sheikh Abdullah of flouting the accepted party policies. And they concluded their memorandum thus:

> ...It is, therefore, with great pain that we have to inform you of our conclusion that the Cabinet, constituted as it is at present and lacking as it does the unity of purpose and action, has lost the confidence of the people in its ability to give them a clean, efficient and healthy administration. (Singh 1983: 159)

The Sadar-e-Riyasat immediately invited Prime Minister Sheikh Abdullah to come to see him as soon as possible. As the prime minister was going to Gulmarg that afternoon, he came to see Singh by noon. When he was enquired of the situation within the government he claimed that everything was fine. When Singh said that he was distressed and concerned about the absence of homogeneity in the cabinet, Sheikh Abdullah had supposedly side-tracked the issue. The Sadar-e-Riyasat made a suggestion to hold a meeting at his residence to iron out the differences, if any, that evening. Sheikh Abdullah was to have mounted an attack on the biased Indian Press for exaggerating the differences in his cabinet. When pressed for doing something for ratifying the situation, 'he stated quite clearly that no internal solution was possible until there was some external solution acceptable to India as well as Pakistan' (Singh 1983: 160). Sheikh Abdullah went ahead on a visit to Gulmarg, having said that.

Karan Singh informs that by then he had made up his mind that Sheikh Abdullah would have to be dismissed. His natural successor, Bakshi Ghulam Mohammad, the deputy prime miniser of the state, made it clear that he would not undertake to run the government if Sheikh Abdullah and Mirza Afzal Beg were left free to propagate their points of views. One gets enough hints that the Sader-e-Riyasat was in the know of the whole development and had been working on a way out with other operatives for some time.

> By the time the documents were ready, it was late evening. The weather was also in turbulent mood; it was pouring, thunder rumbled and jagged shafts of lighting cut through the clouds. I deputed my ADC, Major B.S. Bajwa, to go to Gulmang and deliver the letter to Sheikh Abdullah. A police party also went along with him, but they were delayed by the torrential rain and bad road beyond Tangmarg.... Our gamble was a risky one, if the Sheikh got an inkling of what was happening, he would react ferociously, and our lives may well have been in danger. However, the die was cast.... The Sheikh was totally unaware of the developments.... When the ADC and police

contingent finally reached Gulmang it was late at night, and Sheikh and Begum Abdullah were fast asleep. With some difficulty and much knocking he was awoken and handed the letter and warrant of arrest.... The early hours of the 9th morning they were escorted to a car and driven out of the Valley to Udhampur, where they were kept in detention. (Singh 1983: 163-4)

In the early hours of 9 August 1953, Bakshi Ghulam Mohammad and his colleagues were administered the oath of office of the prime minister and ministers respectively.

Now it is worth recording Sheikh Abdullah's version of that critical night, 8-9 August 1953 at Gulmarg:

It was about four-twenty in the morning, when I heard a tap on the door and saw my private secretary standing outside. He said that the house was surrounded by the soldiers with machine guns and that the Superintendent of Police, L.D. Thakur, accompanied by the ADC of the Sader-e-Riyasat, came in. The latter handed me an envelope from Karan Singh. It contained a letter saying that I had been dismissed from premiership. I was given another envelope which held a memorandum signed by Bakshi, Saraf and Dogra. It said that the signatories had lost their confidence in me. It was first time I was being informed of their differences with me and of their lack of trust in me.... Anyway, Thakur showed me my warrant of arrest. I said I might be given some time to get ready and perform my ablutions and say my prayers. Actually, the order of my arrest had originated in a falsehood. Sadr-e-Riyasat's letter that was handed me along with my warrant of arrest said that the dissension among the cabinet members had caused deterioration in administration and that Sadr's attempts at reconciliation had failed. Hence the dismissal. But this was a blatant lie, for when I had met him on August 8, it was agreed that we would seat together on 10 August and sort out our differences. (Abdullah 1982: 399-400)

Once the news of Sheikh Abdullah's arrest was flashed all over, the new cabinet under G.M. Bakshi had taken over and two of the other ministers, Saraf and Dogra, had taken oath, was radioed to Delhi.

Sheikh Abdullah's Release from the Jail and Re-arrest

Sheikh Abdullah was kept in detention, but there was no move of framing formal charges against him. As a democrat, Jawaharlal Nehru felt bad about it and Karan Singh informs that time and again, he had reminded G.M. Bakshi of it, but Bakshi ignored the reminder on some or other pretext. So much so that on 11 January 1957, J.L. Nehru wrote to Karan Singh: 'My conscience cannot accept anyone being kept in captivity without a trial. I have objected to this so many times in the past and one should have no doubt that I do not like it' (Abdullah 1982: 447). Nehru visited Srinagar for the first time after Sheikh Abdullah's detention in August 1953 last in December 1957 and he gave a vague hint of Abdullah's possible release in near future. Suddenly, on 8 January 1958, D.W. Mehra, the Inspector General of Police, appeared at the detention camp and asked the Sheikh to pack up his belonging for a possible release. When the prisoner refused to travel from Udhampur Jail to Srinagar in the night, he was forced to move to a nearby guest house without any amenities suitable for the ex-prime minister in the night itself. Next day, Kashmir Valley accorded an emotional welcome to the Sheikh Abdullah.

In particular at Duru, where in 1953, more than a dozen of his protesting supporters were gunned down and their burial ground had been turned in a park, there was an unmanageable crowd to welcome him. Sheikh Abdullah halted and addressed them:

> I have been kept away from you for a long time. My opponents cried themselves hoarse claiming that my people had forgotten me. But I would not believe them. They said they had bought your conscience in return for free rice. But I would tell them my people were not saleable.... Those who were intimidating you are themselves cowards. They are afraid for their conscience in uneasy. Do not be afraid of them, follow the truth and goodness, and you will not cower before any power.... History will proudly write that when atrocious methods were used to arouse your baser instincts, your preserve in your principles and defended the honour of your land.

Furthermore, writes Sheikh Abdullah:

> It is just not possible to describe the magnitude of reception. Every gesture of people was indicative of their affection for me, and of their sense of anger, hatred and disgust against the government. A whole edifice of fraud built over the last five years on the blood and flesh of thousands of martyrs with money weapons was washed away in the swirling tide of humanity. (Abdullah 1982: 452-3)

The Indian Press as usual reported that the Kashmiris could not care much for Sheikh Abdullah's release and Bakshi and company sat soundly on the solid rock of public support. Only *Blitz* from Bombay exposed the hollowness of claim and exposed the enormity of mischief: 'This false reporting will prove calamitous to India. The fact is that the Sheikh Sahib was received like a victorious Roman hero.' However, it is reported that having observed the enormity of instant reception from a vantage point, Prime Minister Bakshi turned to his friend nearby and said: 'All my strategy has failed. No one seems to be on my side. Some new methods will have to be devised. Sheikh Sahib will have to go to jail once again.' Mujahid Manjil office and the entire edifice of the National Conference were already usurped by the BBC, the acronym of G.M. Bakshi and his notorious brothers. Bakshi stood for complete integration of Kashmir with India. But he was known to be an unscrupulous politician infamous for corruption and high-handedness (Singh 1983: 47, 57, 87, 91). He and his cronies had captured the entire structure of the political party, the National Conference, assiduously built up by the Sheikh Abdullah and his suffering comrades through thick and thin. Bakshi's regime was notorious for rampant corruption, especially a cousin of his, who controlled the Conference edifice on behalf of the big brother and who has also raised a notorious body, the 'peace brigade', a gang of bullies. So much so that even Karan Singh, after three and half a month of Sheikh's release from the jail, wrote: 'Sheikh Sahib's arrest has further complicated the Kashmir problem; especially when he was making appeals to people to remain peaceful. Things were returning to normal politically. This action taken even when the atmosphere was tranquil is totally unjustified.'

Sheikh Abdullah records that Vijaylaxmi Pandit, Prime Minister Nehru's sister, was on a visit to Srinagar and staying in a houseboat. She desired to meet Sheikh Abdullah and for that an appointment was fixed. When Bakshi's intelligence network reported that to him, he presumed that his misdeeds might be exposed. And he acted fast and got Sheikh Abdullah arrested on 29 April 1958 under so-called Kashmir Conspiracy Case, which was filed on 25 May, in the Court of Special Magistrate of Jammu. Look at Karan Singh's version of the story:

On his release the Sheikh entered Kashmir Valley to a massive welcome, and at once launched into an angry and powerful tirade against Bakshi and the Government of India. Going back on his previous stand that the state was an integral part of India, he insisted that the accession was provisional, and that it could only be settled after the Kashmiri Muslims had exercised their 'right of self-determination'. Despite his undoubted stature and charisma among the Kashmiri masses, the Sheikh was never able to outgrow his Kashmiriyat and become a truly national leader.... It was clear that he had decided to utilize the Plebiscite Front as his main political vehicle for capturing power.... Almost all mosques were used to whip up feeings against 'Hindu India', and Abdullah began touring the valley extensively.... After three and half months it was decided that his activities were compromising the national interest, and he was again taken into custody under the Preventive Detention Act on 29 April. (Singh 1983: 56-5)

The hearing of the case against Sheikh Abdullah and his captive colleagues went on for about six years. Meanwhile there was a bloody border war between India and China, in which India was badly beaten. The entire country stood demoralized on the outcome and it was especially damaging to the prestige and health of the prime minister, Jawaharlal Nehru. Against her known policy of importing defence equipment from the Western countries, India had no choice but to request them for costly armed import for the sake of security. The prime minister was unwell for some time and it appeared that his old fire and dynamism from him was lost. Nehru was said to be always upset with the way the Sheikh Abdullah was imprisoned, released, and reframed and elaborate conspiracy cases were filed against him and his associates. As long as G.M. Bakshi was the prime minister of Kashmir, it was not easy to think afresh. Soon after assuming the office of the prime minister, Sadiq had a detailed consultation with the prime minister on the long incarceration of the Sheikh. A decision was taken to withdraw the conspiracy case against the Sheikh and his associates and, in fact, a petition to that effect was moved in the court of the Additional Session Judge on 8 April 1964. And, in fact, on the same day, Sheikh Abdullah and his colleagues were released from jail. Once released Sheikh Abdullah described Premier Sadiq as an old colleague in the Conference.

Sheikh Released from Jail Meets the Prime Minister and Travels to Pakistan

The Sheikh records in his biography:

When we came out of prison (on April 8, 1964), we were amazed to see a wonderful change in the environment. Large number of people had collected outside the prison to facilitate us. Jawaharlal had sent a special emissary to Jammu with a letter for me. He had arrived two days before but had not been given immediate access to me. The tone of the letter was soft and affectionate. It indicated a great change that had come upon the writer. I was invited to Delhi to be his personal guest so that we could have an informal chat. Since I had decided that I would first go to Srinagar to know the mood of my people and to take stock of the general situation in the valley, I wrote back to say that I could not do so immediately but would be delighted to meet him as soon as I was free from Srinagar.... We decided to stay some time. In the evening the new Prime Minister, Sadiq, came to see me at the bungalow. This was our first meeting after 1953.... The change of heart in New Delhi reflected in the news bulletins over radio stations in Delhi and Srinagar. For the first time since 1953, they were giving a true account of the joyful reception given to us. Bakshi was in Jammu. He had not yet left his official residence. His mother had passed away a few months before. So I thought to go offer my sympathies. We met after eleven years. He had grown weak and was visibly repentant. (Abdullah 1982: 487-8)

About his reception to Kashmir Valley, writes Karan Singh:

Abdullah entered the Valley on April 17 and received a tumultuous welcome wherever he went in Kashmir. There was no doubt that he was the most popular and charismatic Kashmiri leader. His speeches, however, were ambiguous. While on positive side he laid great stress on the maintenance of communal harmony and urged the Kashmiri Muslims to safeguard the life and property of the non-Muslims.... His tours and speeches created a tremendous impact in the Valley. (Singh 1983: 108-9)

Sheikh Abdullah came to Delhi at the end of April and had an emotional meeting with Jawaharlal and stayed with him as his guest. He had prolonged meetings with the prime minister as well as other cabinet ministers and other political leaders. The Sheikh announced that he was visiting Pakistan shortly to have a discussion with President

Ayub Khan and others. Jawaharlal Nehru himself made a statement in the Parliament:

> Sheikh Abdullah is wedded to the principles of secularism and does not want anything to be done to vitiate these in any way. He does not believe in two-nation theory which was the basis of formation of Pakistan. Nevertheless, he hopes that it should be possible for India, holding on to her principles, to live in peace and friendship with Pakistan and thus incidentally to put an end to the question of Kashmir. I cannot say if we shall succeed in this, but it is clear that unless we succeed India will carry the burden of a continuing conflict with Pakistan with all this implies. I hope Pakistan will get rid of its hatred and fear of India. She has nothing to fear from India, unless she herself attacks India. I hope that it may be possible for two countries to develop closer and more intimate relations to the advantage of both. If Sheikh Abdullah can help in bringing this about, he will have done a great service to both the countries. We are prepared to help him in this attempt, but in doing so we must adhere to our principles as well as our basic attitude with regard to Kashmir. (Quoted by Singh 1983: 111)

Incidentally, both, Sheikh Abdullah and Karan Singh, were greatly influenced by Jawaharlal Nehru's personality and his personal charms. While, for Sheikh Abdullah, he was 'an elder brother'; Karan Singh considered him his 'political guru' since he was in his teens. The brothers had similarity of world view, social philosophy, style of politics, and use of politics for the cause of the downtrodden; but they differed on two things – in their political style and the company they kept. But both were sincere secularists and for them politics was a means for achieving social goals. For Karan Singh, Nehru remained an icon and mentor, as there was a marked difference in their age. Between these two adversaries also, there was an irony of fate. The Sheikh was already a rising star in Kashmir politics, when Karan Singh was born to an unpopular Dogra ruler Hari Singh of his third queen, and that too in Cannes in France. The same Karan Singh was destined to play critical roles times and again in the life of Sheikh Abdullah from 1948 to 1964 and naturally their relations were formal and civil.

Mirza Afzal Beg and Sheikh Abdullah went to Delhi at Jawaharlal Nehru's invitation. They were received by Indira Gandhi and others at the airport and were driven directly to Teen Murti House. Jawaharlal was profusely warm to his visitors. They were meeting after eleven years and in between things had changed. When Sheikh Abdullah had seen his host last, he was a moving flame of tulip-face all over, but now things were different. 'His back was a little bent and his face had deep lines across it. The effects of paralysis that had struck him in Bhubaneshwar were there.' Jawaharlal came down to welcome the Sheikh in the porch. He still retained his graceful traits. He expressed his regret to what had happened to the Sheikh, which moved his visitor to tears. The Sheikh told him that he regarded him as his elder brother. And that is why what he had gone through was more painful than it would have been otherwise. After that Sheikh Abdullah mentioned the Kashmir problem in these words:

> To my mind this issue is toughest of all other issues. The Indo-Chinese conflict has made me more convinced than ever that India should deal with its smaller neighbours with generosity and friendliness so that they get a feeling that India means well to them. We can then seek their co-operation in creating a better environment. Pakistan is most important of these countries. It should be possible for us to forge a common defence arrangement and commerce with Pakistan. Just a little while ago, we were one country. Our culture is one. The geographical barriers separating us are artificial. The time has come when India should act generously and sort out the Kashmir problem which is the cause of ill-will between the two countries.
>
> Jawaharlal expressed complete agreement with the Sheikh's above statement. He said it was his desire to find a satisfactory solution to the Kashmir issue in the evening of his life. It seemed I had been chosen by providence to go through the penance so as to act later as a conduit between the two countries. Then it was settled that the Sheikh would travel to Pakistan to persuade President Ayub Khan to come to Delhi so that it could be easy to discuss and solve the Kashmir issue. Jawaharlal said since his health did not permit his visit to Pakistan, if Ayub Khan can come, they would discuss all the possible proposals made by the United Nations and also by our friends to settle ultimately for an acceptable solution. The sincerity of his tone decided me to offer my services. (Abdullah 1982: 499-500).

Prior to going to Pakistan, the Sheikh thought it prudent to meet some notable Indians, who had mass appeal and he thought it advisable to seek their blessings. Thus, he met Chakraborty Rajagopalachari, Jai Prakash Narayan, Vinoba Bhave, President Radhakrishnan and Vice-President Zakir Hussain. All these eminent personalities endorsed

Sheikh's mission to Pakistan. The Sheikh records an emotional scene of his last meeting with Jawaharlal Nehru:

When I saw him off at the airport (on his last trip to Dehradun), he warmly shook hands with me, firmly pressing my hand even in his weakness. His eyes reflected a strange combination of vacuity and seriousness. Who knew this was my last living contact with man with the smell of Kashmir, my greatest friend and also my captor? He walked to the plane and then came back to once again shake my hand. He seem to have a premonition that of his approaching death. Next day, on May 25, 1964, the Sheikh accompanied by Mirza Afzal Beg, Masoodi, Mubarak Shah (of Baramullah), Mubarak Shah Naqshbandi, Chaudhury Muhammad Beghseri and his son Dr. Farook Abdullah and a number of Indian journalists left Delhi for Rawalpindi on a Pakistani plane. The President Ayub had sent his foreign minister, Z.A. Bhutto, on his behalf to welcome the Sheikh at the airport. The guests were put up at the State Guest House and they met the president at his residence, where plenty of warmth was displayed.

In my meeting with Ayub Khan I explained to him at length the background of the Kashmir issue. I told him how Pakistan leaders in their short-sightedness had complicated the issue. He heard me carefully. He admitted that his country had made mistakes. There was no point in raking up the old issues but to remedy the situation. Then suddenly he remarked that a Confederation was no solution to the problem. I started at this. I said I had not suggested any such thing. All I wanted was that he and Jawaharlal meet to discuss all possible proposals including the notion of a confederation as well.... I told him to consider the proposals we had laid before him. I also invited him to come to Delhi for a frank and friendly dialogue with Jawaharlal. Even if no acceptable solution emerged, nothing would have been lost. At least the two sides would be in a better position to appreciate each other's perception. If that eased the tension between the two countries, that in itself would be an achievement. Ayub Khan appreciated my sentiments as Jawaharlal had, and agreed to come to Delhi. A date was fixed, which I conveyed to Delhi. It was stated officially that the meeting would happen in mid-June. My mission to Pakistan accomplished, I looked forward to the summit conference. (Abdullah 1982: 504-5)

But it was not to be. Sheikh Abdullah and party proceeded to Muzaffarabad on 27 May 1964 with friends, officials and journalists. But before they could reach their destination, the news was broken to them that Nehru had passed away and they were advised to return back. Undoubtedly, Sheikh Abdullah was devastated and he took some time to pull himself together. In Delhi he tearfully bid a farewell to Nehru, participated in the funeral procession, picked up some ashes from the cold pyre and brought that to Srinagar to be immersed at the confluence of the Jhelum and the Sindhu rivers. He addressed a condolence meeting on 11 June at Srinagar, in which he broke down several times when he referred to Jawaharlal. He hoped that President Ayub Khan and Prime Minister Lal Bahadur Shastri would pick up the thread of his discussion in Pakistan with the President and make progress on the Kashmir issue.

Sheik Abdullah Goes on Haj to Mecca and Gets Arrested on His Return

Soon the Sheikh would be leaving India on his cherished pilgrimage to Mecca and Medina and leaving behind Kashmir to his colleagues. In February 1965, the Sheikh along with Begum Abdullah went on a pilgrimage to various holy places in Saudi Arabia and visited Egypt and Europe. All through the Sheikh had been meeting with notable world personalities such as President Gamal Abdel Nasser, journalist Mohammad Hussain Haikal (Al-Ahram) of Egypt, Zhon-Enlai (People's Republic of China), famous revolutionary and the President Ben Bella (Algeria) and others. It is alleged that the Chinese Premier had invited the Sheikh to visit his country. And he had accepted the invitation. There was a growing feeling in the corridors of power in Delhi that the Sheikh was trying to internationalize the issue of Kashmir by meeting those dignitaries. So when he returned to Delhi by Air India, he was taken to Bangalore on route to Ootacamund, where he was imprisoned.

Look at what Karan Singh writes on the incident:

> Despite his much professed secularism, it was almost invariably on a religious platform that he enunciated his political policies. Before he left (India) he had succeeded in creating a good deal of anti-Indian sentiments in the valley.... There was an outcry in the press and in parliament (on his meeting with the international dignitaries and allegedly discussing Kashmir issue), and finally the Minister of External Affairs announced that all endorsements on the passports of Abdullah and party had been cancelled except those

necessary for the purpose of Haj. This gave rise to acute speculation as to what his future moves would be. Would he return to face the consequences of his actions or would he continue to operate from abroad? Knowing him, I felt sure he would return. Whether one would agree with his policies or not, there was no doubt that he was a man of courage and determination. It was not for nothing that he had come to be known as the Lion of Kashmir. In the event, the Sheikh, the Begum, Mirza Afzal Beg returned to India on May 8, 1965 were taken into preventive custody by the Government of India and were flown to Ootacamund in South India, where they were ordered to remain within the municipal limits. So for the third time since 1947, Abdullah found himself under detention. His two main failings were his unwillingness to accept that Jammu and Kashmir would have to continue as part of India like other states, even though it may enjoy a somewhat special status in some matters, and also his inability to come to grips with tri-regional character of the state in which the aspirations of the people of Jammu and Ladakh were often contradictory to those of the Valley. (Singh 1982: 129-31)

Sheikh Abdullah was shifted from Ootacamond to Kodaikanal, another hill resort in south India, and he was allotted a bungalow Kohinoor to live in. Soon after that, his wife and other members of the family were moved to be in his company. On some pretext, the authorities prevented Sheikh Abdullah from going for his daily walks. That resulted in a rise in his blood sugar leading to symptoms of diabetes. When the situation became critical, he was shifted to All India Institute of Medical Sciences (AIIMS), New Delhi for a month long treatment. Even when he recovered from his ailment, he was kept under house arrest at 3, Kotla Lane, New Delhi. In all these years, momentous events had happened. First, Pakistan sent infiltrators in Kashmir in 1965, leading to a full-scale war between India and Pakistan. Both the countries claimed they had captured their adversary's territories. There was a ceasefire and an international meet at Tashkent, in which both the countries had to withdraw from each other's territories captured during the war. However, Lal Bahadur Shastri, the Prime Minister of India, died of heart failure next morning in Tashkent on 10 January 1966. Indira Gandhi, the only daughter of Jawaharlal Nehru, succeeded to be the next prime minister in New Delhi.

Then things began to happen in a dramatic ways, writes Sheikh Abdullah:

On 2 January, 1968, Mr. Tandon, District Magistrate of Delhi, unexpectedly walked into my house and handed me the order of my release. It was Eid. I went to Eidgah to offer my prayer. The news of my release had already reached there. People greeted me in large numbers and when the prayer was over, I made a brief speech. I said that my life's aim was to that all people of the subcontinent should be able to live in freedom and peace. So it was important that India and Pakistan should come close and pull down the wall of hatred that separated them. A few days later, I met Indira Gandhi. She had great respect for me as a family friend. I felt happy to see one with common origin with us as India's Prime Minister. Moreover, she was well conversant with the whole process of our freedom struggle. Also, during the two years of rule, she had proved herself to be a person with an open mind and an amazing capacity for decision-making. (Abdullah 1982: 522)

Sheikh Abdullah flew to Srinagar on 4 March 1968 to a great enthusiastic welcome by his admirers.

Kashmir Accord and Thereafter

Sheikh Abdullah had started openly talking that he had no quarrel with Kashmir's accession with India, but he had reservation on the extent of accession (Noorani: 2019; Rai: 2019).[3] Both the parties, Kashmir and India, had reached a certain agreement in 1947, leading to the enactment of Article 370 of the Indian Constitution, which the Indian leaders had violated and thus, there was a degree of parting of ways. If the Act was restored to its original shape, where was the question of differences between the two? Not only that, Sheikh Abdullah reportedly said that if Prime Minister Indira Gandhi was agreeable to that, he was ready to meet her any time as per her convenience. P.N. Haksar, her private secretary, met Sheikh Abdullah at the All Indian Institute of Medical Sciences, New Delhi, where he was undergoing some medical treatment (Ramesh: 2018)[2]. The Sheikh was invited to meet Indira Gandhi. When he went to meet her at her residence, she received him warmly. Smilingly, she said: 'Sheikh Sahib/ forget the past. Let us begin a new chapter'. The Sheikh said, 'If that is what you feel, I extend my hand of friendship. I have been striving after an objective that I hold dear. I have nothing personally against anyone. If we can still move in the right direction that would be great'.

Soon after that, Mirza Afzal Beg from the Plebiscite Front and G. Parthasarthi, the Vice-Chancellor of Jawaharlal Nehru University, New Delhi, and also the son of Gopalaswami Aiyengar, the former prime minister of Jammu & Kashmir, met and hammered out the commonalities. Their report was submitted to the prime minister; then the two: Indira Gandhi and the Sheikh, met in February 1975 with the report. Thus, the understanding reached between the two leaders was announced as a satisfactory way out and this came to be known as the 'Kashmir Accord' (Abdullah 1982: 537; Ramesh 2018: 259-61). In spite of all that, as it is said, there was devil in the details.

Sheikh Abdullah reached Jammu from Delhi on 4 February 1975 and there were crowds to welcome him; overall the atmosphere was easy. The same afternoon, the Congress parliamentary party convened a special meeting in the chief minister's private office, where Sheikh Abdullah was elected unanimously the leader of the parliamentary party. President of Indian National Congress, Dev Kant Barooah, was present on the occasion as well. The out-going chief minister, Mir Qasim, had proposed Sheikh Abdullah's name, and to all appearances the proposal was warmly welcomed. That very day, the Kashmir Accord was placed before the parliament; the entire house called it a capital achievement. The prime minister called Sheikh Abdullah and felicitated him for that.

The Last Phase of Sheik Abdullah

But there were evil omens around. The All India Radio called Sheikh Abdullah's taking oath of office as a great victory for the Congress in its evening news bulletin and repeated it in the next morning news broadcasts. When it was pointed out, it was reported that some lower level employee might have done the mischief. Sheikh Abdullah's chose the persons of integrity from among the ministers from both the parties for his cabinet, which was appreciated generally. The Sheikh records his apprehensions and marshals his inner strength:

> I was internally troubled by the apprehensions about our immediate future. The coup on August 9, 1953 had caused an infection in the body politic (of Kashmir) that had affected every walk of life. After undisputed authority of twenty-two years, those who had caused the infection were now on the run

saddling us with the responsibility of finding a cure to it. I was no longer young and my health showed signs of decline. Yet my hope for Kashmir's bright future remained undimmed. Then I saw a divine providence in my having outlived the tough ordeals I had gone through. The thought gave me courage and I shouldered the new responsibility. (Abdullah 1982: 538)

But the Sheikh had seen plenty of platitudes thrown around that he would not be befooled. He noted:

But the situation seemed somewhat uncanny. Karan Singh's presence on the occasion gave the situation a strange piquancy. It was he who had signed my dismissal from the Prime Ministership on 9 August (1953) and the same man was now offering me a wreath of flowers on my assumption of the same office.

There may be a second opinion on Sheikh Abdullah's decision to revive old National Conference without sounding the central leadership of the Congress with whom he had formed the government. Furthermore, it was further inept of him to invite Presidents of the State Congress and Plebiscite Front to join the National Conference. Howsoever, his ideas might have been noble from his point view, no self-respecting Congress leadership would have accepted the invitation. Sheikh's invitation, in itself, appears sincere: he had written to Mir Qasim:

I write to you and your friends in all sincerity to leave behind all peripheral issues, personal preference and bitterness and join the National Conference and share in its glorious legacy. I am aware that at the moment you are associated with the pre-eminent party of the country. Still, what motivates me to invite you to join the National Conference is the affinity rather than the rivalry between the two parties. And that affinity was the basis on which our party enjoyed the support of the Congress all through our struggle against the Maharaja's autocratic rule. The two parties related to each other so well that it was not thought necessary to merge them. As for the role of the National Conference after 1953 and the decision in 1965 to merge it in the Congress, these were matters of expediency rather than a matter of ethic based politics. Now that a new leaf has turned, and the impediments in the way have gone, we should allow no further delay in reviving our beloved party on which depends the fate of our present and future generations. (Abdullah 1982: 544)

While the leaders and workers of the Plebiscite Front rushed to join the Sheikh's outfit, the Congressmen were reluctant to do so. Soon after that, Mrs Indira Gandhi travelled to Srinagar; she addressed a meeting of the party workers at Emporium Garden and rejected the very idea of disbanding the Congress in Kashmir. By then all arrangements were made for the expansion of the state cabinet by including some 'cleaner' members from both the parties on 25 October 1976. However, it was not to be, as the Congress had decided not to permit its members to take the oath of office. Meanwhile, there was a massive political upheaval happening on the Indian political horizon within the next six months, in 1977. The Internal National Emergency imposed by the Prime Minister Indira Gandhi was lifted; a general election for the Parliament was declared; a considerable number of leaders and cadres of the Congress defected to the opposition; the results of the general election threw up a new ruling party, Janata Party under Morarji Desai.

The Congress party had lost power at the centre for the first time in the electoral history of India and many of its leaders including the Prime Minister Indira Gandhi were defeated in the election to the Loksabha in 1977. In case of Kashmir, it was the National Conference, which got its 50 out of 75 nominees elected to the State Assembly in the year 1977. And that was the time, when the old Lion of Kashmir had a massive heart attack while canvassing in the hill tract of Badgam area, necessitating him to be in bed for about a month and a half. And that was the time Sheikh Abdullah, as the leader of the National Conference Legislators Party, took the oath of office of the chief minister of Jammu & Kashmir on 9 July 1977. One may remember that in 1948, Sheikh Abdullah was the prime minister controlling 72 of 75 of the seats in the Constituent Assembly, which also doubled as the first State Legislative Assembly.

Sheikh Abdullah wrote his biography in Urdu (*Aatishe Chinar*), which was translated into English by Muhammad Yusuf Taing, and he desired that the book should be released to the public on 5 December 1982, on his 77th birthday. But it was not to be; the Sheikh decided to take leave from this world on 8 September 1982. He was a person whose life story is a textbook for a common struggling Indian, who defied all types of adversaries on his way to serve the common man.

A man who struggled and suffered for five decades from his foes and friends alike, but he remained a model of civility all his life. Gentle, polite, decent and dignified, Sheikh Abdullah was more than willing to highlight the positive points of his adversaries. It is difficult to give a label to such a magnetic personality. May be he was a rebel for Maharaja Hari Singh, his feudal associates and his prime minister, M.C. Mahajan. And possibly for Mahatma Gandhi, Jawaharlal Nehru, Chakravarti Rajagopalachari and pre-independence Congress, he was a collaborator in their cause of democracy and secularism. And to cynical Muhammad Ali Jinnah and his Muslim League, he was no less than a traitor to their politics and world view. His biographer has rightly written that Sheikh Muhammad Abdullah was rooted in the past of Kashmir, he dominated the present of Kashmir for five decades in the middle of the twentieth century, and he would continue to pre-figure in the future of Kashmir thereafter too.

Come what may, Sheik Abdullah's name will be etched in the annals of Kashmir history forever. He was a self-made man, who turned a colossus with his sheer sacrifice for the cause of the suffering Kashmiri peasants. His politics was for a cause: that too for common Kashmiris. He was a man of the masses who never cared to cultivate communal politics as a tool to settle scores in politics as others did. He was attracted to sacrifices made by the Congress party and its leaders for the cause of the masses. But he had little time for hair-splitting argumentative politics of the leaders of the Communist Party of India. Similarly, he did not appreciate the detached intellectual involvement of the Congress Muslim stalwarts such as Maulana Abdul Kalam Azad and Khan Abdul Gaffar Khan. But he did admire them for their non- communal politics. In the same ratio, he was repelled by the elitist, pro-establishment and out and out communal style of leadership of the All India Muslime League. In spite of his nationwide image of a fearless anti-feudal crusader with an all-India appeal, Sheikh Abdullah preferred to be the tallest freedom fighter of Kashmir. He suffered so much for two decades in independent India also for his politics for the cause of the common Kashmiris, but he did not stoop low to call names to his friends who had betrayed him. It appears that Sheik Abdullah was born as a crusader for the toiling Kashmiris with whom he lived, suffered for them and died in their cause. He could not complain, though he had suffered massively at the hands of feudal cum the communal gang of Jammu. But it looks these elements untimately prevailed over the destiny of Kashmir. A time comes in every active politician's life at the end, when even the bravest of them finds constant struggle as meaningless and exhausting. It appears that his tired and exhausted body refused to obey his rejuvenated agenda of a 'new Kashmir' (*Naya Kashmir*) at the fag end of his seventh decade of life.

And what a time he chose to depart from this world, when India and Pakistan, both were passing through one of the most crtical moments of their recent history. There was a massive military crackdown on the civilian population of East Pakistan in 1970 leading to a civil war in Pakistan; millions of refugees crossed over to India; advent of the Mukti-Bahini and their counter-offensive on Pak armed forces; Pakistan's attack on India and Indian retaliation leading to surrender of the Pak army to the Indian forces and the emergence of Bangladesh as a new nation state. It saw the end of military dictatorship in Pakistan; emergence of Z.A. Bhutto only to be hanged by Gen. Zia, the military dictator. Similarly, in India too, there was an internal national emergency in 1975; the first non-Congress government was elected to power in 1977, which lasted hardly for two years; re-election of the Congress back to power in 1979 and Prime Minister Indira Gandhi being assasinated by her armed bodyguards on 31 October 1984. There was chaos all around in India, Kashmir and Pakistan; by then most of his contemporary national leaders had already left this world and it was good that the Sheikh Abdullah too was not around to witness alone that depressing scenario of gloom.

NOTES

1. Novel Leaders of New India.
2. P.N. Haksar wrote to the prime minister on June 1972:
   'We have been lacking in subtletey in handling Sheikh Abdullah. A variety of interests have made the task of looking at Sheikh Abdullah, as he is, an exmely difficult one. Neverthless it is imperative to make a fresh start and lead him by hand on the difficult and treacherous road whose ultimate destination is reconciliation.... Even apart from the ... considerations of need for reconciliation, there is an impressive necessity of not keeping

Sheikh Abdullah in our custody and thus having his sekeleton in our cupboard when we talk to President Bhutto and tell him that Kashmir is ours with Sheikh Abdullah in our custody rather than a free man... I mentioned all this to Shri D.P. Dhar several days ago and told him quite frankly that since the original sin of what was done was done in 1953 (Sheikh Abdullah's arrest and dismissal as the chief minister) lay largely with him, he should ponder deeply over the problem of what is to do with Sheikh Abdullah.... I believed that he subsequently spoke to the PM and I was glad to learn from the PM last night that the chief minister of Jammu and Kashmir feels that the Sheikh should immediately be released.... But releasing Sheikh Abdullah is not enough . Before he returns to the valley, the PM must meet the Sheikh Saheb. The meeting is going to be painful, because PM has to show exreme forebearance and listen to his long tales of woes, but the PM should let him unburden himself and then say we must look to the future.... Given this, we can begin step by step, the long journey towards reconciliation, Sheikh Saheb should appoint someone and that the PM should also appoint someone and two of them can queitly talk over.... If it is decided to release Sheikh Saheb in the next 24 hours, Dr Bajaj of the All India Insttute of Medical Sciences (Sheikh Abdullah's doctor) should be instructed to ... that he advise Sheikh Saheb should enter the AIIMS for a thorough check-up ... that Sheikh Saheb should return to Kashmir after he has gone through the check up if he wishes to do so, I think the PM should meet the Sheikh Saheb on 11 June 1972 just on the eve of her departure (for Stockholm).

Haksar's script was played out exactly as he has disctated as the Sheikh himself was to recount in his biography many years later. The only addition to the script was Haksar himself went to AIIMS to meet the Sheikh and give him a bouqet and greetings on behalf of the PM. Sheikh Abdullah was released from prison on 5 June 1972. Ten days later on, on 12 June 1972, Haksar wrote another script for the PM (259).

A few months later, on 26 July 1972, Haksar informed the PM:

I asked G. Parthasarthi if I could give him an assurance which was not to be publicly repeated that we conceded the principle that the relations between India and Jammu & Kashmir were based on the Instrument of Accessession and that once this was conceded, we could then work out the basics of our present relationship. We naturally gave no such assurance and merely stated that the time for seeking such assurance or giving such assurance had not yet arrived and that we should for the next few months concentrate our energy and attention on the restoration of trust and confidence which should be palpable to the people of India.

Afzal Beg and Parthasarthi would arrive at a final understanding on the night of 13 November 1974, paving the way for Sheikh Abdullah to return as the chief minister of J and K on 25 February 1975 after a gap of 22 years. Behind G. Parthasarthi was Indira Gandhi and behind her was Haksar, who had got the ball rolling in the first place in 1972 with his visit to the AIIMS to see the Sheikh (261). (Ramesh 2018: 259-61).

3. In 1947, Sheikh Mohammad Abdullah was reputed leader in the Kashmir Valley (not so much in other region). 'In Kashmir, Abdullah had found the Muslim Leagues's Pakistan idea insufficiently accommodating of Kashmiri distinctiveness with Muslim commonality. The Congress', especially Jawaharlal Nehru's, sympathy and indirect support for the popular movement against Maharaja Hari Singh led by Sheikh Abdullah was manifest. But it turned out that Abdullah was too much of an autonomist for either the League's or the Congress's tastes. He had stood with Delhi as the invading tribes from Pakistan were repelled in 1947; in the Indian eyes, this was a definite Kashmiri rejection of the Pakistani option. However, at no point had Abdullah conceded the Maharaja's accession to be anything but provisional, the final outcome to be decided by a plebiscite, which had been promised by Louis Mountbatten and confirmed by Nehru following the accession. The Delhi Agreement he signed with Nehru in July 1952 ratified Kashmir's autonomy and restricted the Indian Union's jurisdiction to the same limited terms as those in the Instrument of Accession' (Rai: 2019: 26).

Rai 2019, 'History of Betrayals', *Frontline*, 30 August, pp. 25-7.

'Sheikh Abdullah's Regret: There is incontrovertible evidence Abdullah bitterly regretted the accession to India within days of the event. In Nehru's presence he suggested accession to both the countries to a British minister, Patrick Gordon-Walker, on 21 February 1948. At the UN Security Council in January-February 1948, he approached Pakistan's delegates but was snubbed. He complained about this to President Ayub Khan in May 1964.

If it were not Nehru's pledge, Kashmir would not have come to India. It is a part of India only because he backed out of his pledges. He was no idealist but a ruthless hardliner on Kashmir as well as the boundary. India has reaped and still reaps the fruits of Nehru's breach of faith, while Kashmiris refused to reconcile themselves to their fate. That is root of 'the Kashmir problem'. There are some 30-odd pledges on plebiscite by Nehru from 1947 to 1953. Patel concurred publicly' (Noorani 2019: 108). Then five instances of pledge were mentioned (Noorani 2019: 107-8).

Noorani 2019: 'Secret Held in the Archives: A Collection of Documents that throw light on how Indian leaders contrived to keep Kashmir in India', Books in review, *Towards a Ceasefire in Kashmir, British Official Reports from South Asia, 18 September-31 December 1948*, Selected and Edited by Lionel Carter, Manohar, Delhi; *Frontline*, 26 April 2019; pp. 105-9.

REFERENCES

Abdullah, Sheikh Muhammad, 1982, *The Blazing Chinar: Autobiography*, Gushan Books, Srinagar.

Basu, Narayani, 2020, *V.P. Menon: The Unsung Architect of Modern India*, Simon & Schuster, New Delhi.

Noorani, A.G., 2019, 'Secret held in Archives', Book Review: Towards a Cease Fire in Kashmir, British Official Reports from South Asia, No. 18. September-December, 1948; Selected and Edited by Lionel Carter, Manohar, New Delhi, *Frontline*, April 26, pp. 105-9.

Rai, Madhu, 2019, History of Betrayals, *Frontline*, August 30, pp. 25-7.

Ramesh, Jairam, 2018, *Intertwined Lives: P.N. Haksar and Indira Gandhi*, Simon & Schuster, New Delhi.

Singh, Karan, 1982, *Heir Apparent: An Autobiography*, Oxford University Press, Delhi.

Singh, Karan, 1985, *Sadar-i-Riyasat: An Autobiography*, Volume Two: *1953-1967*, Oxford University Press, Delhi.

9

Pu Laldenga and the Mizo National Front

Pu Laldenga was born in village Pukpui in Lushai Hills district of Assam on 11 June 1927 in a family of traditional clan chiefs. During his schooling, he could see the stirring activities of his elders in 1930s-1940s, especially when the British rulers were to leave India for good. He was smart enough to watch his elders conversing with the Superintendents of the district, Major A.G. McCall, and subsequently, Leonard Peters. Naturally, he took interest in the activities of the Lushai Chiefs' Council, which wished to join Chin Hills with their ethnic cousins from the adjoining district of Burma. In fact, his preferred political formation was that of United Mizo Freedom Organization (UMFO) led by another clan chief, Lalbiakthanga. At the age of 17, he joined the Indian Army Supply Corps in 1944. He earned three bars as a soldier, rose to the rank of a Havildar and subsequently resigned from the Forces in 1955.

1940s was an eventful decade for the Lushai Hills district as well. Like Naga Hills district, it was also an 'Excluded Area' in the British province of Assam, which meant, though it was formally a part of Assam Province, it was the Governor of the Province who was responsible for its administration. Its administration was run by the British administrative cadre, who were left on posts for longer period of time with a view to learning about the tribes more closely for an effective administration. However, the provincial government could not pass laws for the excluded districts like the Lushai Hills. Moreover, the district was inhabited by a community which was loosely called Lushais after a dominant clan of the tribe, though there were Lakher, Poi, Chakma, Hmar, Kooki and others on the fringe of the district.

FIGURE 3: PU LALDENGA
(*Source:* https://www.oneindia.com/india/former-mizoram-cm-laldenga-remembered-on-his-death-anniversary-1478401.html)

We have noted above, how powerful were the Lushai chiefs, who worked in close in coordination with the British Superintendent of the district.

Against the wishes of the Chiefs' Councils, the Lushai Hills Commoner's Mizo Union was determined to join the Indian Union. Ultimately,

> 15 August 1947 (the day India became independent) was not celebrated with any fanfare. A suggestion by volunteers of the (Commoners) Mizo Union to have a procession to mark the occasion was resisted by the dissidents in the party. Not a single tricolour was raised anywhere for fear of those advocating independence and incorporation of the district with that of Burma. A meeting was convened on August 14 at Aizawl by Leonard Peters, the Superintendent of Lushai Hills district, which some 50 accredited leaders of the Mizo political parties attended. There they accepted the *fait accompli* of the inclusion of their hills into India, with a demand that they should be allowed to opt out of the Union within a period of 10 years. Moreover, the Chin Hill Regulation and Bengal Eastern Frontier Regulation imposed by the British administration should continue to operate for them. (Syiemlieh 2014: 28)

After his release from the armed forces, Laldenga was appointed as an accounts clerk in the Mizo Hills District Council on the ground of being an ex-soldier. The Council was headed by Chhunga, a commoner, who had suffered at the hands of the Lushai chiefs and he was inspired by what he had heard of the ideology of the Indian National Congress and thus, he and his party, the Mizo Union, preferred joining the Indian Union. But like other tribal leaders from the hill districts of Assam, Chhunga too was deterred by the apathy of the leaders of the Congress in the Province of Assam. It appears that these orientations of the two operatives of the District Council, the head of the Council and his account clerk, led to Laldenga's removal from the council on the charge of financial defalcation, a charge of fudging the accounts. Laldenga would soon begin taking active part in political debates and discussions. He would openly talk about Mizo independence from the apathetic conditions under the Assam administration.

The impatient Laldenga waited for an opportunity, which occurred in the form *mautam*, a type of natural calamity, in 1959. Mizoram is located relatively in the rain shadow area east of the Chittagong Hill ranges. These rugged hills are full of natural bamboo groves all over. These bamboo forests flower wildly every 15 to 30 years, which was last reported in the year 1925-6. These bamboo flowers produce certain seeds which are the favourite food of rats. Within no time, million of rats devour all fruits, flowers, leaves, vegetation, and grains stored in the houses leading to the starvation among the villagers. N.E. Parry, the then Superintendent of the district, reported to have instituted a rat-killing campaign, which resulted in killing of 'half a million of these animals' (Reid 1983: 47) in 1926. Mizos cannot recall a worst calamity than that of *mautam.*

Mautam, Mizo Famine Relief Front (MFF) and Mizo National Front (MNF)

Laldenga may not have been a scion of a ruling Lushai chief, but he retained much of their arrogance and audacity. Moreover, he appears to be resolute, scheming, ambitious and certain of his objectives. He had leadership qualities to attract youth around himself and organizing skills to keep them engaged on the schemes he would propose. Once he lost his job with the District Council, he was looking for something to get involved. He was aware of the District Council Chief, Chhunga's brush with the Chief Minister (CM) B.P. Chaliha. He had learnt that the CM had not responded positively to Chhunga's SOS for assistance to the suffering Mizos during the *mautam*. Immediately, he got busy to organize Mizo Famine Relief Front (MFF), reached various non-government organizations (NGO) engaged in welfare and charity works and formed squads of young men and women to deliver relief materials to the needy people in every nook and corner of the district. Mizos had a sense of relief and thus they could survive two years of trying time during the days of *mautam*. The moment he realized that the phase of relief work was getting over, he was smart enough to change the name of MFF to Mizo National Front (MNF) and got busy with brainwashing the young men and women for a daring political adventure.

Laldenga reasoned with his close associates that in the worst days of their crisis, 1959-61, neither the State of Assam, nor the Indian Union in Delhi, came to their relief and the Mizos were left to die.

So what was the use of being a part of such political structure which did not come to the rescue when the worst of the moment arrived for the community? He reached the conclusion that the only route left to the Mizo was to declare independence from India and prepare to fight for that objective. And for that, the first thing first was to procure arms and prepare the youth to sacrifice their lives for the cause. The District Council chief Chhunga informed the powers to be, but there was no visible response known to him. He kept on filing his reports and praying for the good of the community as a good Christian. Laldenga did attract a band of young men and women, who saw a bleak future for themselves on the face of prevalent extensive unemployment even among the educated people. Laldenga's associates got in touch with a group of Mizo instructors, who were demobilized for some reasons from the armed forces.

Writes the historian of regional insurgency:

> ... a growing number of Mizo youth under a group of tough instructors, men who had been discharged from the Assam Regiment a couple of years earlier. They had been sacked because of a mutiny in the regiment and nursed a sense of grievance against the government (of India) and army. The supporters of the rebel leader Laldenga located this group of embittered but trained men and tapped them to fight the Indian state. In the valleys of the Mizo Hills, they trained the youth to hide in the terrain, crawl through undergrowth, fire at moving targets, master close combat, survive the jungle. (Hazarika 2018: 83-4)

While the training of the cadre was on, Laldenga got busy in collecting arms for attack and subversion from anywhere. And for that he turned to the enemies of the Indian Union: Pakistan and the People's Republic of China. Much earlier in his efforts at insurgency, he first turned to Pakistan for arms and ammunitions. Way back, on the eve of Christmas 1963,

> when Laldenga and two of his associates were detained when they were surreptitiously returning from East Pakistan. They were in jail for a couple of months and released upon an assurance of 'good conduct' and their commitment to work within the Indian Constitution. Laldenga persuaded (Chief Minister, B.P.) Chaliha that all he wanted was to seize control of the district council, which had once tossed him out. (Hazarika 2018: 90)

This raises serious question on the role of the Chief Minister B.P. Chaliha: how could he connive with a dismissed ex-employee against a duly elected head of a constitutional body? However, there was no stoppage of Laldenga's march to defiance and subversion. The

> arms were collected surreptitiously; the first group (of MNF cadre) went to East Pakistan for weapons and returned under Laldenga's command. It was intercepted and Laldenga was captured in 1965. Assam Chief Minister, Bimla Prasad Chaliha, aware of the sensitivity of the Mizos and battling the Naga conflagration at the same time, ordered (again) Laldenga's release. He got little gratitude in return. (Hazarika 2011: 113)

Then they turned to China for the arms. For that, Laldenga depended on his intelligence chief, Vanlalngain, a diminutive, but sharp intelligent man, who was asked to walk across Burma to China. In his own words: He walked to Kachin area in Burma and spent two months with Kachin Independence Army. Then in the company of Kachin scouts, he crossed into China where he met with the officers from the People's Liberation Army. He was there for over four months but did not have much success in extracting Chinese support. That was to follow a few years later. The reasons were simple; the Chinese were smart enough to note that location of Mizoram was not advantageous to them and thus, they did not want to get caught in the embarrassing situation for no obvious return.

There is an intriguing picture of Laldenga. He was the supreme leader of the Mizo insurgency and the rest were his supporters. He had never bothered to put on record, what type of independent Mizoram would be: it will be a democratic system, chieftainship, dictatorship or a theological state. For illustration, Phizo talked of 'Nagaland for Christ'; his Nagaland was to be heaven for the Christians, who would live in free and clean air in the lap of nature, away from 'black dirty over-crowding Indians'. Laldenga simply wanted to drive away or kill the Indians to make Mizoram free and after that? He had no time to think over: possibly Mizo freedom would automatically solve all the problems, if there would be any. However, he does not seem to imagine any problem to arise once the Mizos achieve their freedom from India. Even the MNF structure and its hierarchy was not proposed, planned, discussed and known to the cadre of the forum.

Operation Jericho and the Response of the Indian Union

Once arms were collected and training of the cadre was complete, the leader, Pu Laldenga, launched his secret 'Operation Jericho' on 28 February 1966 against the Indian governmental establishments in Mizoram, 'the Years of Trouble', or Rambuai in Mizo language. In a quick electrifying move all the government establishments were taken over by the insurgents. A large many persons were killed; properties were burnt and looted; especially the followers of Chhunga, the leader of the Mizo Union, were targeted for the reprisal. So much so that 200 cadres of the Union were done to death. With the exception of the Assam Rifles camp on a hillock in Aizawl, the entire township was taken over. So was the fate of other towns such as Surchhip and Lungleh. The entire rural area fell to insurgents as the villagers anticipated that the new regime would care for their welfare promptly. Having done that, the insurgents kept on moving towards the difficult frontiers anticipating violent reaction from the Indian armed forces. Many of them just crossed the eastern and southern borders of the district and camped in the forests of Arakan Hills leaving behind cells of operatives working under well-organized network of female couriers. These couriers would move with bamboo caskets on their back full of rice, vegetables, even meat and other consumer articles for exchanging them with the consumer goods from the villagers. However, they would carry relevant information across to MNF members/sympathizers and would be hiding chits containing coded messages for them.

The State and Federal government were rather surprised to learn the collapse of administration in the far away poorly connected corner of the country. The Chief of the Eastern Command, Fort William, Calcutta, Sam Manekshaw, later Field Marshal, was asked to rush his forces to control the situation. He reasoned with the authorities that a guerrilla force of even 100 or 200 trained personnel could pin down a huge army in a rugged forested unfamiliar terrain of Mizoram. In the absence of a large urban centre, MNF, however, must be collecting food from the network of villages. Thus, it was advisable to deny them access to the villages for seeking shelter and food. And for that experience of regrouping of the villages by the British military in Malaya against the Chinese Communist in 1940s and 1950s was suggested.

As a prompt reaction to insurgency, the 3rd Bihar Regiment of the Indian Army, stationed at Agartala, in Tripura, was rushed on operation Little John to Mizoram. They reached Aizawl, reviewed the situation and found that the Assam Rifles had literally held the fort bravely. They were instructed to reach the beleaguered Lungleh by the earliest, which they did. Mizos of Lungleh remembered the good work done for them by the 1st Bihar Regiment during the Second World War for them apart from fighting the invaders. With least casualty, the Regiment retook the township; succeeded breaking the chain of intelligence network of their adversary and levelled a hillock to turn it into a helipad with the manual service contributed by the villagers from nearby. Within a fortnight or so, Commander Manekshaw landed on the helipad and inspected the field situation and developed a better appreciation of the battlefield.

Re-Grouping of the Mizo Villages

Meanwhile, with a view to breaking the network of rural support base of the MNF, Manekshaw hit upon the idea of regrouping of the villages, which was earlier tried in Malaya by General Sir Gerald Templer (Powell 2014: 12). It had so happened that the British had trained the Malay Communist Party to fight the Japanese during the World War, but after the war the Communists turned onto the British. So much so that emergency was declared in Malaya in 1948. Field Marshal Gerald Templer and General Harry Briggs realized that the answer lay 'not in pouring more troops into the jungle but in the hearts and minds of the people'. Drawing lesson from Chairman Mao that 'the guerrilla fighters, like fish out of water, gasps helplessly until he dies, if he is separated from the local population'. The British resettled the rural inhabitants in new villages to keep them from infiltration by the guerrillas, and opted for intelligence-led rather than large-scale military operations against the guerrilla groups (Powell 2014: 12). The counter-intelligency strategy handbook, written by Templer and Briggs, turned out to be the handiest weapon for such future operations.

On 1 March 1966, fighter jets of the Indian Air Force began pounding Aizawl and around.

> The Indian bludgeoning was not wholly unexpected by the MNF. It had believed that there would be retaliation but not on the scale of the counter-strike that followed, which smashed and burnt villages, molested and raped women, virtually displaced the district's entire population, destroyed property and tortured the elderly and youth. The violence was unprecedented in the history of India and its already nascent struggle against the pro-freedom group in Nagaland which had erupted over a decade earlier. (Hazarika 2018: 96)

The state Chief Minister B.P. Chaliha, who had felt let down by the MNF, its leader, Laldenga, said ominously: The army will move into Mizo Hills. When the army moves, it means what it says. Again to quote Hazarika:

> ...Chaliha spoke of the re-grouping scheme, perhaps officially for the first time, saying that while it was not a new idea, it had also been tried 'with considerable success in some other countries under similar conditions and even at home in Nagaland'.... The Chief Minister added that 106 villages on the Vairangte-Aizawl and Aizawl-Lungleh roads with a population of 50,000 had been re-grouped into eighteen larger villages, known as Progressive Protected Villages (PPV).... The 'hostiles', the political leaders said, reacted sharply to move to cut off supply lines and refuse, attacking the resettlement operations, inflicting 'considerable casualties' on the security forces. This was mainly because the forces had to function in smaller parties than usual for conducting the villagers heavily laden with their possessions to the new centres and could not adopt the necessary tactical measures in all cases. In other words, without air cover or sufficient strength in this ill-advised move to uproot eventually two-thirds of the entire Mizo population in the district, the soldiers were sitting ducks for the guerrillas. And they took their wrath out on the innocents. (Hazarika 2018: 103-4)

With Collapsed Dreams, Laldenga Negotiates with India from Pakistan

When the MNF was struck at Aizawl, Laldenga coolly crossed the international borders to East Pakistan and reached Dhaka, where he was treated well and was housed comfortably with befitting amenities.

He was given all the amenities to communicate comfortably with his field operatives. Soon after, his family would stealthily move to join him in East Pakistan. But this blissful hospitality would be snapped soon with the Pakistani army's crackdown in 1970 on the civilian population of its eastern wing. Subsequently, the Bengali Mukti Bahini, the Bengali freedom fighters, would mount reprisal raid from their safe sanctuary on Pakistani targets. The Pakistani Army would target not only the political organizations opposed to them, but also massacred the common civilians in the street. Desperate Bengalis crossed the Indo-Pakistan borders in droves and took shelter in India wherever they could. Very soon the situation would go out of control for the Pak Army and in desperation they attacked India in December 1971 leading to the Indo-Pakistan War. In the open war, Pakistan lost not only the battle, but also the Bengali-speaking people in its eastern wing. And finally, her 73,000 soldiers, led by Gen. Niazi had to surrender before the Indian Commander General Jagjit Singh Aurora in 1972.

In this gloomy scenario, Laldenga and his MNF associates were advised to run to the hills and forests of adjoining Arakan in Burma through the Kola-dyne river to take shelter. Indians anticipated the move and mounted a chase on the fugitives, but they missed the target by a hair's breadth. At last, the Pakistani operatives safely evacuated Laldenga and company from Chittagong Hills to Karachi just before their surrender. Once in Karachi, it dawned soon on Laldenga that a belaboured Pakistan would have not much interest left in him anymore. And that was precisely what happened. He was shifted to a modest accommodation and his maintenance allowance was also curtailed. Hazarika informs that a long lost Mizo lady working as a nurse in Calcutta, who had married a Muslim army officer against the wishes of her family, was discovered in Karachi. By then, her husband had risen high up in the military hierarchy. The couple helped the MNF contingent to move to Islamabad, the new capital city of Pakistan, where they were well treated for some time.

It is reported that Laldenga was getting bored with inactivity. He demanded money from his patrons to run his government in exile and to mount attacks on India. Pakistanis had seen through the game; they responded by asking the MNF Chief to provide them with the list of individuals working for him and their address so that the money could be transferred. Laldenga did not want that and he responded that the amount should reach him as the chief of the MNF and he would decide where to spend that. In the process, his accommodation and associated facilities were reduced to a bare minimum. Not only that, they were suddenly moved to a smaller house in Rawalpindi, the district headquarter, and (the ISI) began giving their allowance reduced to Rs. 2,000 in a month. Laldenga contacts RAW and reach New Delhi as guest of Government of India.

Within a few months, the atmosphere even in the Rawalpindi house became suffocating for Mizo contingent. Laldenga wanted to reach the Indian establishment. But he needed new travel papers for that, which (the passport) was obligingly issued by Pakistan on the name of Peter Lee, as the Mizos were a burden to them. Peter Lee alias Laldenga travelled to Geneva, where he met with Mr Singhal (the assumed name of Hassan Walia of RAW). He wrote to Prime Minister Indira Gandhi that he was unilaterally calling on MNF to stop operating against the Indian security forces and requested for reciprocal action from the security forces. Moreover, Laldenga made it clear that the Mizoram solution would have to be within the Constitution of India. At last, MNF vice-president, Tlangchhuaka, MNF Party president, Chawngzula, and armed commander, Biakchhunga reached New Delhi in January 1976 along with their boss, Lalgenga.

Laldenga had reached New Delhi on 24 January 1976 and sat with his colleagues with representatives of the Government of India and an agreement was reached on 1 July 1976. Mizoram celebrated 7 July as Thanksgiving Day with prayers and church bells ringing all over the land. But the underground elements rejected it and Laldenga termed it as not an 'agreement' but an 'understanding'. Thus, the insurgency and counter insurgency operations were resorted to once more. Meanwhile there was a new government in New Delhi in 1977. The new government charged Laldenga for indulging in anti-India activities and directed him to leave the country latest by 6 July 1977. He turned to new prime minister's door agreeing to implement 1 July 1976 agreemet, which PM Desai concurred, only to go back on his promise. Ladenga was such a slippery character that between July

1976 and 22 January 1982, he promised as many as 8 times on agreements with the Government of India only to reneged on them (Nag 2002: 262-5).

Mizoram Accord: 30 June 1986

Laldenga had to deliver what he had promised to the Government of India and for that he had to take his colleagues in confidence. But his colleagues, who had taken to the arms, proved hard nuts to be cracked. They were not easily agreeable to surrendering their arms. One of the major problems was that declaration of Mizo independence was never explained by the great leader himself even to senior leaders and field commanders of the fighting forces. Now, the entire district known as Mizo Hills in Assam was in the hands of the Government of India; the rebels were trying to ambush their alleged enemy targets off and on, but ultimately, but for what were they engaged in? The Mizo in general, the way they had suffered through the regrouping of the villages, in which the entire fabric of their social and cultural life was shattered. Old, young, men and women were humiliated for the rebellion, engineered by the MNF, but what did they get for all the sufferings and forbearance? The MNF had to convince their people that the sufferings they had undergone was commensurate with the achievements made through the Accord. On that score there was no consensus. And that was the reason for the delay in completing the negotiation.

Moreover, many of Laldenga's lieutenants, who had saved his life and staked their own existence for him, felt ignored through the rigmarole of the negotiation and began to toy with the ideas of finding their own alternatives. When pressed for what were they negotiating for, Laldenga had nothing in concrete to offer. Historian of the regional insurgency, Sanjoy Hazarika wonders:

> So was it an insurgency or an armed fight for more internal political power, an effort to force the Centre to accommodate the ambition of one man, who had managed to convince many Mizos of the rightness of that ambition, if not cause? This always makes fascinating space for conjecture: Did Laldenga unlike Muivah, the Naga leader, actually truthfully believe in liberation from

India, or was he really interested in settling scores with the Mizo Union, which had tossed him out of an accountant's job in the district council, and was determined to hurt them? (Hazarika 2018: 119)

In late 1970s India itself was in turmoil: a state of national emergency was declared in 1975; it was withdrawn, general elections held, the ruling Congress party was defeated at the polls; as a new political forum, Janata Party conglomeration formed the government in 1977, which collapsed within two years, another leader of the Janata Party formed the government; which resigned without facing the parliament. New National Elections were held in 1979, and the Congress under Mrs Indira Gandhi came back to power, but she was assasinated by her bodyguards on 31 October, 1984 and then her eldest son, Rajiv Gandhi, took over the government as the prime minister. By then the MNF was tired of endless negotiation. On the other hand, the local predicament of the Union Government, Brigadier T. Sailo's Mizo People's Convention was defeated in the General Election of the Union Territory and the Congress party led by Lalthanthawla came to power.

The new prime minister, Rajiv Gandhi, decided to address the pending problem of Mizo insurgency expediously. For that he entrusted his senior colleague, Arjun Singh, to get involved in the negotiation along with others. Thus, the prime minister included army and security chiefs, chief minister, Lalthanthawla, and Chief Secretary Lalkhama of Mizoram of the Union Territory and the Union Home Secretary, R.D. Pradhan in the process. The Congress chief minister Lalthanhawla was persuaded to resign from the post of chief minister for the larger cause; the Union Territory was elevated to Statehood; Laldenga was to be elected as the chief minister; the rebel army was to surrender their arms at an agreed place within the given time frame and then they were to be rehabilitated. Thus, finally the Mizo Accord was signed on 30 June 1986, by R.D. Pradhan, the Union Home Secretary, Lalkhama, the Chief Secretary of the Mizoram Union Territory, and Laldenga, the MNF chief, after ten years of meandering negotiations.

The Mizos, like the Nagas, had demanded integration of all the Zoro people within the state of Mizoram. However, it was never seriously pressed by anybody during the negotiation between the two parties. In these frontier areas, land, which was by tradition, a communal property, was the only known source of sustenance for the people there. Thus, every regional community strives to enlarge their land as much as possible. In such a situation, there are conflicting claims and counter-claims on land in Arunachal Pradesh, Nagaland, Meghalaya, Manipur and Mizoram. In the process the old state of Assam, to which all the above enumerated regions, except Manipur, were part, has boundary disputes with all of them. It is difficult to tinker with the old boundaries among the states and thus, the issue of integration of the claimed ethnic areas from other states is an extremely sensitive issue, which the central government will always be reluctant to undertake.

Laldenga: The Chief Minister of Mizoram

While preparing the ground for settling the Mizo problem, Rajiv Gandhi impressed upon the Congress chief, Lalthanthawla, to co-ordinate his forum with that of Laldenga's outfit to ensure the success of settlement. Laldenga became the chief minister of Mizoram after the Accord. The Union Territory of Mizoram was transformed into a state of Mizoram and election for the State Legislative Assembly was held in 1987 and Laldenga got elected as the chief minister of the new state. Immediately he opened the pandora's box in the name of development. Land in and around Aizawl and elsewhere was allotted for a massive construction of unplanned urban growth. The central government was liberal on the new state in terms of financial allocation and it is alleged that money was used in a big way for various purposes. There is so much haphazard urban growth that the author was pleasantly surprised to learn that a Mizo 'Shahjehan' had got constructed a replica of the famous Taj Mahal on a spur in Aizawl, in which unlike the Mughal Emperor, he resides himself along with his 'Mumtaz Begum'. Naturally, Lalthanthawla and the Congress parted ways with the Chief Minister Laldenga soon. However, Laldenga himself proved to be less than competent for the demand of the office. Some defections happened from his flock of MLAs in 1988 itself and he lost the majority in the Assembly and thus, he had to resign from the post of Chief Ministership in 1988 itself.

By then, he developed some health problems. Ultimately, it was diagnosed as some sort of cancer. He was rushed to London, where he was operated upon for lung cancer, and he died on 7 July 1990, while his treatment was still on. His mortal remains were brought from United Kingdom and were buried with state hounour at a prime location in heart of Aizawl city at Treasury Square, the capital city of Mizoram. Of course, his chief ministership of the state was for a brief period of time. But there is no evidence left behind by Laldenga that he had any clear plans for a better Mizoram for the Mizos. Soon after that, the reign of the governance came in the hands of the former Congress chief minister, Lalthanthawla.

The central government kept its words to financially support the new state. In this context, the author would like to recount an incident indicative of honouring the financial commitment made by the Central government. By then, North Eastern Hill University (NEHU), Shillong used to operate in Mizoram with a Centre of Studies, where about a dozen academic departments were located at Aizawl. The visiting team from the University Grants Commission (UGC), New Delhi, was on its visit to NEHU for assessing its financial requirements for the next five years on the basis of the proposal submitted by the university. When the UGC visiting team came to NEHU in mid-1990s, first the visiting team went to Aizawl to assess the requirements of a new university for Mizoram and then they came to NEHU at Shillong. The Chairman of the team simply informed NEHU authorities that they were instructed to decide financial allocation for Mizoram Centre independently, which was not to be discussed with NEHU, as Mizoram was supposed to have its own Central University, which materialized soon.

Laldenga, the Person, the Leader and His Impact

Laldenga appears to be a typical product of frontier defiance of the centralized state authority. Moreover, as a scion of a chieftain, he appears to have nursed contempt for the commoners and their forum, Mizo Union and its leadership, especially to Chhunga, who headed Mizo Hills District Council, the highest civil authority in the district. In case of Chhunga, Laldenga had a personal grudge against him for chucking him out of the Council for financial defalcation. As an alert functionary of the Council, he was aware of the fact the Congress chief minister of the Province Assam, B.P. Chaliha, was allergic to Chhunga for his political independence. Laldenga used this political allergy between the two constitutional authorities to his advantage, when the time came. He had given enough evidence of his duplicity of character. He would make promises, which he could not honour. Yes, he was certainly the master of strategy so far insurgency was concerned, but in the absence of clarity in objectives of the mission, he confused his cadre at the end in their operation in the battlefield.

Slowly it became obvious to his colleagues that after giving a call for independence of Mizoram and capturing the installations and administrative apparatus, they did not know why and for how long they would live in the bush? Sanjoy Hazarika quotes the reaction of some of senior collagues after a lapse of 50 years:

> So what did Laldenga and his colleagues really want? ... Did they really want the 'development of our beloved Mizo district' or did they want to break away from the Union of India? It appears from the new material that has emerged over the past years that Laldenga was never really interested in a protracted war and was unsure of himself much of the time, seeking to open talks with the Centre even before the insurgency was launched! The new material shows a man who was more concerned about the safety and comfort of his own family than the future of his people or the suffering that they were being put through. (Hazarika 2018: 100-1)

It is a fact that in those dark days of insurgency, Indian State as well used extreme form of measures to counteract the insurgency: strafing from the air, regrouping of the villages, extreme deprivation of common Indian citizens and many other things. But the question remains unanswered: was the insurgency worth its outcome? Yes, both CM B.P. Chaliha and MNF chief Laldenga, played dirty games with people's lives and their miseries and deprivation. One does not know for sure what they felt at the end. But we have a little window on Laldenga's mental frame:

> When the peace accord was signed in 1986 and Laldenga became the chief minister, he was once asked if he would apologize or seek forgiveness for those civilians killed by the MNF and for the casualties suffered in the years

of trouble. 'Why should I' he snapped.… Laldenga seized the opportunity to take his people to the promised land of freedom and equality but only ended up putting them through hell. (Hazarika 2018: 94).

REFERENCES

Hazarika, Sanjoy, 2011, *Strangers of the Mist: Tales of War and Peace from India's Northeast*, Penguin Random House India, Gurgaon.

Hazarika, Sanjoy, 2018, *Strangers No More, New Narratives from India's Northeast*, Aleph, New Delhi.

Nag, Sajal, 2002, *Contesting Marginality: Etnicity, Insugency and Subnationalism inNorth-East India*, Manohar, New Delhi.

Powell, Jonathan, 2014, *Talking to the Terrorists: How to End Armed Conflicts*, Penguin Random House, London.

Reid, Sir Robert, 1983, *History of the Frontier Areas Bordering on Assam: 1883-1941,* Eastern Publishing House, Delhi.

Syiemlieh, David R., 2014, *On the Edge of Empire: Four British Plans for North-East India, 1941-1947*, Sage, New Delhi.

10

Palden Thondup Namgyal, the Last Maharaja of Sikkim

Palden Thondup Namgyal, second son of Sir Tashi Namgyal, the 11th ruler of the little princely State of Sikkim, was born on 3 May 1923 as an incarnation of his uncle, Sidkeong Tulku, the Gyeshe Rimpoche, the Prince, who was a Precious Jewel. He was schooled for monkhood prior to his brother's death and was also recognized as the spiritual head of the two important monasteries of Rumtek and Phodang. As his elder brother and heir to the throne died in an air crash, he was given secular instructions at St. Joseph's Convent in Kalimpong, St. Joseph's College in Darjeeling and Bishop Cotton College in Simla, as the successor to the Namgyal dynasty. After that he joined Indian Civil Service (ICS) probationers' course at Administrative College at Dehradun like princes of other Princely States (Rustomji 1987). His lifelong friend, Nari Khurshid Rustomji, found him to be a complex personality, 'a shy, timorous, lonely and lost' individual (Rustomji 1987: 21). In his considered opinion Sikkim belonged to the Bhutias; the Kazis were, after all, his courtiers; Lepchas were, in any way, the loyal subjects and the rest (of his subjects, read the ethnic Nepalese) were intruders, and thus, responsibility of the protecting power of Sikkim, i.e. the (British or Indian) Government of India. He was stubbornly opposed to any accommodation at the state level with the Nepalese; he took it as the surrender of his dynadtic legacy.

European Style of Upbringing

The Namgyal palace was run on European lines; morning tea was served in bed with breakfast, lunch and dinner as the family meals in the dining room. The Maharaja was punctual and other members

FIGURE 4: PALDEN THONDUP NAMGYAL
(*Source:* https://sikhim.blogspot.com/2008/09/last-chogyal.html)

were expected to be present at the table. It was normal for the royal children to visit the Political Officer at the Residency, which was in those days an Old England, as if, with its fine timber beams, panelled walls, period furniture and lovely garden stocked with homely flowers of England. The Himalayan climate in Gangtok added to the illusion of Europe. Moreover, hot scones, strawberries and cream, cheddar cheese, apple-sauce, and the English illusion was complete. Given this background, the princes were more English than the English themselves. On top of that, English governesses were in attendance in the palace. The Maharaja, Sir Tashi Namgyal, lived a life withdrawn from the humdrum of everyday life. Though educated at Mayo College, Ajmer under the guidance of Tibetologist, Political Officer, Charles A. Bell, he could not forget how his parents spent their years in jail at the little town of Kurseong; his eldest brother was deprived of his patrimony and spent his life in exile in Tibet and how strong-willed elder brother's rule in Sikkim was cut short mysteriously with a heavy overdozes of medicine. So that the make belief world of palace was in reality withdrawn from the immediate reality of the land, which groaned under feudal excessive exploitation. There was a club of two dozen households of Kazis, drawn from the immigrant Bhutias mixed with Lepcha chiefs, who ran the administration on behalf of the ruler. They controlled chunks of big landed estates, did not pay much of the taxes to the palace, charged arbitrarily to their subjects, had imposed a variety of impresse labourers. And on top of it all the Kazi aristocrats maintained their private courts, jails and police force, and comprised the most loyal functionaries, which include relatives, and the influential courtiers of the royal household. But unfortunately the royal family was un-concerned with the fate of its subjects.

Palden Thondup, the Crown Prince or the Maharaj Kumar, was in reality the ruler of the little kingdom right from the 1940s, as his father, the Maharaja, had no interest in running the affairs of the principality. It is said that he was drawn to religious paintings and a type of Buddhist mysticism. And when he found time, he used to drink heavily to the extent of being an embarrassment to others. Meanwhile, the political scenario in India was changing fast as the Indian political parties were agitating for India's Independence. The Second World War had come to an end and there were rumours that the British would grant independence to India and would go back home. In such a situation, the Maharaj Kumar along with his father's brother-in-law and the Bhutan Agent, Raja Sonam Tobgyel Dorji, reached Sir Basil J. Gould, the Political Officer, to plead for continuation of their old relations with the British Crown even if the British withdrew from their Indian Empire. Gould reasoned that that was not possible for a variety of reasons and advised them to prepare their memoranda and proceed to New Delhi to meet the Cabinet Mission sent by the British government. The two delegations did go to Delhi and spent some days there, but it was not possible for them to meet the Cabinet Mission and thus they were advised to go back and wait for decisions on their memoranda. At last, a Note was prepared for the Cabinet Mission on 10 August 1946 and it was sent to the Political Officer of Gangtok, which stated (see Chapter 6).

Apparently, the above note must have been sent to the three ruling establishments of the three Himalayan kingdoms of Sikkim, Bhutan and Nepal and its contents must have been reassuring to the rulers of three principalities to a great extent. And that is why the newly established Government of India signed first the standstill treaties with Nepal, Bhutan and Sikkim and then signed new treaties almost on the same old lines of British treaties soon thereafter. Apparently this was a diplomatic affair, which may not be known to the political activists agitating for the political rights and reforms in the overall administrative structures of three Himalayan kingdoms. Conversely, assured of contents of the Note above, the ruling establishments of the three kingdoms were possibly assured of non-interference from the Indian Union and treated the political agitations for reforms more harshly. And that is how the democratic reform movements in Sikkim and Bhutan, largely by the Nepalese-speaking subjects were suppressed. And similarly, the anti-Rana movement launched by the Nepali Congress was largely supported by the suffering Nepalese and Madesis, which was ruthlessly suppressed by the Nepalese Rana regime.

Palden Thondup Namgyal: The Bhutia Ruler

Coming to Sikkim, the Maharaj Kumar saw himself just as a Bhutia ruler of his little kingdom, and grudgingly accepting the Lepchas as his associate subjects simply because of the fact that if he could not, the very myth that the ancient Lepcha chief having invited the Palden's ancestor, Phuntso Namgyal, to be the ruler of the land and his own descendants would be his loyal subjects would have lost relevance. At times, the Maharaj Kumar of Sikkim appeared defiant to the protecting power. In fact, he took a huge risk by openly organizing the Sikkim National Party (SNP), as an anti-thesis of the Sikkim State Congress in April 1948. In fact, he was headstrong to have an agenda of getting independence for his little fief without thinking of international complications and financial viability. It appears that the Government of India could not actively oppose the move because of the fact that they were not sure of democratic credentials of the Sikkim State Congress (SSC) at that stage. In the process, the Government of India permitted the Maharaj Kumar to blackmail her simply because of the fact that the treaty was signed, by which India was not to interfere in the internal administration of the state. Against an uncompromising anti-Nepali stand of the Maharaj Kumar, the Government of India had to willy-nilly agree to a compromise: the late lamented ethnic party between the two sociocultural blocks of Nepalis and Bhutia-Lepcha: the notorious Parity System. It did not occur to him that while his ancestors were Sikkimpati Maharaja, he had reduced himself to a small fraction of the Sikkimese populace: the Bhutias. On the other hand, in the face of Durbar's opposition, it was a gain for the Sikkimese Nepalese, as at least 50 per cent of them were recognized as bonafide Sikkimese.

With the exception of Tashi Tshering, there was no voice from among the Lepchas or Bhutias, which was heard in opposition to the parity system in the state as a whole. Unfortunately for Sikkim, Tashi Tshering by then was completely discredited as a foul mouth agitator by the vested interests and even his ethnic identity, Bhutia, began to be questioned and he was charged to come from a Sherpa community. The last nail, so to say, to the coffin was his contesting election for the State Council and losing it miserably in 1953. The problem was further compounded for the Government of India because of the fact that SSC did not a have a creditable Bhutia leader to stand against the antiques of Maharaj Kumar at the moment. And what assessment does one have of the SSC leadership from among the Nepalis? Unfortunately, those who were in the helm of affairs were known as the weather-cocks. I have records from 1948 to 1956, of the SSC keeping on passing resolutions and sending delegations to Delhi for merger of its outfit with the Indian National Congress (INC), which were ignored. At last, the President of SSC, apparently a fraternal delegate to the Durgapur session of the INC, was advised by the president of the INC and the prime minster of India not to attend the Congress sessions in future, as it created problems for them with the Durbar. In all these politically muddy waters, two individuals stood consistently and unwaveringly for their chosen politics till the end without changing the sides: Netuk Tshering, a common muleteer, who had joined Sikkim National Party in 1948 and remained a royalist all through his life, and Lhendup Dorji, a scion of the aristocratic Lepcha Khangsarpa Kazi family, who began his career on the side of democracy, and who died as a democrat after a chequered political career in Sikkim. And at last, a grateful Indian Union awarded him with Padma Vibhushan, the second highest civilian decoration of the state.

The most unfortunate aspect of all these developments was that of the complete absence of creditable leaders from among the Lepcha (the Rongs) commoners and Limbus (Tshongs), the two original denizens of pre-Bhutia Sikkim. On the other hand, the Maharaj Kumar of Sikkim refused to share power with the immigrants, which meant all the Nepalis inclusive of the Newar Tikedars, known as the Pradhans, who were instrumental in development of Sikkim for the last many decades. When the populist political demands were made by the demonstrators, barricaders and agitators paralysed the administration, which was in any way minimal and informally in the hands of the Kazi and lessees, there was even an officially inspired whisper to divide already little Sikkim into two: South and West Sikkim from that of North and East on the communal lines and opting for two different course of actions. Moreover, the intelligence sources reported that there was a strong rumour spread by the vested interests in Sikkim West, a stronghold of the SSC, that the Chinese Red Army had freed all the slaves and distributed the lands confiscated from the aristocrats and monks in Tibet; thus, coming of the Communists (Red Army) would not be that bad, a possible propaganda unleashed possibly by the Communist Party of Nepal.

The Maharaj Kumar was determined to make a stand in defence of the Lepcha-Bhutia communities against the democratic aspirations of the Nepalese living in Sikkim. He did not hesitate to play a communal card in his principality for his vested interests: Buddhist Lepcha-Bhutia vs Hindu Nepalese. One may have a look at what he was engaged in 1949: Harishwar Dayal, the Political Officer, informed I.S. Chopra, Ministry of External Affairs, Government of India on 13 October 1949:

> I feel also that the interests these section of population (Lepcha-Bhutia) should be protected. But the war-like pretention of the Maharaj Kumar certainly cannot be tolerated.... His belief that he can look to Tibet for active assistance in a possible conflict with the Nepalis is entirely unfounded. Tibet has too many problems of her own to seek adventure outside her borders.... At present time the persons of the highest authority in this country are particularly interest in their military supplies.... It is foolish as well as objectionable for the Maharaj Kumar to engage openly in party politics by presiding at the meetings of the Sikkim National Party, and it is unfortunate that the advice given to him by me, but also by some of his trusted servants, should have gone unheeded. (Dayal 1949)

Palden wrote to his friend, Nari K. Rustomji way back on 12 April 1949, when he was about 25 years of age:

> I am all for fulfilling the wishes of our Bhutias and Lepchas, real wishes. But I will be sooner damned than let these mean conspirators and job hunters have their way, if I can. We are on the verge of getting our independence of sort like Bhutan and I think we have achieved a miracle in not having to accede (to Indian Union). Out greatest drawback is that the P(olitical) O(fficer) and the Government of India seem to favour the other side and we have to proceed so that we give you people (the Indians) no chance to butt in. The second trouble, which I have a feeling is a common, is the unruly Nepalese element against whom I cannot take action as I would like to have. (Rustomji 1987: 27)

So in his scheme of things, Sikkimese Nepalese did not figure in his domain; and that ultimately turned out to be his undoing, as the events showed in early 1970s. He saw Sikkim in his own image, and stubbornly believed that others must do the same.

Creation of a Make Belief Sikkimese (Tibetan) Cultural Complex

Rustomji joined as the second Dewan of Sikkim in 1954 and found that while Lepchas and Bhutias were worried for their future in the ever increasing demographic profile of the Nepalese in Sikkim, the majority of Sikkimese of Nepalese extraction were denied their basic rights. Writes Rustomji, in his book that 'the Prince, on the other hand, was a strong willed man and was not prepared to yield. In the Nepalese presence he saw a threat not only to the throne and to the age-old culture of the land, but to the survival of Sikkim as an "independent" entity'. Two of them, the Crown Prince and the Dewan, worked out architectural designs that would harmonize more happily with the natural landscape of mountains and forests. Moreover, Rustomji joined Maharaj Kumar in his endeavour to create a cultural renaissance in Sikkim on the Tibetan pattern of architecture, furniture, carpets, and other crafts. They took initiative to revive the traditional dress, language, architecture, religion, social customs, music and paintings of Sikkim.

Unfortunately, the Prince's Tibetan wife died in 1957 leaving behind three small children to take care of. As a lonely widower, he ran into an American tourist, Hope Cooke, in Darjeeling. By then he was 44 years old and Hope was a young girl of 20 years. He decided to get married to her, but it was opposed by the strong lobby of the clergy and aristocracy in Sikkim. However, he managed to have his way and got married in a blaze of publicity in March 1963. The royal coronation was a grandeur affair in 1965 after his father's death in December 1963. The Prince had requested that the ruler's title be changed from the Maharaja to that of Chhogyal (One who rules as per the tenets of Chho, religion). The Government of India agreed to the term to be used informally in Sikkim, but formal change was not permitted as it would have required a change in the document of the treaty between the two. However, the ruler in his enthusiasm, did not stop at just the nomenclature of 'Chogyal' for himself, but added 'Gyalmo' (queen), Gyalyum (queen mother), Sidlon (prime minister) to the former office of Dewan.

The new Maharaja, now the Chogyal, began nursing a dream of

an international image for his little kingdom of Sikkim. In this endeavour, his new queen, nee the Gyalmo was more active with her club of Sikkim Youth Study Forum. This was the time, India and her neighbourhood was very much in the news. The elections to the parliament were were held in Pakistan, in which Mujibur Rahman's Party, Awami League from East Pakistan, came victorious by winning majority of the seats in the parliament. But instead of honouring the people's verdict, the military rulers of Pakistan put him in jail and mounted a military crackdown on the Bengali-speaking Pakistanis who took shelter in India in large numbers. King Jigme Singhe of Bhutan and King Mahendra of Nepal had expired in 1972 and two states in the east and west of Sikkim were run by two young Crown Princes, who were yet to be crowned as kings. Prior to that, Bhutan had become a member of the UNO with Indian sponsorship. In response to the military crackdown on the Bnegali-speaking Pakistanis by the Pakistan Army and consequent upon the flight of millions of refugees into India, the Indian Army in turn crossed the borders and thus was instrumental in the liberation of Bangladesh. This was the time, Sikkim Maharaja, now preferred to be known only as the Chogyal, his American queen and her courtiers from Sikkim Study Forum began openly expressing their desire for independence. Moreover, the protecting power, the Indian Union, was charged of following a colonial policy of maintaining a protectrate on Sikkim instead of leading her to independence. Now Chogyal Palden's visits to New Delhi turned more formal and demanding, which made New Delhi to think afresh on things Sikkimese (Ramesh 2018). And *Sikkim Fortnightly*, edited and published by a more than a loyal ex-soldier, K.B. Thapa, would mention Mr. Namgyal's going to and coming from outside Sikkim, as 'His Majesty's departure and arrivals'. This type of false and hollow personae of the ruler was being created by at least some courtiers with encouragements from the elements closer to the palace.

End of the Game or Dynastic Rule in Sikkim

We have described above how the ruler manoeuvred the practice of ethnic parity between Nepalese and the Lepcha-Bhutias in the functioning of the State Council and the Executive Council to his advantage from 1953 to 1970. The ruler adopted the same partisan role in the 1973 State Council elections: the Royal party, SNP, came victorious on 8 elective seats against 6 of the opposition. There were charges of fraud and electoral malpractices, which were simply ignored and the ruler got busy in his golden Jubilee celebration. By then, the opposition had taken to the street, mass demonstration in Gangtok and elsewhere and there was police firing on the unruly agitators leading to few deaths. And that gave the signal to the people, who took the administration in their hands and civil administration in Sikkim collapsed. Unlike in the past, this time, commoners were so fed up with the affairs of the state, that they chased out police from the police stations and these were occupied by the agitators; civil administration was run by the volunteers of the newly formed Sikkim Congress. Many of courtiers, who were known for their anti-democratic leanings in the past, were hauled up and humiliated publically.

At last, the ruler realized the limits of his options slowly, and once more he had to request the Government of India to take over the administration. The Indian Foreign Secretary, Kewal Singh, paid a visit to Gangtok. He met with the leaders of the Sikkim Cogress and discussed with them their grievances and emphasized the need to end the agitation. The public leaders insisted on establishment of representative government in the true sense of the term. After a prolonged discussion and bargaining, an agreement emerged between the Chogyal, political parties and the Government of India. A tripartite agreement was signed on 8 May 1973 among the leaders of the three political parties (Sikkim Janata Congress, Sikkim National Congress, and Sikkim National Party), the representative (the Foreign Sectretary, Kewal Singh) of the government of India and the Maharaja.

As per the tripartite agreement, a 32 member State Legislative Assembly was elected on the principle of 'one man, one vote' under the supervision of the Election Commission of India. The newly established Sikkim Congress, after merger of Sikkim State Congress, Sikkim National Congress and Sikkim United Front, came victorious on 31 out of 32 seats for which the elections were held in 1974. And the democratic government led by Kazi Lhendup Dorji, the leader of the Sikkim Congress, was sworn in as the first popularly elected chief minister of Sikkim. This was the same Chyakhung Kazi, who was allegedly defrocked at the instance of the palace and all through the ruler had seen to it that he never got a chance to have his due in politics in spite of being elected to the State Council (Das 1983). And the Kazi stoutly backed up by his political party and wife, Kazini Eliza Maria Dorji, was determined to pay Namgyal in his own coin. Once the State Assembly passed a resolution for closer association of Sikkim with the Indian Union and abolition of Namgyal's office, there was nothing left for him in the affairs of Sikkim. Sensing such an eventuality of dire circumstances, his wife, the Gyalmo of Sikkim, Hope Cooke had already left him and Sikkim for good and in course of time, and filed a case for divorce in the USA.

Rustomji records:

> She decided to leave Sikkim, where she had looked for security, position, as well as domestic happiness, to be rewarded by a collapse of all her aspirations and all that she had worked towards.... She was a woman of sensitivity, self-respect and honour. Foolish (she was), yes. And her decision to leave her husband was the right decision, perhaps the first really matured decision of her life. She had discovered that despite all her strivings to strike roots in Sikkim, she was working in unfertile soil. For all her silken brocades and laboured lisping in Sikkimese (or Bhutia), she would never be accepted as of the soil. Her marriage had already shown symptom of breaking up under the strains and tensions of a way of life so divorced from her early upbringing.... (Rustomji 1987: 94-5)

Palden Thondup Namgyal: As a Private Citizen

There was nothing left for him in Sikkim after passing by the Parliament of India the Constitution (Thirtieth Amendment) Act, 1975. Then he had to try to arrive at a financial settlement with the Government of India for the maintenance of his family, which had large many members and dependents. Moreover, his children were being educated abroad, a costly affair in those days. But that too he mucked up and he was running into a daily losing battle with the Governor, Bipin Bihari Lal, and an old batchmate of his in ICS probationers' course at Dehradun. Unfortunately for Namgyal, tragedy did not come alone. He had high hopes from his eldest son, Tenzing Namgyal. But as ill-luck would have it, he met with a fatal automobile accident on 11 March 1978, which was mourned by the Sikkimese at large.

Though Namgyal was then at the mercy of the Government of India, he hired a legal advisor in Bhuwaneshari Kumari, a princess of the Patiala Princely household to plead his case. Naturally, that did not endear him to the power to be. Unfortunately for him, it appears he never learnt politics. As an illustration, he was not very wise to celebrate Lhendup Kazi's defeat in 1979 State Assembly elections, as if Kazi's defeat vindicated Paldent Thondup Namgyal's style of functioning. Similarly, his was not a very sound strategy to celebrate Mrs Indira Gandhi's defeat in the Indian parliamentary elections in 1977 and Morarji Desai's statement on Sikkim's take-over by India, as at last, nothing came out of it for him.

His last few years were spent in deprivation and constant financial difficulties. He had expected if not a lavish, but a reasonable compensation for his family maintenance from the Government of India for his loss of resources after abolition of his rule. For that instead of pleading his case in happy circumstances, he had made the local presiding deity in Gangrok, the Governor, hostile and similarly his obstinacy had not endeared him to the Prime Minister, Indira Gandhi. Thus, if one cares to read his correspondences with his well-wishers, there is a constant reference of the financial worries and delay of settlement of his financial entitlement from the Federal government. He wrote to Appa Pant, a former Political Officer in Sikkim on 26 December 1977:

> … Most of the sources of livelihood including the Private Estates have been usurped, but my expected settlement (has) not reached yet. Recently the dole I used to receive from Delhi pending my settlement has been stopped and I am in acute financial difficulties at Present. (See Baleshwar Prasad Collection, NMML, New Delhi)

At last he met the new Governor, Talyarkhan in June and wrote to him on 4 July 1981:

> Apropos our meeting and your Excellency's telephone yesterday, I write to express my deep concern and fears with the proposals to my settlement. I cannot understand how my claims to the Private Estates have been overlooked without assigning any reasons after the Government of India called for them.

The question of the Palace compound with buildings is yet to be settled as also many other questions given in my notes to your Excellency and letters to the Govt of India, including the separate settlements for my mother Gyalyum and brother J T Namgyal.

Regarding the revenue of the Govt of Sikkim ... in 1974 was more than 2-8 crores. The Privy Purses of the ex-Princes of India were on annuity and If I am considered on the same lines, then I should be given the capitalized value of the same and not just one years' due. I should also be given interest on the amount from the year 1975 in which the settlements should have been made.

As regards my acceptance of Rs. 57.65 lakhs, I accept the same in cash Rs. 17.65 lakhs and the remainder 40 lakhs in bonds very reluctantly with reservations subject to my claims being sympathically considered; as I feel grave injustice has been done to me and my family. I would seek an appointment with Her Excellency the Prime Minister so that I may plead my case for a just and sympathetic consideration. (see N.K. Rustomji Collection: File No. 37: NMML, New Delhi)

May it be, but as if he had time to settle for the above claims, however genuine they may have been. The author happened to be in Gangtok and decided to call on him at the palace possibly in Septemer 1981. The author was ushered in an ordinay unkempt enclosure to wait for. Soon enough, he came twitching his eyes. Mine was a courtsey call and I requested him to write his biography. I asked him what he was doing those days. He responded that he had his family affairs to worry about and there were a number of dependants on the royal household, who needed to be supported. When I requested him for permission to write his biography, his response was: 'Who will read my biography?' I reasoned with him that his biography would be useful for the regional history and would as well be a precious document on the role of the Namgyal family in history of Sikkim. He responded that he hardly had time to do that. I volunteered to take dictation from him. He laughed and the matter ended there and then. He appeared tired and his voice was hardly audible, as he spoke in a sing-song manner with effort. When I came out from the audience, I learnt from Nirmal Chandra Sinha, the former Director of Namgyal Institute of Tibetology, Gangtok that he was suffering from throat cancer.

At last, he was flown to New York for treatment of throat cancer, as his voice was choked and barely audible. His end came on the morning of 30 January 1982. His body was brought to Gangtok and a befitting state funeral was organized at the royal crematorium in Gangtok on 19 February 1982 attended by a number of dignitaries and a large many villagers from different parts of Sikkim. His friend for more than 40 years, N.K. Rustomji, wrote P.T. Namgyal's obituary on 14 February 1982, which only he could do:

> It was his misfortune that, try as he might, he could not get the people to understand that small can be beautiful. Nor could he allow himself to be convinced that others did not see Sikkim as he saw her, that Sikkim's existence was, for the rest of the world, a non-event. His principles might have been unrealistic and all wrong, but he was not prepared, to the very last, to compromise with them. He was intoxicated by his passion for his land and people. (Rustomji 1987: 160)

Palden Thondup Namgyal: The Person and His Make-Belief World

P.T. Namgyal's lifespan of 58 years may conveniently be divided into three broad phases: the period of blissful youth (1923-47), the period of Intrigue and manoeuvre (1947-73) and the period of struggle for survival (1973-82). His lifespan looks like a normal graph, in which the line slowly rises from left to the peak and then drops down to a sharp decline. It will be instructive to examine the three phases briefly.

The Period of Youthful Bliss

We have noted above that he was born as the second son of the Sikkim ruler, Sir Tashi Namgyal, and was trained to be an incarnate monk of the Tibetan spiritual order known as Gyeshe Rimpoche, the precious jewel. However, he was also sent to the Christian mission schools in Kalimpong, Darjeeling and Simla for secular education. He loved horses and riding on them and going on galloping for a distance. The palace was run on the European lines: everything had to be on time and in proper formal order. The children were largely taken care of by European governesses and later by the resident Political Officers, who not only cared for their upbringing, education and manners, but also their marital alliances to an extent. In P.T. Namgyal's case, Sir Basil J. Gould, the Political Officer from 1936 to 1946, appeared to have played a major role in his political socialization. This happened specially when his elder brother had died in an air crash and then Palden was to succeed him as the Crown Prince of Sikkim, and who was to be groomed for the office of the Maharaja. Slowly, but steadily, the period of youthful bliss was perceptibly altered to the phase of intrigues and manoeuvre. This was apparently a phase in his life of a novice green horn colt, which was indulgently ignored by all concerns.

The Tibetologist Gould like his predecessors saw Sikkim as an Indian state of Tibetan heritage. And he had initially inspired the two cousins, Palden and Jigmie Dorji (of Bhutan), to form a Buddhist federation of Tibet, Bhutan and Sikkim. Their Tibetan uncle, who was a high-up in the Tibetan government of His Holiness, the Dalai Lama, was roped in the scheme of things initially, but ultimately it did move fast enough. As an alternative, he advised the two cousins from the Himalayan kingdoms to travel to Delhi with their memoranda and plead for their case to the Cabinet Mission sent from Great Britain, with the result that status-quo was maintained in the three Himalayan kingdoms Sikkim, Bhutan and Nepal at last.

The first Indian Political Officer at Gangtok, Harishwar Dayal and Sir Tashi Namgyal, the Maharaja of Sikkim, signed the Indo-Sikkimese Treaty, 1950 at Gangtok on 5 December 1950. This treaty was in line with the 'Instrument of Accession', signed by other princely states of British India with the Indian Union after Indian indepencence. Like the other princely states of India, Sikkim too signed the treaty surrendering its defence, foreign relations and communication to the Indian Union and considering her location on sensitive borders, it agreed to its status as an Indian protectorate. Once assured of continuation of the old order of Namgyal rule, Palden got busy in espousing the cause of Sikkim as an independent Bhutia kingdom at any cost. Apparently, he had no concern for the sufferings of his subjects under the oppressive feudal system and he got busy in manoeuvring the newly established multi-ethnic Sikkim State Congress. Unfortunately for him, Palden Namgyal took the Treaty as a binding only on the Indian Union and he got busy espousing the cause of Sikkim's independent identity.

Period of Intrigues and Manoeuvre

Palden was specifically advised by the same Political Officer, who would sign the Indo-Sikkimese Treaty, 1950, not to initiate any move to form a political party as the Crown Prince to encounter the Sikkim State Congress. But he went ahead and established the Sikkim National Party in April 1948 by presiding over the meet for the purpose as an 'anti-thesis of the Sikkim State Congress' (SSC) with the avowed objectives of opposing its three-point charter of demands. His political party, euphemistically called 'the king's party' was run by the Kazi aristocracy, Bhutia commoners and a smattering of some Lepchas and Nepalese. The party was to run even on the palace stationery to a large extent. Palden's one-point programme was to prove that the SSC was a Nepali party and thus, he justified his antics of forming an out and out Bhutia party in SNP for safeguarding their given cause. In this endeavour, he got indirect support from the lukewarm attitude of the Political Officer's to the SSC, as New Delhi was uncertain about the ascendency of Nepalese politics in that part of the country. But Sikkim State Congress was in reality a multi-ethnic organization, which took up the cause of the toiling masses through it mass campaign. So much so that there was a *gherao* of the palace in 1949 and the Maharaja had to take shelter with the Political Officer (Sinha 2019).

Soon after that he manoeuvred with the offices of the Dewan and the Political Officer and an artificial and unjust arrangement was stealthily hammered between the two ethnic blocks: Lepcha-Bhutias and the Nepalese. It was decided that all political representation would be shared equally between the two ethnic blocks: Lepcha-Bhutia combined and Nepalese at large. This system of ethnic parity came to be known as the Ethnic Parity System. The President of the Sikkim State Congress, Tashi Tshering, was opposed to the move and had not authorized his representatives to sign any document, but to report the outcome of the meet to the party forum. But the representatives of the two parties (SNP and SSC) were made to sign the final document presented to them and thus it was a fate accompli. When Tashi Tshering opposed the move, he was ousted from the party, he had founded. More surprises were in for them; when the election to the State Council was held in 1953, all the candidates of the King's party were elected on the Lepcha-Bhutia seats and the representatives of the Sikkim State Congress got elected on the Nepalese seats. This game of ethnic intrigues continued for the next 20 years. So much so that every voter in the politically illiterate state had six votes to cast. Moreover, an intricate procedure of the counting of the votes was in place. Thus, whatever the parties opposed to the king's doing would be permitted to take part in the elections, but the result was the same: the king's party would be elected and the Senior Executive Councillor would invariably be a nominee of the king's party. Every step was taken to manipulate the system to deny the majority population of Sikkim to its rightful share in the governance of the state by one man, P.T. Namgyal, first as the Maharaj Kumar and then as the Maharaja nee the Chogyal. That crude display of *laissez faire* act of one man was exposed in the mass upsurge of 1973, which upset his apple cart for all times to come.

Phase of Struggle for Survival

From 1973 onwards turned out to be the beginning of his end. He was known to be an obstinate, headstrong and non-compromising character in his resolve. These aspects of his character came haunting to him in his lean period of life. He was immensely distressed that the Government of India let him down by standing with the majority of the people, the Sikkemese of Nepali extraction, in the hours of his distrest. But he forgot that he and his American consort went on espousing the cause of claimed international personality of Sikkim without taking the 'protecting power' into confidence. Moreover, he went on flouting the wishes of the Government of India not to ignore the democratic aspirations of his own people all through the 1950s and 1960s. So he should blame himself, if anybody to be held responsible for his misery. His daily struggle for the cause of his rule led to his hangers-on parting ways with him. Someone put a claim on the land adjacent to the palace and managed to get it transferred in his name legally. Another hanger-on staked a claim on a prestigious hotel owned by him and had it. A third one claimed his two cinema halls located in the same building complex in the main market place in Gangtok and became the proud owner of those properties. Now

Namgyal was engaged in fighting a losing battle with the Government of India for his throne, estates, title and assets. Unfortunately, he had few sympathizers and still fewer friends in place to help him out of the mess he had created for himself.

He was made to sign the merger documents in a desperate situation without any condition for making provision for his maintenance and that of his family and dependents such as his old mother and sick younger brother, J.T. Namgyal. While he was struggling for negotiating an honourable settlement for himself and his family, he should not have exposed himself to the ongoing political developments at the state and national levels. With passing of time, he turned to be a sick man who required prompt medical treatment, but there was no money on hand for that. His children were being educated abroad, which cost money. Meanwhile his American wife had filed a divorce case against him in far away in New York. But try as much as he could, there was no money coming on time to help him out. In spite of all his efforts, compensations for his private properties were not settled to his satisfaction. And for that he was equally responsible to an extent. For illustration, he had made claims for developing copper mines in Sikkim. But it is a known fact that the Government of India helped to develop copper mines in Sikkim, but copper ores were negligible, of poor quality and its extraction was abandoned as costly investment. Was it a state enterprise or a private one? If it was a private one, did he pay for it? His correspondences with the friends were full of financial worries in those years of late 1970s. Slowly and slowly, the number of his visitors decreased and there were fewer persons to correspond with him at the end. Deliverance came not belatedly when he breathed his last in far away New York on 30 January 1982. Posterity would recall his ceaseless efforts to maintain that Sikkim was essentially a Bhutia kingdom on Tibetan pattern and its integration to India might add to the Indian plurality, but not to its Hindu ethos and he remained unconvinced till end that Sikkim belonged to India.

REFERENCES

Baleshwar Prasad Collection, Nehru Memorial Museum & Library, (NMML), New Delhi.

Das, B.S., 1983, *Sikkim Saga*, Vikas Publishing House, New Delhi.
Rustomji, N.K., *Collection*, NMML, New Delhi.
_____, 1971, *Enchanted Frontiers: Sikkim, Bhutan and India's North Eastern Borderlands*, Bombay, Oxford University Press.
_____, 1987, *Sikkim: A Himalayan Tragedy*, New Delhi, Allied Publishers.
Sinha, A.C., 1991, *Bhutan: Ethnic Identity and National Dilemma*, Reliance Publishing House, New Delhi.
_____, 2001, *Himalyan Kingdom Bhutan: Tradition, Transition and Transformation*, Indus Publishing Company, New Delhi.
_____, 2019, *Dawn of Democracy in the Eastern Himalayan Kingdoms: Nepal, Sikkim and Bhutan in Mid 20th Century*, Routledge, London.

PART D

Performance

11

Indian Strategy of Accomodation and Defence against the Dissenters

We have noted earlier in Chapter 2, how the British had divided their Indian Imperial possesion into two dominions of India and Pakistan on the ground of the religious affiliation of the people. Moreover, the newly independent Indian state was struggling with the problems of integrating of the princely states of various sizes into a cohesive Indian political structure. So far the princely state of Jammu & Kashmir was concerned the Indian establishment was banking on the popularity of Sheikh Muhammad Abdullah, an associate of the Indian National Congress party, who was a secular and anti-feudal politician in his outlook. The ruler of the state, Sir Hari Singh, was toying with the idea of independence for his principality. With a view to expediting the Muslim majority princely state to merge with it, Pakistan sponsored raids, arson, and attacks on Kashmir on 22 October 1947. The Maharaja took steps towards joining the Indian Dominion by signing the instrument of accesssion and India took Pakistani invasion seriously by mounting armed counter-offensive to recover the lost territories. On the other hand, so far as Nagas' alleged independence on 14 August 1947 was concerned; the Indian Dominion did not take it seriously to begin with. It was considered as an adventurous act by some small number of misguided elements of the tribes from the distant eastern frontier of the province.

Indian democratic system is based on consensual approach. Right from the beginning, there was a consensus in the Indian Constituent Assembly that the federating Provinces must be autonomous for administering themselves and at the same time, there must be a strong Federal Authority to develop her potential resources and keep the country united against the internal sabotage and external aggression. With a view to dealing with the dissenters, a three-prone strategy was evolved:

(A) constitutional accommodation to the maximum level to the various ethnic, linguistic, religious and underdeveloped communities and people,
(B) an effective armed defence against to those, who violently opposed the Indian Union on some or other grounds and,
(C) negotiating a common ground to work with the dissenters within the constitutional frame work adopted by the country.

In the first strategy, the constitutional mechanism was used to entertain all types of regional, local, and disadvantageous socio-cultural sections by providing constitutional and financial support from the federal government. At the same time, the country was determined and well-prepared to eliminate any violent effort from any corner of the country to its constitutionally established authority. And lastly, the Government of India did not hesitate to sit together with the dissenters to bring them round to work within the legal framework of the Constitution.

A: Constitutional Stipulations

1. *Constitutional Provision for the Special Status to the Scheduled Districts of Assam*

Considering the historical and geographical backwardness of the hill tribes of Assam, constitutional provision for the Sixth Schedule for the Scheduled Tribes of Assam was made, which provides exclusive rights of the scheduled tribes on their land, natural resources and ethnic traditions, which will be governed by the their customary laws and practices. And with a view to administering those aspects, it was envisaged that the five Scheduled Hill districts would elect their scheduled tribal representatives for administering their district councils. Among the five scheduled districts of Garo Hills, Jaintia and Khasi Hills, Lushai Hills, Mikir Hills and Naga Hills districts, the last one, the Nagas of the Naga Hills district, rejected the provision of the district council along with the entire constitutional edifice. The Nagas had boycotted the district councils because of the fact that 'they had allegedly declared their independence after the withdrawal of the British colonial power from India'. The district councils were elected in rest of the hill districts of Assam for the next two decades till the two districts were promoted to the statehood. And even after the statehood of Meghalaya, the district councils go on functioning as before in that state.

Though the institution of the Hill District Council could not function to the best of the expectations of people concerned in many cases, but those of the communities, which remained uncovered by the provision of such councils, have been demanding creation of the district councils even in the plain areas with demographically mixed population of Assam. So much so that the state of Assam had been creating district councils like fast food kiosks in the plains of Assam. As a special consideration, the citizens of the region were exempt from paying the income tax to the Union government. Moreover, considering the weak infrastructural resources in the difficult mountainous terrain of the frontiers states, the Union government gives 90 per cent grant in aid to these frontier states.

2. *Granting of Special Status to the Jammu & Kashmir and the Princely State of Sikkim*

Once the Maharaja of Jammu & Kashmir signed the instrument of accession on the subjects of defence, communication and foreign relations with India in last week of October 1947, Indian forces mounted a defensive invasion to secure its territories from the invaders. The State Assembly was authorized to frame its own constitution; jailed popular leader of the National Conference, Sheikh Abdullah, was released and elevated to be the office of Premier of the state and the Maharaja continued to be in the office as the head of the state on behalf of the Indian dominion. The invasion of Jammu & Kashmir by Pakistan was taken to the United Nations Organization (UNO), where it continues to be on its agenda for the last more than seven decades. The Maharaja of Sikkim and the Political Officer of India in Sikkim signed the Indo-Sikkim Treaty on 5 December 1950 at

Gangtok. Considering the special location and cultural uniqueness of the principality between, Nepal, Tibet, Bhutan and Darjeeling, India agreed to its status as an Indian Protectorate to be ruled by the Maharaja Sir Tashi Namgyal. As per provision of the above treaty, the Government of India would be responsible for the defence, foreign relations and communication and the ruler would be responsible for internal administration of the principality.

3. *Creation of the State of Nagaland in 1963*

All through 1950s Naga Hills district remained politically disturbed, as the Nagas had boycotted the State Assembly and Parliamentary Elections held in 1952 and 1957. Once the Naga National Council (NNC) mounted their boycott of the democratic process and resorted to non-cooperation with the authorities, the state intervened with a view to providing security to the section of the Nagas, who had opposed the NNC demands. Thus, the armed forces were pressed in operation with a view to establishing normalcy for common people. In a topographically difficult and forested territory, even the defence forces were exposed to harsh treatment unleashed by the insurgents. Thus, an unusual step was taken by the parliament to pass a controversial act, the Armed Forces (Special Protection) Act (AFSPA), 1958. This Act remains to be one of the most draconian and controversial acts in India. So much so that some five decades after its enactment, a five-member commission was appointed, presided by Justice B.P. Jeevan Reddy to

> suggest how the act could be made 'more humane'. The Commission submitted its report, which was not to the liking of the government. Enquired of the fate of the Report of the Commission, one of the former members of the Commission got the reply: 'The Governments may come and the governments may go, but AFSPA will remain (in operation)'. (Hazarika 2018: 4-5)

The armed forces made the plea that as the insurgents violated all the established legal practices, it would be impossible to mount anti-insurgency drives without violating the normal legal practices in the insurgency bound areas. Thus, the things became so hot that N.N.C.

leader, Z.A. Phizo was smuggled out of Nagaland to East Pakistan, from where he went to London with a view to seeking international support for the cause of the Naga independence.

Meanwhile a group of Nagas formed a parallel body, Naga People's Convention (NPC) to the Naga National Council and came out with a clear roadmap for their future. The Convention met thrice and hammered out their charter of demands to put before the Government of India. They proposed to create a separate state of Nagaland within the Indian Union, in which they would participate in the democratic process. Moreover, they suggested the integration of Naga inhabited areas from adjoining districts into the new state. The Government of India passed the 13th Amendment Act to the Indian Constitution with a view to creating the first ethnic state of Nagaland in 1963. Accordingly, the State of Nagaland was inaugurated by the President of India in December 1963. The first State Assembly Elections were held in February 1964 and the first democratically elected governmen was sworn in office. However, a section of the Nagas owing allegiance to the Naga National Council (NNC) was not reconciled and they continued their subversive activities in and around the state of Nagaland in the region. Since then, there has been an elected state government and an active insurgency mounted by another set of the Nagas simultaneously in the state of Nagaland and its adjoining areas.

4. *North-East Region Re-organization Areas (Reorganization) Act, 1971*

The State of Assam declared Assamiya as the state language, which was opposed by a large section of the ethnic groups, tribals and none-tribal alike in the state. Unfortunately, the history of state language in Assam had been controversial since the British took over Assam in 1826 after the first Anglo-Burmese War. Considering that the Assamiya was the dialect of the Bengali, the British introduced elementary education in Assam through the medium of Bengali, which was opposed by the Assamese at large as well as American Baptist Christian Missionaries working in Assam. In course of time, the mistake was corrected by introducing Assamiya in the primary schools in the state as a medium of instruction.

Within no time, Assamiya emerged as the lingua franca of the state even among the farthest tribal corner of the frontiers. It may even be remembered that Bengali was the language of the two districts of the Barak Valley in the western part of Assam. Moreover, Bengali professionals were spread through the nook and corner of the state. In such a situation, the decision of the state government declaring Assamiya as the state language was opposed by many people leading to a prolonged anti-Assamiya language agitation. The hill districts, which were mainly inhabited by the scheduled tribes, who had received their elementary education in their mother tongue in the schools run by the Christian missionaries, organized themselves in All Party Hill Leaders Conference (APHLC) to oppose the move of the state government. The language movement took virulent shape for a long period of time. The Hill districts and districts of the Barak Valley remained disturbed for most of the time in the 1960s, which the central government could not avoid. The Union Government appointed the Patskar Commission in 1960s with a view to finding a way out of the stalemate in the province. The Government of India gave a serious consideration to the report of the Commission and passed the North-East (Re-organization) Act, 1971 by introducing the 22nd Amendment to the Constituion.

The North East Re-organization Act envisaged establishment of a regional developmental entity known as, North Eastern Council at Shillong as an apex body for the creation of inter-state human and infra-structural amenities. Furthermore, in the year 1972, the State of Meghalaya was created out of Garo Hills and United Jaintia and Khasi Hills districts of Assam. Two Union Territories of Manipur and Tripura were elevated to statehood and the Union Territories of Mizoram and Arunachal Pradesh were stipulated to be accorded statehood in the near future. Though the state of Nagaland complained that creation of NEC was as if the old practices of Assam state was being brought back in another name. However, the NEC was able to create various technical, professional, and academic institutions for manpower training in the region. Moreover, inter-state road connectivity and electric power generation and transmission lines were special gifts of the NEC to the region. Meanwhile the State of Assam was caught in another socio-political fever, anti-foreigners agitation by All Assom Students Union (AASU) in 1979.

5. *The Tripartite Sikkim Agreement, 1973, 35th Amendement Act of the Constitution of India, 1975 and Merger of Sikkim in the Indian Union*

After the fifth general election to the State Council in Sikkim in January 1973, there were protests by the political parties against the electoral malpractices. The Maharaja ignored them and got busy in celebrating his 50th birth anniversary. That led to anger in the public and they launched an extensive agitation against the partisan politics of the regime. Soon thereafter, the administration collapsed and the ruler requested the Government of India to take over the administration to establish the rule of law. With a view to creating a general administrative framework, a tripartite agreement was hammered out and signed on 8 May 1973 at Gangtok among the 15 leaders of three political parties, who were agitating for the reforms, the Maharaja of Sikkim and the Foreign Sectretary of the Government of India.

Before a fresh election was to be conducted, the demand for 'one man, one vote' (universal adult franchise) was conceded to the Sikkimese. A State Legislative Assembly with 15 Lepcha-Bhutia and 15 Nepalese and a seat for Scheduled Castes and another for the Buddhist monks was conceded. The election to the State Legislative Assembly was held in 1974 and the Sikkim Congress came victorious out on 31 out of 32 seats. Powers to the Legislative Assembly were already defined and office of a chief minister with a cabinet of ministers was envisaged prior to the election. However, the ruler was not convinced with these stipulations. The chief minister designate, Lhendup Dorji Kazi, was equally unwilling to take oath of office from the Maharaja. While this issue was being sorted out, the ruler was invited by the Government of Nepal to attend the crowning ceremony of Prince Birendra Bir Bikram Shah as the king, an unusual and unprecedented development. The Maharaja was advised against attending the Nepalese celebration, but he managed to attend it and used the occasion at Kathmandu to air his unhappiness on the

Sikkimese development to the international media. When he came back home, he had to face a hostile welcome in Sikkim and thus, the State Assembly passed a resolution abolishing the institution of Namgyal dynastic rule. Moreover, a plebiscite was conducted hurriedly in which more than 97 per cent subjects of the principality voted to do away with the monarchy in Sikkim. All these happenings in Sikkim led to the Government of India enacting the 35th Amendment Act to the Constitution of India in 1975. This enactment provided for the end of dynastic rule and creation of a state of Sikkim in the Indian Union (Sinha 2008: 247-8).

6. *Creation of State of Mizoram, 1986*

Mizo insurgency led by MNF leader, Pu Laldenga, was at a low key after the emergence of Bangladesh out of East Pakistan in 1972. The President of MNF wrote a letter to the prime minister of India expressing his allegiance to the Indian constitution and offered to negotiate the conditions for the settlement of the Mizo problem. Unfortunately, the negotiation between the two parties went on for many years. It so happened that the armed wing of the MNF, fighting from their external hideouts, was against the terms of the settlement. At last, views of the MNF chief prevailed over the dissenters and an agreement between the Government of India and the MNF was signed in 1986. The Agreement envisaged elevation of the Union Territory of Mizoram into statehood as per Special Provision of the 35th Amendment to the Indian constitution. Laldenga became the chief minister of the State of Mizoram jointly sponsored by the Congress and the MNF. Thus, the two decade long insurgency in Mizoram came to an end and since then, this is one of the most peaceful states of the Indian Union in the Northeast region.

7. *Creation of State of Arunachal Pradesh, 1987*

Soon after that, it was turn of the Union Territory of Arunachal Pradesh. Thus, 55th Amendment to the Constitution of India was passed in 1986 and a new state of Arunachal Pradesh was created with an elected Legislative Assembly and the chief minister to preside over his cabinet of ministers. Since then, the state of Arunachal Pradesh has regular elections for the state assembly and the elected cabinet led by its chief minister administers the state for the last three decades. Similarly, Arunachal Pradesh has been electing her three representatives to the Indian parliament regularly.

B. Defensive Measures for the Territorial Integrity of the Indian Union

1. *Steps for Securing Kashmir from Invasion and Raids from Pakistan in October 1947*

One of the sacred duties of the Indian Union has been to safeguard the territorial integrity of the Union. Once the Maharaja of Kashmir had signed the Instrument of Accession to India in October 1947, the Indian armed forces moved fast to regain the lost territories of Kashmir to Pakistani raiders. However, that happened within two months of Indian independence, when even the armed forces were divided between the two dominions haphazardly and they were still commanded by the British Army Officers. That was also the time when even the divided armed forces were yet to recover from their long involvement in the Second World War. Moreover, the war was fought on the difficult terrain under the shadow of Karakoram mountains in the north-western Kashmir. As there was limited time to recover the lost territories in a logistically difficult region, India gambled by mounting air force to reach armed forces on time to overtake the raiders. Forward march of the raiders to Srinagar was blunted and India began pushing the raiders back. But by then, the north-western flank of Kashmir was lost to Pakistan for ever. And since then, a UNO sponsored ceased fire is on in operation between India and Pakistan stretching for the last seven decades.

2. *Anti-Insurgency drive in Naga Hills District of Assam since 1950*

We have referred earlier how Naga National Council tried to pre-empt Indian independence on 14 August 1947, which was aborted by the Vigilant Deputy Commissioner of the Naga Hills district, Charles

Pawsey. But the Naga movement turned strident under the leadership of Z.A. Phizo, who took successively more and more militant and non-compromising stand with the Indian Union. They resorted first to civil disobedience, and when they were opposed to by a section of their own folk, they turned violent against the leaders championing the moderate stand to a series of murders. The state administration of Assam intervened, but the situation demanded harsher treatment with possibly superior forces and for that the armed forces had to be involved leading to further confrontation between the NNC and the Government of India.

3. *Passing of the Arms Forces Special Power Act (AFSPA), 1958*

We have discussed the circumstances how the provisions of AFSPA 1958 were enacted by the Indian parliament to fortify the sagging morale of the armed forces operating among the civilians under the adverse circumstances in Naga Hills. Soon after that, the operational area of the AFSPA was extended to Manipur and adjoining regions of Nagaland. As various shades of insurgencies appeared in Manipur, Mizoram and other districts of Assam such as United Liberation Front of Assom (ULFA), armed forces moved in those areas operating under the provisions of the AFSPA to contain the onrush of unrest effectively. Naturally, when two opposite sides fight to finish the war of attrition, there would be accesses, which could not otherwise be defended. Justice Jeevan Reddy Commission was appointed to study the operation of the AFSPA. But reports of the Commission had not been implemented as yet.

4. *Anti-Insurgency Drive in Mizo Hills District of Assam, Air-strafing on the Rebel Hide-outs and Re-grouping of the Mizo Villages 1966*

The district level officers were holding a meeting in the Deputy Commissioner's chamber on the fateful 28 February 1966 at Aizawl, the day MNF launched its 'Operation Jericho' by killing all of those present in the meet. After that it was almost a cake walk for the insurgents to take over all the government establishments in the town except a little hillock, where the Assam Rifles was located. It appears that the news was something like a serious bolt to the already belaboured

Government of India. The Commandant at the Eastern Command, Calcutta was pressed to act, and act fast before it became too late. Considering the topographically undulating terrain of the district, where a large many foot soldiers could be tied down in the long drawn flushing operation of the underground forces, air force was ordered to strafe the rebel hide outs. Indiscriminate air dropping of the incendiary bombs reduced Aizawl and other inhabited villages to ashes. But taking advantage of meandering topography, MNF foot soldiers vanished into the thin air of the hills, but populous settlements were raised to the ground. However, the initial success of MNF cadres made them bold enough to 'hit and hide' on the newly already harrassed solders from the plains. And that led the security forces to adopt a device adopted by the British forces in Malaya to flush the Communist insurgents out of their hideouts. The device was a very cruel, inhuman and anti-environmental exercise, in which a number of villages were uprooted and their entire population was ordered to settle down by the road side colonies, created by the forces to be guarded under their surveillance. They were provided some food and drinking water, but were prohibited to go to their fields to cultivate their land and forests to hunt games and collect roots and fruits for their normal consumption. This exercise of re-grouping of the villages along Silchar-Aizawl road and Aizawl-Lungleh Road created untold hardship and ecological havoc for the Mizo society for all times to come.

C. Exploring the Avenues for Settlements of Political Problems

Negotiation is the easiest way to solve a problem but it is not so easy to to accomplish it in reality. Noted negotiator, Jonathan Powell, writes:

> It is far easier to start a negotiation than it is to end one successfully. Armed groups may be inclined to open a peace process because of the legitimacy and publicity it bestows, but they generally move by consensus and would rather talk indefinitely than face up to difficult compromises necessary to reach an agreement. They often prefer the airplane to circle endlessly rather than land. Finding a way to conclude successfully is the Holy Grail for negotiators.

Powell continues: 'Why do some talks conclude successfully and others fail?' Enumerating the reasons for that he identifies the factors that determine success or failure:

> the nature of the organization (with hierarchical groups having an advantage over groups that cannot control their members' actions); the nature of the leadership (groups with a strong leader having an advantage over those that are decentralized); and the nature of public support for the cause (where groups with constituencies who tire of violence are more likely to compromise).... While all these have an influence on success or failure, the key factor is the ability to close a deal: can the two sides be pushed into an endgame and into making difficult decisions? One way of forcing a decision is to set a deadline, but establishing one that people really believe in is not always so easy.... Deadlines can thus be both a solution and a problem. Certainly setting deadlines can put the credibility of the mediator on the line. (Powell 2014: 243-4)

We have below four case studies, a success story of the Mizo Accord and two cases of failures from Nagaland: the Shillong Accord, 1975 and the Negotiation between the GOI and the NSCN, 1994 to 2020 and another one (the first one) of uncertain consequences.

1. *Kashmir Accord between the Sheikh and Indira Gandhi: February 1975*

Sheikh Abdullah was under house arrest; had been unwell for some time and he was being treated in All India Institute of Medical Sciences (AIIMS), New Delhi in February, 1972. P.N. Haksar, Private Secretary to the Prime Minister Indira Gandhi, met the Sheikh and informed him that the PM would like to meet him. Subsequently, the Sheikh was released from captivity on 5 June 1972. He met the prime minister and she suggested to him to forget the past and work together with her. Two leaders instituted a Committee consisting of Mirza Afzal Beg and G. Parthasarthi to suggest the modalities between the two to work together. The discussions were concluded and the two leaders met in February 1975 and decided to work together on the basis of the recommendations of the Committee. This came to be known as the Kashmir Accord. Sheik Abdullah reached Jammu on 4 February 1975 and the same evening he was unanimously elected the leader of the Congress Parliamentary Party in the State Assembly in the presense of Deb Kant Barua, the President of the Indian National Congress party.

Sheikh Abdullah invited equal number of members of the Plebiscite Front, Kashmir (a forum floated by Mirza Afzal Beg with doubtful credentials) and the Congress Legislative Party to join him in his cabinet of ministers. This did not go well with the Congress party. Moreover, Sheikh Abdullah decided to revive in Kashmir his old war horse, the National Conference, which was apparently not to the liking of the Congress party. The invited members of the Congress Legislative Assembly were first reluctant and then decided not to join the Cabinet with Sheikh Abdullah. It was an unpleasant development for everybody, which vitiated the political atmosphere in the state. As the National Conference was being revived, signals were sent that the Congress party should stop functioning in Jammu & Kashmir. This was not acceptable to the Congress, which was made public in a meeting at Srinagar by no less a person that the Prime Minister, Indira Gandhi, the tallest leader of the party. However, things were changing fast at the national scene: a national emergency was declared on 25 June 1975; many opposition leaders were arrested; emergency was at last lifted in February 1977 and a general election to the parliament was declared; the Congress party including the prime minister was defeated. While Sheikh Abdullah was electioneering in the hilly region in Kashmir, he suffered from a massive heart attack and was confined to the bed for more than a month. He did recover, took the oath of office of the chief minister of Jammu & Kashmir, but he was no more the same firebrand Sheikh Abdullah any more. And the Indian National Congress and former Prime Minister, Indira Gandhi, too were having a tough time as their adversaries were trying to settle their old scores with her. In the process, no due attention was given by anybody to honour the commitments made in the above Accord.

2. *Signing of the Shillong Accord between NNC and Government of India, 11 June 1975*

The Governor of Assam and Nagaland, L.P. Singh ICS, who had been the Home Secretary, the Government of India, was well aware of the affairs of Nagaland for the last many years. He was approached by some well-meaning church leaders and philanthropists such as Rev.

Langri Ao and Gandhian social worker, M. Aram for the ongoing agony of the Nagas. Shri Singh encouraged them to continue their efforts to reach other leaders so that a meaningful dialogue could be negotiated with the NNC operatives. Thus, a liaison committee was formed to reach the various shades of public opinion in Nagaland. Z.A. Phizo's youngest brother, Keviyallay, who participated in the discussion leading to the Accord and he was one of its signatories, 'had kept him (Phizo) abreast' (Steyn 2016: 156) with the development leading to the Accord. There were only two points in the Shillong Accord: willingness on the part of the underground (Nagas) to accept the Constitution of India and the arms with the underground were to be brought and deposited at a place at an agreed time. And then the government was to rehabilitate the surrendered rebels. There were five signatories from among the undergrounds and the Governor L.P. Singh signed the document on behalf of the Government of India on 10 November 1975 at the Rajbhavan, Shillong.

While in the know of the whole development of the discussion, Phizo was unenthusiastic about the Accord as it did not acknowledge any role for him and his forum, NNC in the future dispensation. Within no time, armed wing of the underground issued threatening rejection to the Accord from their hideout located abroad. The dissenters within the Underground led by Isak Swu, Shangnyu Shangwang Khaplang and Thuengaling Muivah denounced the NNC and its leadership, especially of Z.A. Phizo in clear terms. Not only that, they came out of the NNC and formed a parallel militant and socialist political organization, the National Socialist Council of Nagaland (NSCN) in January 1980. In the year 1988, S.S. Khaplang parted company with I. Swu and T. Muivah and formed his faction of NSCN and remained committed to fighting for the Nagas' cause. Since then, it is the NSCN led by Swu and Muivah, which has been calling the shots in the Naga insurgency. Thus, the Shillong Accord died a natural death immediately and if at all, it remains only on paper: within no time both the parties forgot about it. Why did it fail so miserably within no time? Should there be a need to analyse its collapse with patience? However, it appears that while Governor Singh was in a hurry to show results, the NNC signaturies did not take their armed fighting wing into confidence before signing it.

3. *Signing of the Mizo Accord between the Mizo National Front and the Government of India, 30 June 1986*

For about a decade Pu Laldenga sat in Delhi as an honoured guest of the Government of India and tried hard to bring his cadre to the negotiating table, but the illusive accord was not clinched almost for a decade. Then the Prime Minister Rajiv Gandhi stepped in; he entrusted the delicate negotiation to the senior and experienced Congress leader, Arjun Singh, and kept an eye on the progress of the matter. On the other hand, Pu Laldenga also shrugged off complacency and managed to persuade his reluctant and recalcitrant Johnny's fighters from among the followers. At last, the Mizo Accord was signed by the Home Secretary, R.D. Pradhan, Government of India, Lal Khama, the Chief Secretary, Government of Mizoram and Laldenga, the Chief of the Mizo National Front (MNF), on 30 June 1986. The Union Territory of Mizoram was elevated to statehood and 90 per cent of all funds to the new state would be as grant-in-aid from the Centre. The MNF rebels surrendered their arms and weapons and agreed to abide by the Indian constitution. The Government of India on its part had agreed to rehabilitate the MNF returnees and as well, and provided monetary compensation to them. Among the other things, the government saw to it that the NEHU campus in Mizoram acquired the status of a Central University (Hazarika 2018: 119-20). Why did the Mizo Accord succeed where others fail? The answer lies in the following: Realization of the Government of India to clinch the agreement and acceptance of the MNF leadership that armed struggle had reached a dead end.

4. *Talks and Negotiations between the Government of India and the National Socialist Council of Nagaland (NSCN), 1994-2020 and their Failure*

Prime Minister Narasimha Rao took the initiative to break the deadlock between the Nagas (NSCN) and the Government of India in 1993 and contacts were established between the two for a possible negotiated settlement of the problem of Naga insurgency (Hazarika 2011). By then, NNC was reduced to irrelevance in Naga politics, as its support base had been divided between the Nagas for India and the Nagas with allegiance to NSCN. Even NSCN itself was split into two factions: I. Swu and T. Muivah led NSCN (I-M) and S.S. Khaplang led NSCN(K). Both the factions claim to struggle for independence of the Nagas from India. The first faction led by a Sumi leader Swu and a Tankhul Muivah had an image of being non-compromising in its ideology and ruthless in its field operations invariably from alien lands. The Khaplang faction, operating from north-eastern corner of Nagaland, the home of the Hemi sub-group of Konyaks, the largest Naga tribe, to which the leader belonged, spread in India and Myanmar, was a dominant force in the area. Some fifty years back, the leaders of the two factions: I. Swu and T. Muivah and S.S. Khaplang, had worked together and laid the foundation of the NSCN, but once they parted company, they turned out to be the worst enemies of one another.

The duad put three conditions for beginning of the negotiation with the Government of India: one, the negations would be only with them and it would be in no case with that of the S.S. Khaplang's faction of NSCN; two, the powerful Chief Minister of Nagaland, S.C. Jamir, was to be removed from his position as he was an insurmountable obstacle to the problem; and three, the Indian Army must stop its alleged connivance with the Kuki tribe of Manipur in their anti-Naga operations (Hazarika 2018: 64-81). If the Government of India would accept the above conditions, that that would amount to handing over an alleged greater Nagaland on the platter to the NSCN led by the duad of Swu and Muivah. Naturally, no government in Delhi would agree to such demands made by them. However, the negotiations did start in 1994 and continued till 2020 stretching nearly two and half a decade. In between, credit goes to the Indian political system that passed through the periods, when there were four prime ministers (Narsimha Rao, Deve Gouda, I.K. Gujral and Atal Behari Vajpai) ranging from about two years to four years in the office and the next five prime ministers (Vajpai, Manmohan Singh (twice) and Narendra Modi (second term, which is ongoing)) in the next 25 years. And they continued the dialogue with NSCN all through.

A dramatic episode happened in 2015, when Isak Swu was hospitalized in the Fortis Hospital, Delhi with serious kidney ailment and his conditions began deteriorating. Prior to that, he had confided to a friend: 'I want to sign something before I go'. He desired that he would like to leave his legacy for the Nagas. Hurriedly a draft of preamble to the agreement was prepared and the old man managed to sign it from his hospital bed with the help of his wife. 'And it was this statement that was taken to N. Ravi, the interlocutor (to the Negotiation) and Muivah for their signature at the Prime Minister's official residence at 7 Race Course Road on 3 August 2015' (Hazarika 2018: 79). A year down the road, Isak Swu died in 2016. At one point of time, NSCN submitted the 31 points memoranda, which was thrashed out to a couple of tricky and sticky issues, which no Indian government would like to touch. It was made clear to the NSCN that no Indian Government would ever consider giving sovereignty to Nagaland. Similarly, demand for a greater Nagaland was a non-starter as other adjoining states to Nagaland are opposed to that. All the three neighbouring states of Nagaland, Manipur, Assam and Arunachal Pradesh, were determined not to part with their territories to the Nagas, as they advanced equally logical arguments in their favour to retain them for themselves. A proposal was under consideration that overlapping linguistic and cultural areas across the state boundaries may have their cultural, lingual and even primary educational bodies to be funded by the federal government. But this issue got stuck on the ultimate control of those cultural and educational bodies. However, there was the ceasefire operating in Nagaland and the NSCN cadres were holding their fort in a designated camp in Nagaland.

This prolonged negotiation was testing the patience of the common Nagas. Naga Mothers Association demanded acceleration of the negotiation. The Church leaders came forward once more pleading for lasting peace in the state. The apex body of the non-governmental organizations (NGO) simply asked the two parties to sign the terms of agreement. Meanwhile, fed up of paying arbitrary so-called taxes to multiple legal or illegal authorities, the citizens came out in the street and called for a public strike in the state againt the arbitrary extraction of money. By then, former interlocutor of the Indo-Naga Negotiation, N Ravi, had taken over as the Governor of Nagaland, who expressed disapproval of extracting excessive contribution from the common citizens by the insurgents. The NSCN came out publically against the Governor's statement and claimed that as a political organization, they had every right to demand from the Nagas to pay taxes to them for their upkeep. The NGOs also demanded from the NSCN to come out of endless negotiation and sign the agreement.

The NSCN leadership made a statement that the Government of India must agree to their demand for a separate flag and a constitution for the Nagas, which was out rightly rejected by the Government of India. Moreover, the Government of India had already issued a statement that the Negotiation must come to an end latest by 31 October 2020, which the other party resented. The NSCN reacted sharply that they were being cajoled to sign the agreement and then the Government announced the end of the negotiation with the NSCN (*The Asian Age*: 7 October 2020). These developments after a decade long negotiation between the two parties have been very frustrating for the common man in the street and against their anticipation of a bright peaceful future. Similarly, people at large in India, and all the more in the State of Nagaland, were dismayed as to what had the two sides been talking for more than 25 years if they had nothing to offer in common at the end?

The Naga insurgency has been the oldest ethnic movement, which independent India confronted and it continues to exist inspite of the constituonal provision, armed confrontation and prolonged negations. After all, why did all these efforts fail? Manoeuvring a negotiation into the endgame and reaching a lasting agreement requires skill and luck. Powell says that

> You need to be able to push the parties to their real bottom lines and bridge the gap between the two bottom lines, often by way of constructive ambiguity or by coming up with an imaginative solution that enlarges the context of an intractable stand-off where the two sides are locking horns. The key turning point is when the armed groups finally sees the prospect of political success and realizes its weapons are an obstacle rather than the key to success. If the two sides can see the attempts of the spoilers to derail the negotiations and escape the trap of the zero-sum game while carrying their constituency with them, then there is a prospect of success; but still it is far from inevitable that a negotiation will end with a successful agreement.... Signing an agreement is not the same as making peace. An agreement does not make the two sides

trust each other indeed they have an agreement precisely because they don't trust each other. It is only when they both start delivering on the promises they have made by implementing the agreement that trust begins, gradually, to develop. The hard work therefore starts once you have signed the agreement which is simply what 'enables the process to begin. (Powell 2014: 278-9)

The Government of India presumes that they have solved the problem of Kashmir after signing the Kashmir Accord, 1975 with Sheikh Abdullah. Even before that Prime Minister Indira Gandhi and President Zulfikar Ali Bhutto of Pakistan had signed the Simla Agreement on 2 July 1972 'to settle their differences on the Kashmir dispute by peaceful means'. It is obvious that the newly independent Indian Union desires a strong federal government in the capital to concentrate on development of the resources for the betterment of the citizens, which would be instrumental in removing age-old backwardness of the peoples and regions. There were communities with various sets of disabilities, which come in the way of their socio-political equality with one another. With a view to removing those disabilities within a time frame, constitutional provisions were made for certain sets of people, like scheduled castes and scheduled tribes. We have enumerated above the various steps undertaken to accommodate various frontier regions within the state structure. Second, there were communities led by their leaders within the defined territory of India, who dreamed of their separate destiny for them and took to arms against the Indian Union. They had to be paid in the same coin to make them as examples for future generations. Here we have examined the cases of Nagaland and Mizoram. Third, when the communities with ongoing conflict with the federal government approached for a negotiated settlement, the initiative was seized upon and dialogues held. Again, the case of Mizoram Accord presents the shining example of positive dialogue leading to an end of the decade long insurgency and emergence of a peaceful state of Mizoram.

There is also an intriguing example of stalemate on the decade-long negotiation between the Federal government and the NSCN in the case of Nagaland. One lesson is clear from the above presentation that if the ideological wing is supreme within the insurgent organizational structure, the negotiated settlement is likely to be feasible. It has been noted that the armed field operatives, who naturally survive in the most hazarduous environ, fall in love with them and do not appreciate the logic of ideological negotiations and possibly lack of commitment to lead a normal life of freedom. Perhaps they refuse to see life beyond the glamour of underground illegal armed confrontation. Thus, it was a tragic obstinacy on the part of the two negotiating parties to stick to their known stands and thus their failure to discover a common ground for the settlement of the mother of all the insurgencies in the north-east India' and let the people suffer as before.

'No more talks with the NSCN I-M, up to them to sign or not': Government finalizes Naga accord 'draft', rejects flag demand', writes the Indian Press in 2021.

Ignoring the National Socialist Council of Nagaland (I-Muivah)'s defiant posturing and demands, the Government of India has decided to go ahead with its plan to sign a peace accord with all other armed groups and civil society organizations of Nagaland soon. Security sources admitted that a section of NSCN led by its Secretary General Th. Muivah has not given their final consent for signing the peace accord, but asserted that the ball is now in the NSCN's court to take call on signing the peace accord as all the other stakeholders have approved the 'final draft agreement' aimed at bringing an end to decades-old insurgency in Nagaland.

Disclosing that negotiation between the Naga rebel groups on all issues have concluded, sources in the Ministry of Home Affairs told *The Asian Age* newspaper that a consensus has been created for signing the peace accord and a draft agreement has been finalized. The prime minister's envoy in the talks and the Governor of Nagaland R.N. Ravi is in New Delhi to finalize the draft agreement, and security sources said that talks between the NSCN(I-M) leadership led by its general secretary Th Muivah and Intelligence Bureau (IB) officers concluded about ten days back. Pointing out that for the last ten days no meeting was held between NSCN I M and IB officers, security sources that a section of the Naga rebel leaders have been trying to create confusion that the talks are still going on. Asserting that the demand for a separate flag and constitution for Nagaland has been rejected once again in the negation with IB officers, security sources admitted and said that the NSCN has been trying to buy time by raising rhetorical issues, but the Government of India has made it clear that they cannot prolong peace talks any more as consensus has already been created on all the Naga political issues.

The security sources said that this would be the first time that the civil society groups would also be signatories to a peace accord signed with armed groups. NNPGs, a group of seven Naga tribal insurgents, 14 Naga tribal Hohos and Nagaland Gaon Burah (GB) Federation would also be signatory to the peace accord. Security sources said that a section of leaders in the NSCN may be isolated in Nagaland if they continue to defy the mood of civil society groups which is mounting pressure for an early solution to Naga political issues. Apart from rehabilitation of armed cadres after surrendering arms, the final draft agreement also proposes two autonomous councils – one each in Manipur and Arunachal Pradesh – besides the mechanism of transfer of power by holding general elections in the state. The number of Lok Sabha and Rajya Sabha seats would also be increased to facilitate more representation to Nagas at the Centre' (*The Asian Age*, 7 October 2020). Naturally, NSCN leadership sharply reacted to the above decision of the Government of India. But the above claim of the Indian Union fails to make any sense, as no 'peace accord' has been signed by anybody till 31 March 2021. It is obvious that the Indian Union adopted constitutional, defensive and negotiating steps to accommodate demands of the frontier dissentors as much as possible.

REFERENCES

Hazarika, S., 2011, *Strangers to the Mist: Tales of War and Peace from India's Northeast*, Penguin Books, New Delhi.

Hazarika, Sanjoy, 2018, *Strangers No More: New Narratives from India's North-East*, Aleph, Book Company, New Delhi.

Powell, Jonathan, 2014, *Talking to Terrorists: How to End Armed Conflicts*, Penguin Random House, London.

Sinha, A.C., 2008, *Sikkim: Feudal and Democratic*, Indus Publishing Company, New Delhi.

Steyn, Pieter, 2016, *Zapuphizo: Voice of the Nagas*, Routledge, Taylor & Francis Group, London.

12

Collaborators, Rebels and Traitors

Were the Dissenters Collaborators, Rebels or Traitors?

Who are these dissenters who did not agree to be the part of Indian Union? First, they are individuals, who identify themselves strongly with 'their unique territories and peoples'. Second, they are those leaders who had visions for a prosperous future of their people and their land under their leadership. And last and more significantly, they were individuals who led the groups or organizations formed by them, which dared to stake claim to lead their people for those cherished objectives at all costs. In other words, strong identification of the leaders with their people and the land, clarity of their vision for a prosperous future and a determination to sacrifice for those lofty ideals were essential attributes for the determined dissenters. We shall examine the four dissenters and their background, which have been discussed earlier and look afresh on their attributes to understand their personae.

We have discussed above four cases of dissension from four different frontiers of the Indian Union. The Indian Union claims to be a multi-cultural, multi-ethnic, multi-religious, and a multilingual plural society from the very inception of the polity. In fact, two of the dissenters, S.M. Abdullah and P.T. Namgyal from the north-western and northern frontiers respectively, happily collaborated with the Indian national leadership in building the Indian plurality to begin with. However, their collaboration was based on their understanding that the Indian state would go on honouring their internal autonomy indefinitely. They failed to realize the fact that the Indian Union had made so much investment in men and materials in defense of Jammu

& Kashmir and maintenance of a façade of protection in a hostile environ to Sikkim and will not let it go away from India that easily. The moment these two leaders realized that their autonomy was being eroded, they opposed the Federal moves in their own way and for that, they were ready to suffer and they did so. So much so, that Sheikh Abdullah was imprisoned twice by the Indian Union for long periods of time without trial. At the end, both of them turned out dissenters of the Indian Union. Unfortunately, they failed to appreciate that for the Indian Union, 'the terms of accession' were the first step for the consolidation of the princely states into the Federal Indian Union. Moreover, Sheik Abdullah appears to have overlooked the sacrifices of men and materials to save Kashmiris from the rampaging invaders sponsored by Pakistan and expected that India would let him play his autonomy gamble indefinitely along with Pakistan.

When Sheikh Abdullah was imprisoned for long many years, even many of his associates deserted him and joined the Federal ruling party and they ran the state government. But Sheikh Abdullah maintained his stand on the merger of Kashmir as not a final decision on the plea that Kashmir had joined India only for three subjects (defence, communication and foreign relations) and for the rest it was an autonomous entity. At the fag end of his life, he signed an agreement with the Federal ruling party in 1975 and got elected to the office of the chief minister of the state. He died at a ripe old age in 1982 as an Indian and was buried in Srinagar on a prime location. Similarly, Palden Thondup Namgyal died of throat cancer while pleading for honouring Sikkim's internal autonomy and an honourable financial rehabilitation to the former ruling family and was cremated at Gangtok in his ancestral cremation ground with state honour. However, these two leaders maintained till last breath their stand on internal autonomy and their limited accession to the Indian Union.

Z.A. Phizo from the eastern frontier appears to be a rebel entrepreneur even before the British had left their Indian Empire and he got engaged in building a case for Naga independence by all means, fair and foul. While he happily ignored the Naga ethnic diversity of all types, he began emphasizing differences with the rest of India on racial, linguistic, demographic, and religious grounds as a strategy of political expediency. He turned even unscrupulous in his enterprise by resorting to armed conflict; smuggling arms and ammunitions from the regimes hostile to India; sending his cadres for training abroad in subversion and guerrilla warfare and at last, he smuggled himself first to Pakistan, then Genoa in Switzerland on forged travel documents and at last to the United Kingdom on another set of false travel documents. And from there he got engaged in garnering international support for the cause of Naga independence. He lived in the United Kingdom for the next long thirty years as a known rebel, where he expired in April 1990. His mortal remains were brought to Kohima, the provincial capital of the Nagaland, where he was given at last a final resting place. In his own word, he was born as a Naga and died as a Naga. However, the Indian stand had been that India had inherited him from the British Empire as an Indian and he died as an Indian traitor by his numerous acts of omission and commission. However, a set of Nagas including Phizo never accepted themselves as the Indians even before Indian independence. They claim that they had declared their independence on 14 August 1947. In fact, Phizo never claimed to be an Indian. Then how could he be termed as an India traitor. In fact, he was a unique rebel of his own type.

Pu Laldenga was a typical rebel, who took to arms against the Indian state, which he was serving and crossed to East Pakistan with some of his associates for seeking support. However, when Pakistan lost its eastern wing and Bangladesh was created as an independent country, he travelled stealthily to Karachi, the Pakistani metropolis, where nobody had any use of and interest in him and his insurgency. He was pragmatic enough to realize that his game of insurgency was up. And another realization dawned to him that there was no alternative but to surrender to the Indian state, which he did. The Government of India brought him back, rehabilitated him and his associates once his cadre surrendered their arms and joined the civil society in the state. Soon thereafter he would be elected as the chief minister of Mizoram, which he could not manage to rule for its full term of five years. By then, he had developed a serious aliment and he was flown to London for treatment, where he breathed his last in October 1990. Subsequently, like Phizo a few months earlier, his mortal remains were brought back home from London and a grand last farewell was given to him at Aizawl, the capital city of Mizoram.

Dissenters' Political and Organizational Structure

1. *The Location of Concerned State/District on the International Borders and Real or Alleged Support from the Neighbouring Foreign Countries*

Kashmir was one of the 'units' 'K' in the very conception of the idea of PA'K'ISTAN, which was ultimately claimed by M.A. Jinnah, the spokesman of the All India Muslim League, on the basis of its being a Muslim majority princely state. However, the ruler of the state was a Hindu Dogra from the Hindu majority Jammu region of the state, who was toying with the idea of independence for his kingdom after the departure of the British from India. With a view to hastening the process of ultimate taking over Jammu & Kashmir, Pakistan instigated trained tribesmen and some of its ex-soldiers to raid and invade the Valley of Kashmir. Naturally, it resulted in its merger with the India and India mounted counter attack to defend Kashmir against the invaders. But Pakistan continues till date her known policy of open moral, political, and armed support from across the borders to Kashmiri dissenters. There have been three wars, apart from the so-called tribal raids in 1947, between the two countries in 1965, 1971 and 1998 mainly on the issue of Kashmir. Because of this historical legacy, Kashmir continues to be a 'disputed territory' between the two countries in spite of Sheikh Abdullah's efforts to acquire support from both the countries for Kashmir's autonomous status. Thus, willy-nilly, Indian operation in Jammu & Kashmir cannot be completely autonomous because of extraterritorial interference from Pakistan.

Nagaland: The Naga insurgents were trained, armed and provided sanctuary in its territory since 1950s till date by the People's Republic of China, an ideological adversary of the democratic Indian Union, across the porous borders of Burma. Whenever the Indian security forces would mount serious armed counter-offensive on the Naga insurgents, they would swiftly cross over to China across the porous Indo-Burmese international borders. Unfortunately, the Burmese regimes ever since 1948 have never been in effective control of their mountainous and forested territories between India and China. Thus, external intervention in Naga insurgency, which denies autonomy of action to the Indian state, is one of the reasons of its longevity, frequently referred as 'the mother of all the insurgencies in the Indian Northeast region'. Thus tacit support of the Naga insurgency by China from across the porous international boundary is one of the key factors of its continuity.

Mizoram had a limited support from East Pakistan by arming, training and providing sanctuary to MNF cadre from 1962 to 1970. But once Bangladesh came into being in December 1972, Mizo National Front became politically an orphan organization. Though the leadership of the organization with their families was evacuated to Pakistan, but their hosts had neither resources nor will, nor the utility for the MNF insurgents in the changed geo-political scenario of the region any more. Even maintenance allowance to Laldenga and the leadership was drastically curtailed. Thus, the MNF leadership had no way but to turn to the Indian Union for reconciliation and be a proud member of the Indian federal structure.

So far Sikkim was concerned, but for a little noise from Nepal, there was no murmur of any external support from anywhere when the Indian state took steps to integrate it into the Indian Union. In fact, the last ruler should not be termed as a rebel. He was a real dissenter in the sense that there was a difference of opinion between him and the Government of India on the status of the state. While the last ruler presumed that but for defence, foreign policy and communication, Sikkim was an independent Bhutia entity as his patrimony, which was never recognized. On the other hand, at last in 1970s, the Indian Union began treating it as if it was another princely state, which had similarly signed the Instrument of Accession on those three subjects. None of the neighbours of Sikkim, Nepal, PRC (Tibet), or Bhutan took any anti-Indian posture on the issue of Sikkim's merger with India.

2. *Leadership*

Among all the four, Z.A. Phizo was the most charismatic leader, who led Naga armed insurgency to the extent of physically eliminating the dissenters to his approach and he created a near Naga nation and remained an almost non-compromising rebel till his end. Incidentally, he was a failed entrepreneur up to 40 years of his non-political life. His dictatorial and messianic style of leadership of the NNC did not endear him to many members in his political outfit, NNC (and thus some prominent among them were physically eliminated), but his ruthless pursuit of Naga nationalism against all odds turned him into an iconic status to many of the Nagas.

Sheikh Muhammad Abdullah tried to seek the support from both the countries, Pakistan and India, unsuccessfully to create an independent Kashmir. Unfortunately for him, neither of the two had any interest in Sheikh Abdullah's stipulation. Unfortunately, for both Sheikh Abdullah and the Indian establishment, the Instrument of Accecession on three subjects was a transitory affair. While the Indians believed that they would be able to convince the Kashmiris to merge the state with the Indian Union, Sheikh Abdullah believed that but for the three subjects (defence, foreign relations and communication) Kashmir was independent or at least autonomous for many years. Though at last, he publicly accepted accession to India as a fact, but that was to be limited only to those three issues. However, much water had flown down Jhelum since 1947. His friends in the Indian National Congress wished him to emerge as the secular face of their party at the national level, but Sheikh Abdullah preferred to remain a Kashmiri peasant leader at heart till the end, who unlike in the Kashmir Valley, had limited appeal in Jammu, Ladakh, and the northern Shia Muslim regions of the state.

P.T. Namgyal saw Sikkim nothing but as his patrimony, which he had inherited from his ancestors, and he strongly believed that come what may, he would continue to rule his little kingdom just as his ancestors did before him. For him, it was as if a biblical truth, in which others had no interest. The most tragic situation was that while he made some noise for an international status of Sikkim (which it never had), he presumed that the Indian Union would remain committed to his interpretation of the relationship between the two entities.

Laldenga appears to have been a clumsy small-time regional rebel, who took advantage of an extremely isolated and infrastructurally backward region and he double-crossed the Assam state leadership and the Mizo Union's tribal leadership. Perhaps for his false sense of significance and over-confidence, he did not care for the sacrifices made by his people and the cadre of the MNF for an impossible objective of independence, in which nobody had any interest. Moreover, there is evidence that he cared more for himself and his family's comfort rather than the basic needs of the armed fighters. It appears that he continued to act arrogantly as a traditional Mizo chief's descendant ('Lal'), who did not care much for a commoner Chairman of the Mizo Hills District Council in Chhunga.

3. *Support Base*

All four leaders had their political parties under their control because of their personal styles of charisma. So far as Sheikh Abdullah was concerned, his political forum, the Muslim/National Conference, was basically an exploited Kashmiri peasants' political party with formal but ineffective branches in other regions such as Jammu, Ladakh and small princely states in the north. But it was basically a peasants and artisans' party under the leadership of educated Kashmiri Muslims and Brahmins. But it was the Sheikh, who was the most charismatic leader amongst them, who had risen from an ordinary shawl weavers' family. He and his family had suffered hardship at the hands of the ruthless and archaic administration of the Maharaja living in a false sense of vanity. Unlike most of the leaders of his time, the Sheikh did not appear to have cultivated his clique in his party as he was the undisputed leader of the forum.

P.T. Namgyal had floated in 1948 his own political party, the Sikkim National Party (SNP), as an antithesis of the populist Sikkim State Congress (SSC). Though the party had its own formal structure, but it was a Bhutia party controlled by him entirely. Its leaders had limited support even among the courtiers, and its leaders were largely self-seekers. The leadership of the SNP was hand-picked by the ruler. The moment he ran into trouble with the Government of India, SNP collapsed as an organization like a house of cards in the absence of the support from the Durbar.

Phizo and Laldenga controlled the old Naga National Council and Mizo Famine Relief Front (subsequently renamed as Mizo

National Front: MNF) respectively and turned them more and more militant by pursuing an out and out aggressive anti-Indian agenda and strategy. Both of them gave a call of tribal solidarity against alleged ethnic exploitation by the Assamese Hindus, and thus Indian plainsmen. Both of them harped on religious and racial differences between the tribes and the bulk of Indian population in the plains. Once they gave the call for insurgency, they created an armed cadre of militants, who were organized in squads of fighters on the guerrilla basis. Once the Indian state sent its armed forces to quell the insurgency in the districts, NNC and MNF guerrillas took advantage of the undulating topography, melted in the thick vegetation, crossed the international boundaries and went underground to mount the counter offensives. The two guerrilla forces found easy shelters in the familiar terrain and warm ethnic embience from across the borders.

4. *Leaders and their Ideological and Organizational Background*

Sheikh Abdullah was the most educated among the four of the dissenters. He had an MSc Degree from Aligarh Muslim University and he had imbibed a socialistic ideology with a view to ameliorate the drudgery of the poor and exploited Kashmiri masses. In spite of his having the requisite educational qualification for the advertised posts, his candidature was rejected more than once for a job in the feudal administration of Kashmir. He turned out to be an effective public orator who could enumerate endless indignities heaped upon the helpless Kashmiris by the autocratic feudal regime. He could easily arouse passion against the ruthless feudal regime of the Hindu Maharaja amongst the suffering Muslim Kashmiris, who would instantly assemble to hear tales of their sufferings from one among them. He courted arrest more than once, which further added to his popularity. But his political party was faction ridden: one group opted for Pakistan and moved to the so-called Azad (Occupied) Kashmir after October 1947; another one was a leftist one with tenuous links with the Communist Party of India (CPI); still another faction belonged to those of them who desired to have good times by siding with the new rulers of the independent India, the Indian National Congress. And it was they who deserted the Sheikh Abdullah and formed the government behind his back.

Palden Thondup Namgyal claimed to be an incarnate ruler, who was far away from the hurly-burly of life of the common people. He was not supposed to move among the commoners, rather to rule over them as a sacred and ordained incarnate ruler. Once the myth of his hallowed status was blown out, he was left alone to himself pleading to the powers to be for granting satisfactory maintenance for himself and his dependents. The worse thing happened to his political forum, which he had floated some three decades back against the sane advice given by the then Political Officer. The forum simply vanished into the thin air leaving him to take care of himself.

Phizo and Laldenga gave calls to insurgencies in their respective districts inviting state's armed intervention. Their ideologies were based on ethnic, racial, religious and economic grounds and they invariably referred to their faith in Christianity as a marker against Hindu India. Though many of their cadre courted arrest, but a major chunk of their followers went underground and organized themselves into armed fighting squads. Soon they were trained by foreign armed forces. They would be provided with lethal armaments and were organized as guerrilla fighters, who could specialize in operating in difficult mountainous terrains against the much larger and more resourceful forces of the government with impunities. And they appeared to be equally versatile in the game of infrastructural sabotage by sneaking in the plain districts.

5. *Conflict between the Ideological wing and the Field Operatives Like Trained and Armed Fighting Forces*

The main leaders of the two forums of the Hill Districts remained unchallenged organizationally because of their personal qualities of leadership. The masses understood the leaders' concerns for them and followed their call and they even blindly joined the movement. Once the state government moved the armed forces to suppress the insurgency under the harsh AFSPA provisions, NNC and MNF first went underground and then organized their resistance in various ways from their hideouts. The most obvious among them was a cadre of trained guerrilla squads, which proved more effective as an army of resistance from their jungle hideouts. They would soon receive training in China and Pakistan and would be adequately armed by them and when they would be chased by the Indian security forces, they would be provided with clandestine security. Some of the trained guerrillas developed expertise in reaching the international illegal arms bazaar and in smuggling those arms across the porous international borders to their home base. These armed operators turned so powerful at times that they would challenge the authority of the ideological leadership.

That's what happened to Z.A. Phizo and his NNC after signing of the Shillong Accord in 1975. Phizo's biographer Peter Steyn records that Phizo's brother, Keviyally, had kept him abreast of the developments at Shillong. He considered himself so crtical to the Naga problem that he presumed

> there had always been a possibility that India might, at the last minute, be magnanimous in victory and invite him to return unconditionally. No such invitation ever came, not even a sounding out by the Indian High Commissioner's office in London. Just an arrogant silence. However, Phizo maintained that the sovereignity of his nation rested ... with Almighty God, the NGA National Council, and the Naga Federal Governmet in that order. (Steyn 2016: 157)

Incidentally, Phizo had forgotten that since 1957, the world and India had changed a lot. His alter-ego, Nehru, had died a decade back; India had fought two wars with Pakistan under two new prime ministers and was instrumental in the creation of Bangladesh; and nearer home, the Naga Hills district, now the state of Nagaland had three general elections and had its own chief minister with a cabitnet of ministers. Moreover, India had a dynamic prime minister Indira Gandhi, who was more decisive and pragmatic in her approach.

Soon after that, the armed wing of the leadership, Isac Swu and Thuengaling Muivah, challenged the NNC for signing the Accord. They denounced Phizo and the Accord as a sell out to the Nagas' cause and they founded their own outfit, the National Socialist Council of Nagaland (NSCN) in 1978 to continue with the armed struggle of the Nagas. They organized their new outfit on Marxist ideology and gave their movement a colour of the exploited class struggle against an oppressive Indian state. It is the NSCN which began calling the shots since then in Nagaland and within no time, NNC, the old forum of the Naga insurgency, turned out to be irrelevant. The NSCN reorganized themselves as a lethal guerrilla force in the hills and kept on harassing the well-armed and organized forces of the Indian Union.

For many years since 1993, they held negotiations with the representatives of the Government of India for solving the problems of insurgency within the ambit of the Indian constitution. However, the talks broke down in the beginning of 2021 in spite of Naga popular support from multiple stakeholders. One may remember that in the same way, the armed wing of the MNF almost rebelled against the ideological wing of MNF led by Laldenga and refused to join the negotiated settlement. They were manoeuvred by their opponents at last and a negotiated Peace Accord was signed between the MNF, Government of Mizoram and the Government of India in 1986 ending about two decades old insurgency in the state of Mizoram.

The Variety among the Dissenters

A. *Collaborator*

Collaborator is a person who works with another or other persons for achieving some common objectives. It is said to be a positive attribute in a person, who makes a common cause with like-minded people. In this category, two dissenters, Sheikh Muhammad Abdullah and Palden Thondup Namgyal, qualify to begin with, right from 1947. Sheikh Abdullah sided with the Indian National Congress and the Government of India as both of these institutions wished to end the rule of the Maharaja Sir Hari Singh's unbridled autocracy against the common people. This was the stand of Sheikh Abdullah against the All India Muslim League's communal agenda and Pakistan's open sponsorship of raids on populace, rape of women, arson against the state and private installations in the north-western part of Kashmir. He accepted Kashmir's status as an Indian state only on three subjects, which was agreed upon by the Maharaja: Foreign relations, Defence and Communication. And on the rest of the subjects, he considered

Kashmir to be autonomous to take its own decisions. He had no hesitation on pleading for the Indian case on the dispute of Kashmir in international forums such as the United Nations Organization. However, he was also all for independence of Kashmir, co-sponsored by both India and Pakistan, a possibility on which both the countries did not show any interest. It appears that at the fag end of his life, he believed in internal autonomy of Kashmir before his end came. However, it appears at the end, he had come to appreciate willy-nilly the stark reality of Kashmir being an Indian state for good.

P.T. Namgyal, the Crown Prince of Sikkim, was happy to accept the Instrument of Accecession on the subjects of the foreign relations, Defence and Communication and the Indian recognition of Sikkim's internal autonomy to begin with. And he was happy to accept Sikkim's status as an Indian protectorate. And for the next twenty-five years, he enjoyed his autonomy and largely went along with the Indian stands on most of the issues of his concern. However, the Indian establishment was very clear in their intentions right from the beginning that the 'Instrument of Integration' was a temporary arrangement to begin with and it was the first stage for the princely states for their final absorption in the Indian Union. And that's exactly what happened in 1969, when the privileges allowed to the former rulers of the princely states were unilaterally abolished by the Indian Union. The moment, P.T. Namgyal was made aware of the fact that Government of India would act to honour the resoluition of the State Legislative Assembly to abolish the monarchy in Sikkim, he rose in rebellion and did fight against the mighty Indian state machinery only to lose everything at the end.

Rebel

The term, rebel, is taken originally from Latin, *rebellis*. A rebel or a rebellious person is one who openly resists authority, or opposes any control. It is also referred to an attitude: 'to feel or show strong aversion: as his mind rebels at the prospect of such drudgery'. So far as Laldenga was concerned, he was unabashedly an Indian rebel leader. He was possibly a small-time local operator from a distant frontier of the Indian Union looking for an opportunity to take advantage of achieving his personal ambition. Unfortunately, he was callous enough to ignore the might of the Indian state. He could not visualize the calamity he was inviting for his unfortunate people. Unlike Phizo, he was not a well read man who could debate on the merits of his rising intellectually. He had decided to settle his score with his boss, the Chairman of the District Council, who saw the calamitous consequences of Laldenga's misadventure. Similarly, once he found out that his benefactor Pakistan, who had given him support and asylum, was soundly defeated by India, he had no hesitation in reaching to his other enemies, the Indian authorities, with a signed letter of terms of surrender.

The Indian authorities were magnanimous enough to accept him as a repentant Indian and provide him with the highest elective post in the Indian state of Mizoram. Moreover, his fighters were rehabilitated as much as possible and the status of the district was raised to statehood within the Indian Union. Administratively, he was not a very successful chief minister of the state under his charge. Among four of them, he was the only Indian rebel, who fought against India, surrendered at the end, was rehabilitated and given chance to function as an honoured politician, in which he had limited success, but he died as a proud Indian national.

Traitor

Webster's New World Dictionary refers to a traitor as one, who betrays, or a person who betrays his country, cause, friends, etc., and the one who is guilty of treason. What about Z.A. Phizo? Was he a collaborator, a rebel or a traitor? He was certainly not a collaborator, as there is no evidence that he ever thought of collaborating with the Indian Union at any level. In the same way, as he had never accepted the Indian political reality in terms of Naga Hills district/Nagaland as an Indian state, he cannot be called as an Indian rebel. Similarly, if he had not accepted the Indian reality of Nagaland, may be he could be called an Indian traitor, or traitor to India. Again it will be difficult to provide a logical answer to his status as a dissenter. However, in his style of thinking and functioning, the so-called declaration of Naga independence (?) on 14 August 1947 was the only justifiable ground on which the legitimacy of their rebellion/insurrection was based. But, and there is a big BUT. Their so-called declaration of Naga independence was not known to any formal or external body outside Naga Hills. Moreover, when the British left India in 1947, the district of the Naga Hills was an integral part of the province of Assam, which became a part of the Indian dominion at the time. In this way, Nagas' declaration of their 'Independence' remains as a myth. On the other hand, the inhabitants of the district, who were the Nagas, became Indians by the British Act of Indian Independence. In this way, India may consider Phizo's acts as rebellion and traitorous to the Indian interests. But Phizo never claimed to be an Indian. So the issue remains open. At the most he was a unique rebel of his own type.

An answer to Phizo's call to independence was provided by John H. Hutton, ICS, and former Deputy Commissioner of the Naga Hills district for over a decade. He was not an ordinary mortal; rather he was the Chief Secretary of the Province of Assam and the famous ethnographer on the monographs of the Nagas; was a professor of social anthropology, Cambridge University; progenitor of the Naga Club in 1918 and the original author of the idea of Crown Colony for the hill communities of British India and Burma. Moreover, it was he who championed the Nagas' cause all through his three decade long career in Assam. Hutton reasoned:

> It seems to me that by the formation of the state of Nagaland, protected as it is by a clause in the Constitution of India, the Nagas have in fact got more than they might have expected or even desired – complete internal home rule financed by the Indian government; indeed they have won their way. (Steyn 2016: 118)

Moreover, he 'described his former 'subjects' as head-hunters who if left to themselves, would return to 'the state of savagery in which the British had found them'. His advice to the Government of India was to 'offer a thumping reward to anyone bringing the head of a rebel. In that way this independence nonsense will soon be brought to an end' (Steyn 2016: 142).

At last, what do we learn from the above scenario and sacrifice of the people led by four dissenters to the Indian democracy and plurality? It looks as if the Sheikh never forgot the atrocious indignities heaped upon the Kashmiri Muslims by the autocrat and communal regime of the Dogra rulers. But he forgot that he had limited support base in other regions: Jammu and Ladakh. And he saw the same symptoms in Delhi's efforts to integrate Kashmir into the Indian Union instigated by the old Kashmiri Brahmin and Dogra ruling cliques. Unfortunately for him, his pet project of an autonomous/independent Kashmir did not create any interest in both the countries. It is unfortunate that while the Congress expected him to emerge as a leader of the community and a socialist leader at the national level, he preferred to be encaged in his Kashmiri political ghetto. Of course, he was certainly a self-made mass leader of the Kashmiri peasantry, and he tried to weigh other Muslim Congress leaders as a failure, because they did not have a mass public base as he had.

Phizo was pathologically anti-Nehru from the very beginning, as Nehru saw Naga insurgency as a local problem of law and order. For Nehru, Phizo was a frontier dissentor from a small tribe, who was possibly misguided by the British bureaucrates and Christian missionaries. Phizo kept on charging Nehru without proof that he was a Brahmin communalist, determined to convert the Nagas to the Hindu caste of untouchables. The problem was that while Phizo saw himself as a liberator of his people and 'nation', Nehru did not see him as more than a local obstinate tribal nuisance. Phizo's tirade against Nehru was out of proportion as a political opponent, as the comparison was absurd so were his charges on Nehru.

The tragedy of P.T. Namgyal was that he saw himself as the independent ruler of the little Himalayan principality in the last quarter of the twentieth century, in which nobody had any interest. In our understanding Laldenga was an opportunist local rebel, who rightly objected to the administrative apathy of the Government of Assam and took to arms to settle his scores with his alleged opponent, Chhuanga. Unfortunately for him, drawing lessons from the Naga insurgency, the Government of India reacted rather harshly by strafing on the rebel hid-outs and regrouping the villages along the roadways causing untold misery to the common people. On this score also, nobody can grudge the Indian action, as the Federal government was duty bound to defend its land and people.

These dissension emerged from the four frontiers from among the Muslim majority Kashmir; Buddhist ruled principality of Sikkim, American Baptist Christian Nagas from the Naga Hills and Presbyterian Christian Mizos from the south-eastern corner, Mizo Hills districts of Assam. How does one view the Indian plurality and democracy in such situations? Our analysis presents a mixed picture of the scenario. While functioning of Sikkim and Mizoram states under the duly elected leadership of the two states provide a resounding success story of the Indian democracy, the other two states, Kashmir and Nagaland, are known for projecting not a resoundly positive scenario. As the social scene in both the states continues to be unsettled because of trans-border intervention, establishment of law and order is the first priority of the administrators of these states. Thus, our democracy suffers because of limited loyalty of the electorate and rampant corruption of the ineffective administrative machinery. So much so that these two states continue to have two parallel regimes simultaneously operating 'for the people': a formal administrative one and an informal underground insurgent crowd.

In such situations, how does one remember the four dissentors today? Two of them, P.T. Namgyal and Sheikh Abdullah, died in 1982, other two, Z.A. Phizo and Laldenga, expired in 1990 in London. The mortal remains of all four of them were honourably consigned to the last rites as per their ethnic and religious practices in their respective states. Their memories have already collected some dust in course of time, no doubt. By and large, not many persons remember fondly P.T. Namgyal in Sikkim. With the decline of rebel glamour of the NNC and subsequent rise of NSCN, Phizo too is taken as an old story. Sheikh Abdullah unfortunately has been appropriated by the family, which runs the National Conference as if it is a family business. With the decline in the fortunes of the National Conference, which does not present a cohesive picture of its fighting force, the new generation have almost forgotten Sheikh Abdullah in the cacophony of factional politics of the state. And among all of them, it is Pu Laldenga, who is still remembered fondly by a faithful forum, the Mizo National Front, which has frequently ruled the state for the last 35 years.

Looking Ahead

Has the time come for the Indian Union to look back at the frontiers afresh with confidence? Should India celebrate her achievement in frontier management and feel confident enough to relax its guards on them? Why it is so that the frontier states are invariably happy and comfortable with their local and regional political parties, which may not last for long organizationally in comparision to their alignment with the national political parties? Conversely, why is it so that whenever the 'national political parties' extend their olive branches in the frontier states, invariably they tend to lose them the moment they lose their power at the centre? Ethnically, the states in north-east India present a different sociocultural set-up. Why is it so that the rate of conversion especially to Christianity has increased among the scheduled tribes in the region with their getting politically closer to the Indian general scenario for the last many decades? Should the religious conversion to Christianity be seen as a part of the nation wide process of political modernization of the electorate like that of urbanization, industrialization, professionalization, politicization, and the like?

One may like to consider the Indian Union after the 1972 war with Pakistan and liberation of Bangladesh in a different light. A new type of confidence appears to have emerged to face the problems head on. The leftover agenda of integrating the principalities in the Indian Union was completed with the integration of Sikkim in 1975. The Government of India took intiative to sign the Shillong Accord with the NNC in 1975 and in the same year Prime Minister Indira Gandhi and Sheikh Abdullah signed the Kashmir Accord to make a new beginning in the state. The next year MNF supremo Laldenga was parked in New Delhi to convince his cadre to join the Indian Union as honoured citizens, which was accomplished after a decade. So in spite of the above efforts, the Indians still have a lacerated Kashmir and a groaning Nagaland in agony. One may obviously reason that they are because of the trans-border interventions in affairs of Kashmir and Nagaland. Thus, we may note that there is a national fatigue with the affairs of Nagaland and Kashmir. And India possibly has to live with them till the opportune moments and visionary leadership arrive on the scene for their termination.

There is another aspect of the reality. It is a fact that the Indian Union went out of its way to accommodate Nagas, Mizos, Sikkimese, Kashmiris, and other frontier communities by granting them statehood in the Union and providing them with lavish gant-in-aid amount for their healthy upkeep. However, among the two and half a dozen federating states of the Indian Union, there are about a dozen small frontier states. Are these really equal to the states such as that of Uttar Pradesh, Maharashtra, Karnataka, Madhya Pradesh and the like? Conversely, will there ever be a Lok Sabha member from Nagaland, Mizoram, Sikkim or other frontier states to dream of becoming the prime minister of the Indian Union? Then, the issue remains that even this symbolic provision of states' equality is devoid of meaningful political content. Not for nothing, thus these frontier states will continue to welcome the denizens to their august Raj Bhawans for most of the time from the the police service, intelligence wing and armed forces to adjucate over the functioning of their 'vibrant democracy'.

REFERENCES

Powell, Jonathan, 2014, *Talking to the Terrorists: How to End Armed Conflicts*, Penguin Random House, London.

Steyn, Peter, 2016, *Zaphuphizo: Voice of the Nagas*, Routledge, London.

Webster New World Dictionary, Macmillan & Co., London, 1963.

Index

Abdullah, S.M./Sheikh Muhammad 19, 22, 40, 84, 88, 91, 177-225, 265, 267, 276, 283, 286-7, 289, 291-6, 301-2; Sheik Abdullah goes on Haj to Mecca and gets arrested on his return 215-17; Sheikh Abdullah in Political Ferment 286; Sheikh released from jail meets the prime minister and travels to Pakistan 211-15; Sheikh Abdullah's release from the jail and re-arrest 208
Adams, Philip Francis 101
AFSPA 71, 72, 268, 274, 294
Air force strafed of Mizo villages on 1 March 1966 107
American Baptist Missionaries in Nagaland 47, 53, 58, 69, 145, 269, 301, 304
Angami village (like Greek city states) 51
Anti-feudal agitations, formation of a popular government and its dismissal (Sikkim) 129-31
Anti-insurgency drive in Naga Hills District of Assam since 1950 273-4
Antrobus, H.A. 48
Ao, W. Chubanungba 60: wrote the memoirs 60
armed conflict between Bengalis and Pakistan Army 90, 251
Ash, Timothy 21
Assam Company 47
Azad, M.A.K. 29, 30, 191, 200, 205, 221

Background to Sheikh Abdullah's arrest and incarceration 200-3
Banerjee, Sir Albion 180
Basnet, L.B. 132
Birth of All Jammu and Kashmir Muslim Conference 184-6
Bordolai, G.N. 31, 103, 150: visits Aizawl in April 1947 and sixth schedule was extended to them 103, 266
Borpujari, H.K. 58
British Indian ethnic policy after 1857 25-6
British policy of divide and rule 26-8
British sell Kashmir to establish a satellite Dogra ruling dynasty 81-4
Bruce, Charles 58
buffer state 15, 18

Chaube, S.K. 101
Chhunga's peace mission to Laldenga in 1965, 106, 228-30, 232, 236, 240-1, 296
Christianity and Naga world 57-62
Churchill, W. 27
Clark, Rev. Bro. Edward Winter 58
Clow, Sir Andrew G. 57
Colson, Elizabeth 62
Creation of a make belief Sikkimese (Tibetan) cultural complex 250
Creation of Lushai Hills District in Assam 94
Creation of North and South Lushai Hill District 97-9
Creation of state of Arunachal Pradesh, 1987 272-3
Creation of state of Nagaland as a State in Indian Union 72-4
Creation of the 18 Progressive Protected Villages (PPV) along the roadsides 107
Creation of the Naga Club and Coupland Plan for the Crown Colony 52-7
credentials of the Indian Union 22
Crown Colony 52, 54-7, 100, 164, 209
Curzon, Lord Nathaniel 24

Dalhousie, Lord 81
Damant, H. 64, 65
Dean, Riaz 24
Dewan, Maniram 48
dissenters 15, 16-20, 22, 30-2, 40, 55, 56, 166, 167, 187, 239, 265, 267, 283, 286, 287, 289, 290, 293, 299, 302, 303
dobhashis language interpreters, 53
Dorji, Kazi Lhendup 122, 134, 252

Elwin, Verrier 51
Emergence of NSCN 74
enactment of Article 370 of Indian constitution 217
End of the British rule 100-3
End of the game or dynastic rule in Sikkim 251-3
European style of upbringing 243-6
excluded hill districts 55

Field Marshal Auchinleck 87
foundation of the Kazihood 116, 119
frontier areas/regions 15-22, 30-2, 40, 55, 56, 166, 167, 239, 265, 267, 283, 287, 302, 303

Gandhi, M.K. 26, 30-2, 38, 69, 81, 152, 187, 189-97, 200, 212, 221
granting of special status to the Jammu & Kashmir and the Princely State of Sikkim 267
great game in the Himalaya 105
Guha, Amalendu 118
Gulab Singh annual tribute to the British 81, 82, 191

Hari Singh abdicates on 20 May 1948 89
Hari Singh's delusion of independence 83
Hazarika, S. 104-6, 110, 153, 159, 173, 234, 235, 237, 241
history of the present 21
Hutton, J.H. 52-5, 60, 100, 154, 166, 167, 299

Imkongliba 71, 162

imperial obsession 16
independence of Naga Hills district 69
India took the issue of the invasion of Kashmir by Pakistan to the United Nations Organization 199
Indian Independence Act 1947, 33
Indian National Congress 17, 25-32, 35, 68, 73, 91, 104, 106, 111, 112, 127, 188-95, 200, 202, 218-24, 228, 239, 241, 246, 248, 265, 276, 277, 279, 291, 294, 296
indigenous Nagas 47
instrument of accession 35, 86, 91, 224, 257, 273, 290

Jenkins, Captain 49
jhumming (rotational hill cultivation) 51
Jinnah, M.A./ Muhammad Ali 26-32, 36, 87, 188-90, 202, 221

kalobhari 121
Kashmir Accord between the Sheikh and Indira Gandhi: February 1975 276-7
Kashnir Accord and Thereafter 217-18
Kevichusa 54, 69, 150, 153
Kwarteng, K. 81-4

Lalbiakthanga 102, 226
Laldenga, Pu 20, 21, 104-12, 226-42, 272, 279, 288, 291, 292, 294, 296-302: expired of lung cancer in London, 240; negotiate with GOI, 110; Negotiates and becomes the State Chief Minister of Mizoram 110; Negotiates with India from Pakistan 234; shifted to Karachi 235; the Person, the Leader and His Impact 240; The Chief Minister of Mizoram 239; slipped off to East Pakistan 108
Lalship (chieftainship) 101
Lho-mon-tshong Gsum, 118
Longkumer, N. 59
Looking ahead 302
Lushai Hills District Council 103
Lushai Hills turned into Mizo in 1954 103-4

Makes good breakfast 33
Mautam 100, 104, 228, 229
Menon plan 32
merger of Sikkim in May 1975 136, 252, 271
Mizo Accord 279, 238
Mizo Famine Front 104
Mizo National Front (MNF) 104-6, 226, 229, 279, 301
Mizo Union 101-4, 106, 228, 232, 238, 240, 291
Mountbatten, Lord 31, 32, 84, 89
Muivah, T. 78, 169-72, 237, 278-81, 284, 295
Mukherjee, Shyama Prasad 203: in the Kashmir Imbroglio 203
Mullard, S. 113

Nag, Sajal 21, 152
Naga Hills District Tribal Council 54
Naga Hills was a scheduled district 70

Naga People's Convention (NPC) 71, 162, 163, 269
Nagaland Peace Mission 74, 165
Nagamese 51
Namgyal, Palden Thondup 20, 21, 123, 124, 127, 243-51, 253-65, 287, 294, 296: the person and his make-belief world 256; as a private citizen 253
Namgyal, T. and Y. Dolma 116
Namgyal, Tashi 121, 122, 124, 243, 245, 257, 268
national boundaries 19
Nawab of Junagadh 38
Nehru and Thakin Unu 72
Nehru, Jawaharlal 28-30, 35, 68, 69, 71, 88-91, 105, 130, 151-8, 164, 174, 175, 186, 186, 187, 198-224, 260, 295, 300: sent army to the Naga Hills 71
NNC organized a plebiscite on the issue of Nagas' independence 72
Noorani, A.G. 90, 224

Operation Jericho 106, 164, 232, 274, 304
Owen, L. 23
Owen, R. 25

Padmasambhava 113
Pakistan 17, 19, 26, 27, 31, 33-8, 71, 85-110, 139, 160, 161, 173, 186, 189, 190, 193-6, 211-16, 222, 224, 230, 231, 234-6, 251, 265, 267, 269, 272, 273, 283, 287, 288-90, 293-9, 302
Pakistan attacks Kashmir, accession to India and Sheikh's release 193-7
Pakistan invades Kashmir, 24 October 1947 85
parity system (ethnic), 131, 247, 258
Patel, Sardar Vallabbhai 37, 38, 85, 87, 89-92, 164, 197, 198, 199, 202
Patrick, French 27
Patterson, George N. 116
Pawsey, Charles R., 48, 53, 148, 150, 154, 158, 166, 245, 273
Pemiyagtse (Pemiyangchi) monastery 119
Phizo, Z.A. 19, 21, 53, 69-71, 74, 75, 143-75, 231, 269, 274, 278, 287-95, 298-302: moves to centre stage of Naga insurgent politics 155-60
political status of the eastern Himalayan kingdoms 123
Pope Alexander VI 57
Powell, Jonathan 275, 276, 282
Preamble of the Indian constitution 19
princely states 17, 25, 30, 33, 35, 36, 39, 40, 136, 243, 257, 265, 287, 292, 297

Rai, C.D. 61, 130-1
Rao, Narasimha 279
Ray, Sunanda Dutta 135
Reid, Sir N. Robert 54: and coupland plan for crown colony 54, 55, 57, 101, 164
Reid, Walter 26
Rustomji, N.K. 21, 124, 125, 133, 150, 243, 249, 250, 253, 255, 256

Sakhrie, T., 54, 68, 70, 71, 157, 159, 173, 174: Sakhrie's murder on 18 January 1956 159
Sanyo, Visier 51, 62
Scott, James 103
Scott, Michael 74, 154, 161, 165, 166, 174
Sema, Hokishe 162, 163
Shillong Accord 74, 75, 163, 167, 167-76, 277, 278, 295, 302
Shillong accord, diminishing role of Phizo in NNC and emergence of NSCN, 74
Sikkim National Party 128-30, 132, 248, 252, 258, 292
Sikkim State Congress 127, 129, 130-32, 139, 247, 252, 258
Sikkim Youth Study Forum 151
Sikkimpati Maharaja 121, 247
Simon Commission 53, 55, 67, 100-1: crown colony, and end of the British rule 100
Singh, Dalip 79
Singh, Karan 21, 85-6, 88, 92, 198, 202, 204-8, 211-12, 215, 219
Singh, L.P. 74, 167-9, 277, 278
Singh, Maharaja Gulab 81
Singh, Maharaja Hari 83-6, 89, 91, 92, 182, 192, 196, 198, 212, 221, 265, 296: abdicates the dream of independent Kashmir 89
Singh, Maharaja Ranjit 79, 81
Srinagar 195: Maharaja's capital 195
Steps adopted by the Indian union to consolidate the country 36-40
Steps for securing Kashmir from invasion and raids from Pakistan in October 1947 273
Suhrawardy, H.S. 30, 31
Sukhim (Sikkim), 119

Tea plantation in Assam 47-9, 58, 94
Thanksgiving Day 236
The arrest of Sheikh Abdullah 205
The Bhutia ruler 124, 246
The British moves to the Naga hills 62-7
The Cabinet Mission Plan of 16 May 1946 30-2
The crown prince 92, 125, 128-30, 132, 198-9, 245, 250, 257-8, 297
The Kashmir Muslim Conference was changed to National Conference on 24 June 1938, 187
The last British viceroy: Lord Louis Francis Mountbatten arrives at the scene 32-3
The last phase of Sheik Abdullah 218-22
The ruler overplayed his game and lost the Principality (Sikkim) 134-6
The ruler reacts to impending British withdrawal from India (Sikkim) 122-3
The tripartite Sikkim agreement, 1973 271-2
The variety among the dissenters 296-301
Treaty of Titaliya 121

Tshering, Tashi 122, 125-6, 127, 129-31, 247, 258

Wasteland rules of 6 March 1838 49

Wavell, Lord 28, 31, 33, 56, 191
White, J.C. 121
With collapsed dreams, Laldenga negotiates with India from Pakistan 234-7